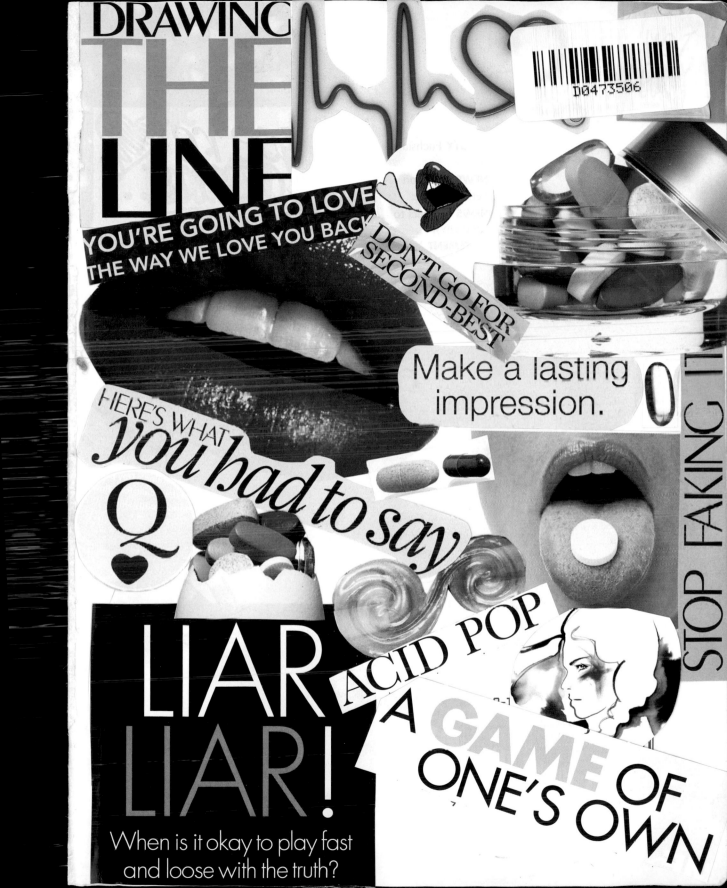

Essential Guide Series

THE ESSENTIAL GUIDE TO DATA WAREHOUSING

Agosta

THE ESSENTIAL GUIDE TO TELECOMMUNICATIONS,
SECOND EDITION

Dodd

THE ESSENTIAL GUIDE TO NETWORKING

Keogh

THE ESSENTIAL GUIDE TO DIGITAL SET-TOP BOXES AND INTERACTIVE TV

O'Driscoll

THE ESSENTIAL GUIDE TO HOME NETWORKING TECHNOLOGIES

O'Driscoll

THE ESSENTIAL GUIDE TO COMPUTING:
THE STORY OF INFORMATION TECHNOLOGY

Walters

THE ESSENTIAL GUIDE TO RF AND WIRELESS

Weisman

Sex addiction is *so* 2010. These days, an increasing number of men and women are seeking help for a different type of dependency – one that turns words like "I love you" into a dangerous drug.

LOST

CONFUSED UNSURE

UNCLEAR

PERPLEXED

SORIENTED BEWILDERED

Woman on-the-go

Today's woman is determined, efficient, quick. When the pace slows, when things get tough, she navigates her way with the nimble gait of an amazon. As far as trends are concerned, she's always ahead.

LOVE BUGGED

SECRETS OF THE

LOVE HUTS

IJ   07458

Library of Congress Cataloging-in-Publication Data

Keogh, James Edward, 1948-
    The essential guide to networking / Jim Keogh.
        p. cm.
    ISBN 0-13-030548-0
        1. Computer Networks—Management. 2. Business enterprises—Computer
    networks—Management. I. Title.

TK5105.5 .K46 2000
658'.0546--dc21

                                                                00-055796

Editorial/Production Supervision: *Vanessa Moore*
Acquisitions Editor: *Miles Williams*
Editorial Assistant: *Richard Winkler*
Manufacturing Manager: *Alexis Heydt*
Art Director: *Gail Cocker-Bogusz*
Interior Series Design: *Meg Van Arsdale*
Cover Design: *Bruce Kenselaar*
Cover Design Direction: *Jerry Votta*
Project Coordinator: *Anne Trowbridge*

© 2001 Prentice Hall PTR
Prentice-Hall, Inc.
Upper Saddle River, NJ 07458

The publisher offers discounts on this book when ordered in bulk quantities.
For more information, contact:
    Corporate Sales Department, Prentice Hall PTR
    One Lake Street
    Upper Saddle River, NJ 07458
    Phone: 800-382-3419; FAX: 201-236-7141
    E-mail: corpsales@prenhall.com

Printed in the United States of America
10   9   8   7   6   5   4   3   2   1

ISBN 0-13-030548-0

Prentice-Hall International (UK) Limited, *London*
Prentice-Hall of Australia Pty. Limited, *Sydney*
Prentice-Hall Canada Inc., *Toronto*
Prentice-Hall Hispanoamericana, S.A., *Mexico*
Prentice-Hall of India Private Limited, *New Delhi*
Prentice-Hall of Japan, Inc., *Tokyo*
Pearson Education Asia Pte. Ltd.
Editora Prentice-Hall do Brasil, Ltda., *Rio de Janeiro*

"I'm comfortable with my body because I view it as a powerful machine."

CONTACT US

MALE HEARTACHE IS AN ICEBERG OF PAIN. WHAT YOU CAN SEE IS ONLY A TINY PART OF THE STORY.

42% of us have wanted – at one time or another – to seek treatment for a mental health issue, yet more than one-quarter never did.

NO MORE SEARCHING.
NO MORE GUESSING.

LOVE IS
LA GAME
A GAME

5   Networks: Connecting over a Wide Area   145

PART 3   PREVENTING AND FIXING
NETWORK PROBLEMS   247

8   Network Reliability and Security   249

Preface

Computer technology seems to completely change every 18 months, and network technology is leading this change. Stop and think for a moment how much you depend on network technology. If you're like me, you probably have a difficult time answering that question because networking is something you don't see and most of us don't touch.

Yet if I asked you how many times you send and receive e-mails every day or how many hours a day you surf the Internet, then you probably would have no difficulty answering. E-mail and the Internet are just two ways we use networking technology every day.

Now for the million dollar question: Do you know how networks work? Take your time answering. Remember, you still have your "lifelines" available. If your answer is no, then you're reading the right book.

Most of us know little or nothing about networks unless we work closely with the technicians who maintain them for our company. However, we're forced to interact with network technology whenever the network goes down, leaving us disconnected from our files and e-mails.

A help desk technician talks network mumbo jumbo to us as he or she tries to get us back online. It's tough to admit, but even the office guru probably doesn't have a clue about what the technicians are doing. I know this for a fact because I was one of those office gurus—and that's the reason I wrote this book. I hung around with networking professionals for about a year and discovered networks interested me enough to become an expert. I'd rather be on the complaining end of a call instead of having to track down a problem in the miles of network cables and the hundreds of network devices that keep data flowing through my company.

To help you understand networks, my objective when writing this book was to make the text plain, simple, and easy to understand. As you read through this book and develop your own understanding of how networks work, I think you'll find that I met my goal.

I begin with basic school science that illustrates how an electronic signal is generated. Don't worry—I purposely left out math problems. If you can turn a light switch on and off, then you'll be fine.

After that, I lead you on a clear, straight path that takes you to local area networks and wide area networks technology and a rare look behind the scenes at the Internet. Your journey will be peppered with a few humorous stories that I picked up while I was writing this book.

The last few chapters are devoted to the business side of networking, and I take you on a tour of the movers and shakers who decide how networks operate. You'll recognize a few of the companies as those that are the pride of tech stock traders. Many are not household names, yet have a dramatic role in network and Internet technologies. I'm sure anyone who has remotely followed tech stocks will enjoy this look at the networking industry.

If you're a network technician or want to become a Microsoft Certified Systems Engineer, then don't read this book. Instead pick up a copy of my *Core MCSE Networking Essentials*, which is a Microsoft Certified-approved study guide designed for studying for the certification tests.

If you're a nontechnical person interested in learning more about networks, then read this book. It's the best way to learn about networking without having to sift through technical stuff you don't need to know.

This book is ideal for anyone who is responsible for administrating network services for an organization and for salespeople, law firms, research organizations, marketing personnel, human resources professionals, project managers, networking managers, and high-level administrators. It will give you the knowledge you need to effectively communicate and understand networking language. And as we evolve farther into a network-centric world, the importance of such a skill is going to be increasingly more apparent and important.

Part 1

Technological Fundamentals

You probably have a friend like Rudy, who needs only a grocer's calculator and brainpower to solve any problem. Rudy insists computers can never outsmart humans and to some extent he is correct—at least for the foreseeable future.

Rudy is always quick to prove that he can outsmart any self-proclaimed computer whiz. At the beverage cart he once watched a young programmer pay $1 for lemonade. Rudy then proceeded to take from the cart a cup, some ice, a few packets of sugar, and a packet of lemon juice used to flavor tea. Then he made his own lemonade—at no cost, of course.

He laughed when a coworker bought software to make personalized greeting cards. Rudy personalized greeting cards too, but using old technology and never paid a cent for them. On Valentine's Day, Rudy borrowed a few sheets of colored paper and painstakingly folded each sheet into the size of a traditional greeting card. Then he drew a simple but effective drawing on it and added his own personal saying. He folded another sheet into a perfect envelope. No one could tell the difference between Rudy's card and one produced by computer.

Rudy's common sense approach couldn't deliver the greeting card to anywhere in the world at nearly the speed of light however. Real computing power is needed to achieve that, and you'll learn how your thoughts are sent on a thousand mile journey through wires in Part 1.

I've put aside the scientific babble and tossed out formulas you'd expect to hear when learning about technology. Instead I present you with a clear and concise understanding of how information is transmitted over a computer network. Math and formulas are fine if you are going to design a computer network from scratch. However, they make understanding how computer networks work unnecessarily complex for most of us.

Part 1 of this book covers the basics that you need to know to understand the workings of a computer network. The basics are covered in the first two chapters. Chapter 1, "Networks: A Look Back," presents the historical foundation of today's networks, and Chapter 2, "Networks: Basic Concepts," explores the science in network transmissions.

Computer networks are based on a long history of technological advancements. The first chapter provides a thumbnail sketch of these roots and pays particular attention to explaining the technological concepts that became the building blocks of today's networks. I purposely left out when and where these advancements occurred since they tend to be less important than how the technology works and the role it plays in today's computer network.

Chapter 2 begins your ground up exploration of how computer networks work. You'll begin your journey by learning how an electronic signal is formed and how information is translated into the signal. You'll complete your basic understanding by the end of the chapter and know how your thoughts are sent electronically to a distant computer in a fraction of a second.

Once you have the basics under your belt, you'll have the necessary background to explore how computer components operate and how they are linked together to form a network.

1 Networks: A Look Back

In this chapter...

Rarely does anyone stop and think of what happens when we communicate over wires or the airwaves to remote places. You sit at work or at home and link your computer to the Internet, then send e-mails to colleagues and friends. Literally faster than a speeding bullet your e-mail zips over telephone wires, beams up to satellites in some cases, and arrives at its destination practically anywhere in the world.

Internet communications are the latest in a long line of engineering marvels that let us translate our thoughts into electronic signals. In this chapter, you'll explore the basics of communication as you visit the inner workings of:

- telegraph networks
- telephone networks
- broadcast networks
- component networks
- mainframe networks
- PC networks
- the Internet and World Wide Web

REALITY CHECK ....

Most of us rarely give telecommunications more than a passing thought whenever we pick up a telephone or surf the Internet, yet with the magic of technology we are able to stay connected to relatives, buy items online, and convert our homes into our offices.

The speed of telecommunications hit home with me the day my daughter moved to Bermuda on a three month auditing assignment for Arthur Andersen. We stayed in touch through daily e-mails. One day, a couple of seconds after I clicked the Send button, I received a call. It was my daughter, asking me to clarify something in my e-mail.

This made both of us stop and think. My e-mail traveled from my office in Brooklyn to my Internet Service Provider in Hackensack, New Jersey. From there it traveled to Arthur Andersen's central e-mail server in Chicago before finally arriving at my daughter's computer in Bermuda. Of course, those are the known stops. E-mail travels along the Internet, which consists of public and private telephone networks and any number of unseen special computers called servers.

Tech Talk

Servers: A computer on a network dedicated to providing a specific function to other computers connected to the network. For example, an e-mail server is a computer that manages the transmission of electronic mail for networked computers.

Then, the public telephone system transmits e-mails and other communications over cables and through a network of satellites. All this technology occurs behind the scenes and provides us with a reliable and seamless line of communication.

Network technology is changing the way most of us do business. I've been writing books for more years than I admit. I started with an electric typewriter—you remember seeing these machines in old movies. Manuscript pages were written and rewritten on paper, and a bottle of Wite Out and carbon paper were the only tools that helped to ease the pain of correcting text and reproducing pages.

A 500-page book required the author to generate about three reams of paper; two reams to send to the publisher and the other as a protection copy in case the U.S. Postal Service lost the manuscript.

The publisher made five or so copies using a copy machine and then distributed these to various editors who reviewed, commented, and made handwritten changes to the manuscript. Each corrected copy was copied several times and then sent to the author, who was responsible for consolidating changes into the manuscript.

Thanks to the benefit of network technology, this laborious process no longer exists. Manuscripts are rarely printed. Instead, they are stored in word processor files, which are then electronically transferred to the publisher over the Internet. Copies of the manuscript are made, but these are electronic copies of the word processor files, not usually the printed manuscript.

Editors receive the electronic manuscript over the Internet, which allows an editor to work from home or on the beach. Comments and changes are made directly to the electronic manuscript. The author reviews these changes on the computer screen before the production editor electronically consolidates changes into one file. The production department transforms manuscript pages into typeset pages of a book and those files are sent over the Internet to the printer. A minimal amount of paper is used; in fact, most of the paper used in the production process, is needed only when the book is finally printed.

The rapid evolution of electronic communication has changed our lives, although we tend to take these changes for granted. It has become second nature to click a few buttons on our computer and connect to the volumes of information and services available on the Internet. E-mail, electronic bill payment, electronic commerce, and online information are quickly replacing the way we conduct business and interact with friends.

Speed forward a few decades. Your grandchildren will be asking you, "What is a telephone?", "What is a television?", "What is an office?", or "What is a store?".

These questions may seem absurd today; however, your children may not remember telephone party lines, black-and-white television, vinyl records, or a time when only large corporations owned computers. Party lines were common 50 years ago. Black-and-white televisions were common 40 years ago. Vinyl records were still around 30 years ago. And it wasn't until 15 years ago that personal computers became affordable.

Looking back in time provides a foundation for understanding and appreciating developments that lead to today's technological advancements, much of which we take for granted. Let's take a trip back to when networks and telecommunications were in their infancy and explore how these building blocks gave birth to the high-speed networks we have today.

FRONTIER LAND...

Networks and telecommunications have a long history that began with the expansion of the American West, the discovery of electricity and electromagnets, and a spark of ingenuity to harness the power to transmit words beyond the loudest shout.

Movement to open the western territory in the1800s stretched the capability to communicate over long distances. Horsepower in the form of stagecoaches and the pony express was used to manually transfer written messages to outpost communities. It took weeks before a message could reach the East Coast.

With the building of railroads, cable was strung alongside tracks and a clever way was invented to saddle our words on electricity so our messages traveled over the cable. This was the first telecommunications network: the telegraph.

Tech Talk

Cable: A cable consists of two or more wires shrouded in sleeves to insulate them from the elements.

Western movies foster the image of the telegraph network by depicting an older gentleman in a visor translating an apparently random set of clicks into words. He would then encode his own words into clicks. Like us, the pioneers probably thought little of the technology that made all this possible. Yet the science behind the telegraph is fairly easily to understand.

Tech Talk

Electromagnetism: the phenomenon that changes a metal bar into a magnet when electricity travels over a coil of wire wrapped around the bar.

The telegraph is based on electromagnetism. When the coil is charged with electricity (Figure 1.1), one end of the metal bar becomes positively charged and the other end negatively charged. Opposite charges attract each other. You probably remember performing this experiment when you were in school.

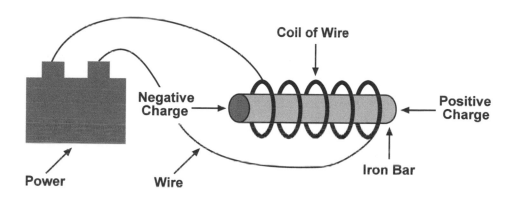

Figure 1.1
An iron bar becomes magnetized when electricity flows through the coil.

A telegraph network consists of a power supply, such as a battery, a cable, a receiver, and a transmitter (Figure 1.2). A telegraph receiver is composed of two metal bars, one of which is an electromagnet. A telegraph transmitter is a switch.

Electricity flows from the battery and over the cable when the switch in the transmitter is closed. The switch is called the telegraph key and controls when electricity flows over the wire. Once the metal bar in the receiver becomes magnetized, it is attracted to the other metal bar in the telegraph receiver, causing a click. The bars separate when the switch is open, causing the metal bar to demagnetize. A telegraph operator would make a tapping sound occur at telegraph stations along the telegraph cable by opening and closing the telegraph key.

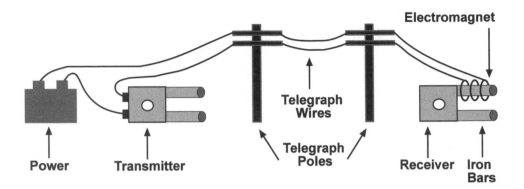

Figure 1.2
The iron bar on the receiver becomes magnetized when the transceiver
switch is closed.

We've heard the clicking of a telegraph in the movies, and to most of us the tap-ping was meaningless. Early developers of the telegraph had the same reaction. They could cause a click to occur at a remote location, but they needed a way to make those clicks meaningful.

Samuel Morse solved this problem by creating the Morse Code. However, in-stead of assigning a meaning to the click, he assigned a meaning to the pause between two clicks. A short pause was called a dot and a long pause was called a dash.

Morse assigned unique pattern of dots and dashes to each letter of the alphabet. A telegraph operator used the Morse Code to translate a message into dots and dashes, which was then sent over the telegraph wire. Telegraph operators along the network heard the clicking and deciphered the dots and dashes back into a message.

Each message began with an address of a telegraphic station and the name and ad-dress of the recipient of the message. At that telegraph station, it was the telegraph oper-ator's responsibility to ensure that the message was delivered to the proper destination.

Addresses used in the telegraph network are not much different than addresses used on today's computer networks. Each computer on a network is assigned a unique address, and software on the network translates and delivers the message (as you'll see in the next chapter).

"Watson Come Here"

The telegraph was cumbersome, to say the least. A message needed to be told to a telegraph operator who required special knowledge of Morse Code to transmit the message to a remote destination. Also, there was no sense of confidentiality.

Something better had to be invented. A new technology was required that lowered the technical skills necessary to transmit messages so a telegraph operator was no longer required. Alexander Bell's telephone was the solution.

Today all of us take the telephone for granted. A bell rings and we pick up the handset and begin talking. The telephone has become our lifeline. It enables us to keep in touch with friends and relatives, to summon emergency services in times of trouble, and allows telemarketers to interrupt our supper. Even in the direst times of a power outage, amazingly, communications engineers are usually able to keep telephones working.

Like the telegraph, the technology used to capture and transmit our voices over a cable seems baffling, yet both technologies are similar. Both use magnetism to encode a signal over a cable.

The telephone converts sound into electrical energy that is transmitted over a cable. The electrical energy is then converted back to sound. A telephone has a transmitter, which we recognize as the mouthpiece of the phone, and a receiver, which is the earpiece. The telephone transmitter is a microphone and the telephone receiver is a speaker that uses technology similar to that found in a recording system.

Tech Talk

Microphone: Translates sound waves into electrical waves.
Speaker: Translates electrical waves into sound waves.

Before we can fully appreciate how sound is transmitted and received across a telephone line, we need to understand sound. Anything can be set in motion. This is called vibration. Vibration causes a sympathetic vibration of air molecules that surround the vibrating object. That is, as the object vibrates so does the air around it.

Tech Talk

Sympathetic vibration: With each vibration, the vibrating object pushes the air molecules surrounding the object causing the air molecules to vibrate at the same rate as the object.

Vibration causes a wave to form in the air molecules similar to waves we see in water. A wave is measured by the wave's height and the number of waves that occur per second (Figure 1.3). The height of a wave is called the wave's amplitude and the number of waves per second is called the wave's frequency.

You cannot see the wave in air molecules, but you can see a similar phenomenon by vibrating a utensil in a dishpan of water. Every movement of the utensil causes a similar movement of water molecules that form waves in the water.

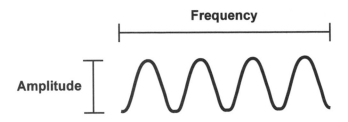

Figure 1.3
The number of waves per second is the wave's frequency.

Air flowing through our vocal chords causes our vocal chords to vibrate, which causes the air molecules surrounding our vocal chords to also vibrate at the same rate. Anything within the surrounding area of the air molecule will be set into sympathetic vibration by air molecules, including our eardrums. This enables us to hear the sound.

The microphone inside a telephone vibrates at the same rate as our vocal cords, which is the basis for transmitting our voice over the telephone cable. The microphone consists of a felt-like material, similar to the membrane in our eardrums, that is connected to a magnet. Vibrating air molecules cause the felt-like material to vibrate, which causes the magnet to fluctuate the flow of electrical current in the telephone cable (Figure 1.4). These vibrations occur at the same amplitude and frequency as our voices. Power to the telephone line gives the wave the energy to reach the end of the telephone cable, where the wave is converted to sound waves by the telephone receiver.

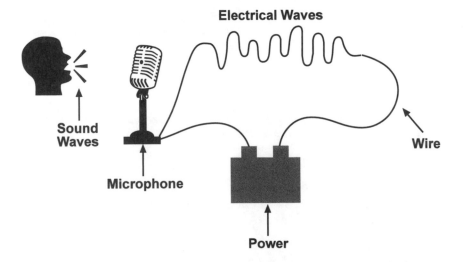

Figure 1.4
The microphone translates sound into electrical waves.

The telephone receiver consists of the same elements as the microphone. Fluctuation in the electrical current is detected by the magnet in the receiver, which causes the felt-like material in the receiver to vibrate at the same amplitude and frequency as the fluctuation in the electrical current (Figure 1.5). Air molecules surrounding the felt-like material are set in sympathetic motion. Anything near the air molecules, such as our eardrums, vibrates at the same rate, enabling us to hear the voice over the telephone.

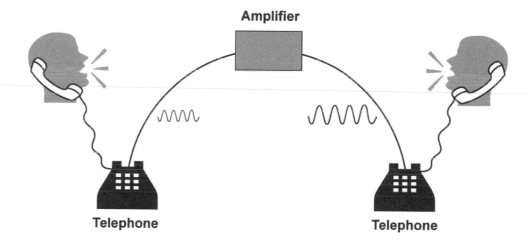

Figure 1.5
The mouth portion of a telephone handset acts like a microphone.
(Redrawn with permission from Prentice Hall. Comer, Douglas E. The Internet Book. Englewood Cliffs, NJ: Prentice Hall, 1997, p. 19.)

Telephones are connected to a network of cables to form the telephone network. Each telephone is connected to the network and is identified by a unique number that we know as the telephone number.

Tech Talk

Network: An interconnection of devices to form a pathway on which to exchange a signal encoded with information.

The Tale of the Number

Demand for telephones outpaced the telephone company's ability to assign each telephone a unique number. Until the 1960s, customers were offered the option of a private telephone number or one shared with other customers. These were known as a private line and a party line, respectively. Of course, a private line cost more and there was a waiting period until someone else surrendered a telephone number.

Tech Talk

Party Line: This is similar to today's extension telephone except the extensions were located in different houses.

A call made to a party line could be answered by anyone whose phone was assigned the same number as the number that was called. You can imagine the conflicts that arose from such arrangements. Only one party could use the line at a time. Others who shared the same telephone number waited until the line was free. However, this didn't prevent anyone with the same number from listening into another's phone conversation. The telephone company reassigned the eavesdropper to another party line to resolve conflicts.

The patience of people who used party lines gradually wore thin and the telephone company found it necessary to derive a permanent solution to the problem by redesigning the telephone network into many smaller networks linked together into larger networks. This is the same concept that is used today with computer networks.

A small telephone network is called an exchange, which is represented by the first three digits of your telephone number. Every exchange can have 10,000 unique telephone numbers from 0000 through 9999.

Tech Talk

Telephone Exchange: A subnetwork of the telephone network used to connect telephones located within the same area.

Whenever an exchange exhausted unique telephone numbers, the telephone company created a new exchange. Until the 1980s, most customers had one telephone per household, so the demand for telephone numbers stabilized when population growth stabilized. However, demand once again increased in the 1980s when customers requested a second telephone line, called a teen line.

Tech Talk

Teen Line: A second telephone number assigned to a household typically used by teenage family members and used to reduce competition to use the family's main telephone number.

Another growth in demand for telephone numbers occurred in the 1990s when customers wanted additional telephone lines for their computers so they could surf the Internet. The telephone company kept pace with demand by using the time-proven method of dividing the telephone network into more exchanges.

The vast number of exchanges are held together by a sophisticated series of switches that route a call to the proper telephone. The technique is straightforward. A telephone call begins with a caller dialing a telephone number. The first three digits indicate the exchange and the last four digits represent the number of the telephone within the exchange.

Each exchange has at least one switch. The telephone number is sent to the switch in the caller's exchange. The switch determines if the exchange of the incoming call is the same as the caller's or different.

If the call is made to a telephone within the exchange, then the switch reads the last four digits and connects the caller to the proper telephone. However, a different exchange will cause the switch to retransmit the call to a larger, regional network, which relays the call to the proper exchange (Figure 1.6).

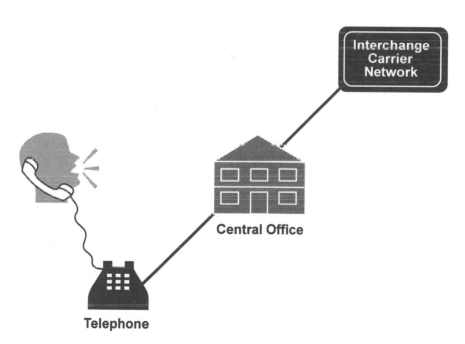

Figure 1.6
The local exchange connects telephones to the long distance telephone network. (Redrawn with permission from Prentice Hall. Dodd, Annabel Z. The Essential Guide to Telecommunications. Upper Saddle River, NJ: Prentice Hall, 2000, p. 97.)

Techniques used to organize the telephone network into subnetworks are carried over to computer networks. Computer networks are also divided into subnetworks, connected with various switch-like devices, which you'll learn about later in this book.

You're on the Air

The telegraph and telephone networks opened a new world of communications that enabled communities to grow beyond the distance they could see and the distance their voices could travel. The same goes for the nation's economy.

Yet there was still one major hurdle that hindered free flow of communication: a cable. A cable was the electronic pipeline that delivered words across vast lands. Telegraph sets, then later telephone sets, that were connected to cable could tap into the words transmitted over the network. But without a cable there couldn't be long-distance communications.

Economics played a crucial role in the expansion of the communications network. Telegraph and telephone companies were willing to lay cable to a community only if they benefitted economically from the installation. That is, a community needed to be a center for business before any thought was given to bringing the network to that community.

Communities lacking commerce were left without access to the network and therefore without modern means of communication. Likewise, communities surrounded by natural barriers, such as rivers and oceans, that inhibited cable installation also couldn't take advantage of the new media.

These barriers were overcome with a new technology called radio, developed by Guglielmo Marconi. Radio was able to transmit and receive sound without using cable. It seemed miraculous at the time—and even today. Stop and think: radio in your home receives sound created in a far-off land without any cable connection.

Radio isn't a miracle, but is instead based on science and the wave phenomenon used in telephone technology. Before trying to understand how radio is able to transmit and receive information over the air, you need to closely explore the wave phenomenon.

As discussed earlier in this chapter, waves are measured in height called the amplitude, and the number of waves per second are called the wave's frequency. Waves are also categorized by frequency in the electromagnetic spectrum (Figure 1.7).

Tech Talk

Electromagnetic spectrum: organizes frequencies of waves into ranges called a spectrum. For example, sound as we know it is actually a spectrum within the electromagnetic spectrum. That is, sound is a range of frequencies that our ears can detect.

Waves within each spectrum have similar characteristics. Sound waves can be heard over short distances that are not obstructed by solid objects. Radio waves cannot be heard but can be transmitted over longer distances and are not normally affected by solid objects such as a wall. You'll learn more about the electromagnetic spectrum later in this book when you explore wireless networks.

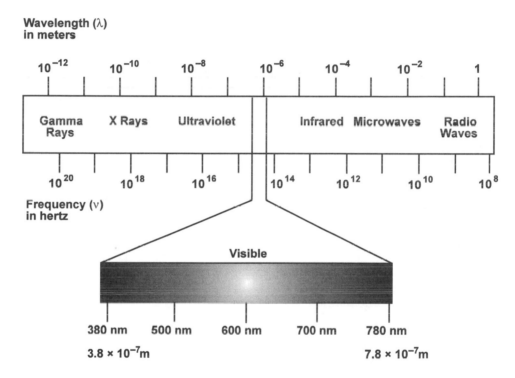

Figure 1.7
Frequencies of waves are categorized in the electomagnetic spectrum. (Redrawn with permission from Prentice Hall. Brown, Bursten LeMay. *Chemistry: The Central Science*, 8th ed. Upper Saddle River, NJ: Prentice Hall, 1999. p.156.)

Marconi's challenge was four-fold: capture sound, encode the sound on radio waves, broadcast the radio waves over long distances, then translate the radio waves back to sound. If this could be accomplished, then communication would no longer be limited to the length of a cable.

The technology for converting sound to an electrical signal and an electrical signal back to sound was known and used in the early telephone system. A microphone translates sound to electricity and a speaker translates electricity to sound. However, the frequency to transmit the signal over a cable wasn't in the radio spectrum. This meant the signal couldn't be transmitted over the air.

Radio transmission requires a signal be generated at a specific frequency within the radio spectrum and transmitted over the air to a radio receiver tuned to the same frequency. Marconi had to find a way to vibrate an object at a radio frequency. The solution was found in nature in the form of a crystal.

Tech Talk

Crystal: A chemical formation of molecules in a distinct pattern. (Salt is a crystal that we come in contact with every day.) When certain crystals are charged with electricity, the crystal vibrates at a consistent frequency and some vibrate within the radio spectrum.

Air molecules around the crystal vibrate sympathetically, similar to the way our vocal cords vibrate the air. And similar to our voice, the distance over which the signal can travel depends on the energy used to generate the signal.

Our lungs provide the energy for our voices. The more air that is forced through our vocal cords, the farther our voice travels. Electricity provides the power for radio waves. Therefore, the more electrical power used to cause the crystal to vibrate, the farther the signal will travel through the air.

Radio transmission also requires an invisible cable that information can travel over. The invisible cable is called a carrier signal, which is the frequency generated by the crystal.

Tech Talk

Carrier Signal: A radio signal that is transmitted at a consistent frequency used to establish a connection with a radio receiver.

Sound is transmitted over the carrier signal by circuitry that changes a characteristic of the carrier signal. This concept is difficult to appreciate, but imagine a still pond. If you vibrate a stick in the water at a consistent frequency, you'll notice a steady frequency of waves in the water that correlate to the movement of the stick. This is similar to a carrier wave (Figure 1.8).

A person at the other end of the pond notices the consistency of the waves. The height and frequency of the wave remains unchanged. Now imagine that you place information on the wave. Both of you agree that everything is fine as long as the height of the wave remains the same. However, help is required if the wave height increases. You can increase the height of the wave and still maintain the wave's frequency by using more power when vibrating the stick. The same number of waves per second occurs, but each wave is taller than the original wave.

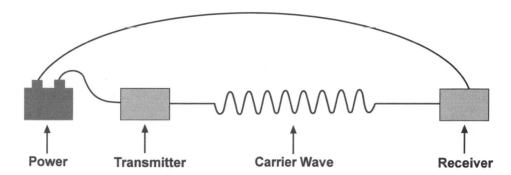

Figure 1.8
A carrier wave is a signal that maintains a communication link when information is transmitted.

    The same basic concept used in the pond example occurs with radio transmission. Both the transmitter and the receiver are set to a specific frequency. The transmitter opens the communication channel by sending a carrier wave. Circuitry in the transmitter modifies the carrier wave based on the sound received by a microphone.

    Circuitry in the receiver is able to differentiate between the carrier wave and the modified carrier wave and translates the difference into the transmitted information. The signal containing the information is sent to the speaker so sound can be reproduced (Figure 1.9).

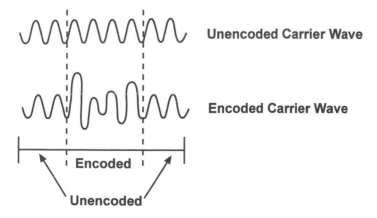

Figure 1.9
Transmitted information is the difference between the carrier wave and the transmitted wave.

Distance and terrain limit radio transmissions. Likewise, there are practical limitations as to how far a message can be broadcast. For example, there is a limit to the amount of energy that can be used to transmit the radio signal. Technicians were able to overcome this problem by linking radio stations to form a network of stations.

Cable and relay stations networked radio stations. A relay station is known as a repeater. The retransmission process strengthens the signal so the transmission can be received at a greater distance. This concept common in radio technology is also used in computer networks to transmit computer data a great distance over cables and over the air, as you'll see later in this book.

Tech Talk

Repeater: A device that receives a radio signal from a distance radio station, then retransmits the signal to other repeaters and radio stations. Retransmission introduces new energy to power the signal for longer distances.

Television

Shortly before World War II, scientists were able use enhanced radio transmission technology to send pictures into living rooms around the world. We call this television. Television plays a critical role in the history of networks and computers since television technology is used in computer monitors.

Images on a television screen are composed of a series of tiny dots similar to the way photographs are printed in the newspaper. Hold a magnifying glass up close to a newspaper photograph and you'll notice that the picture is really a group of dots. As you hold the picture farther away from you, the dots seem to disappear and trick your mind into seeing an image.

Tech Talk

Pixels: Picture elements used to create an image on a television screen.

Pixels are created by a stream of electrons fired from an electron gun located at the back of the monitor that hit a coating on the back of the picture tube. When an electron connects with the coating, energy from the electron causes the coating to glow. This is similar to a dot that makes up a printed picture.

Electrons are tiny and cause only a tiny portion of the coating to glow, giving the appearance of a dot on the screen. As the electron gun zigzags across and down the screen, the glow remains visible until the electron gun retraces its path back to that position.

The glow isn't like a light bulb that remains lit until the power is turned off. Instead, the glow immediately begins to dissipate once the electron gun moves on. However, the glow remains visible long enough for the electron gun to return to the position.

Scientists had the challenge of controlling the firing of the electron gun. If they could meet the challenge, then the technology used to print pictures could be used to display pictures on a television screen.

Scientists turned to radio technology for the solution. Characteristics of a radio wave could be encoded to send a signal to a receiver to fire the electron gun. Once the electron gun was fired, a dot appeared on the television screen. Nothing would appear if the gun wasn't fired. By properly encoding the transmission of the television signal, a scientist could broadcast a picture to distant receivers.

But how could an image be encoded into a radio wave? The answer came with the invention of the television camera. Circuitry in the television camera scanned an image in the same sequence as the electron gun in the monitor that moves across and down the screen. The image captured by the camera is reproduced on the television screen by circuitry that controls the firing of the electron gun (Figure 1.10).

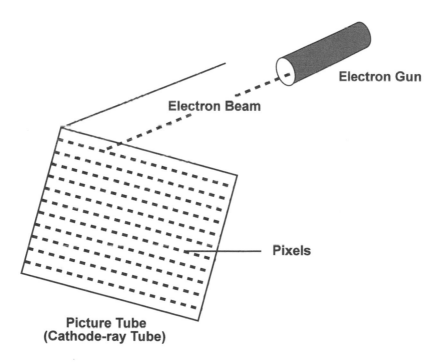

Figure 1.10
An electronic gun in the rear of the cathode-ray tube shoots a stream of electrons, causing pixels to appear on the screen.

Tech Talk

Scanning: A method of dividing an image into a series of pixels, each of which are encoded into a radio wave.

Radio waves provided the means to transmit the television signal and range in frequency from 10 kilohertz to 300,000 megahertz. However, those signals could interfere with radio broadcast. The Federal Communications Commission (FCC) assigned a new range of waves for television broadcast. This is called the television spectrum.

Tech Talk

Hertz: One complete cycle of a wave.
Kilohertz: 1,000 Hertz.
Megahertz: A million Hertz.

The television spectrum, like the radio spectrum, is limited by the distance the signal can be transmitted and by terrain. If you're located beyond the range of the television transmitter, or a mountain range sits between your television set and the transmitter, then you are not able to receive the broadcast.

Technicians overcame these limitations by creating a television network. Although the term television network conjures thoughts of companies such as NBC, ABC, and CBS, the term actually refers to a communication channel that transmits a signal over long distances.

Tech Talk

Communication channel: An electronic pathway over which a signal travels, similar to a highway.

Television networks created a communication channel using repeater technology similar to that used to create a radio network. A television repeater is a receiver and transmitter that is placed at the fringe of the transmission range of the television broadcast signal. The repeater receives the broadcast signal then retransmits it, thereby increasing the range of the broadcast in a similar manner to technology used to form a radio network. This enables a broadcast signal to be transmitted across the country by using a series of repeaters to form the network.

By the late 1940s, corporations recognized the commercial viability of television technology. The Federal government, through the FCC, regulated the industry by issuing broadcasters assigned frequencies within the television spectrum and areas of the country within which they could broadcast their television signal. These regulations reduced the likelihood that signals would interfere with each other.

Each broadcaster was responsible for creating television programs. As the industry matured, broadcasters such as NBC shared their programming with other television stations. In the first days of television, all broadcasts were live and were distributed to affiliated television stations using a repeater network to form their television network. Today's television networks still use repeaters along with other technology, such as satellites and cable networks, which we'll explore later in this book.

The Hidden Network

You probably realize by now that a network consists of two or more devices linked electronically to exchange a signal. Telegraph, telephone, radio, and television are examples of networks. However, there is another kind of network that is invisible to most of us. This is the network used to connect components inside our computers.

A computer is a black box—or maybe green or orange if you have an IMac. It is a box of wizardry that seems to baffle most people. However, computers are not complicated to understand because they are composed of a handful of components:

- the CPU, which is the brain of the computer

- memory, where information is stored temporarily until the computer is turned off

- the monitor, where images are displayed

- the keyboard and mouse, used to input information

- the hard disk drive, where information is stored permanently

- devices such as a printer, a scanner, a modem, a network connection, and even a camera

Components are linked by thin wires etched into the circuit board. The group of etched wires is called a bus. You can think of the bus as the telegraph and telephone cables or the broadcast signal of a radio or television station. The bus forms the network inside the PC.

Tech Talk

Bus: A collection of wires etched into a circuit board used to transmit information among electronic components.

The design of the PC's internal network took a cue from historical mainframe computers, which required a room to hold similar components. In a sense we can say that the old mainframe computer room is similar in functionality to the main circuit board, called the motherboard, in today's PCs.

The CPU of the old mainframes consisted of circuits within a four-foot or so square cabinet. Memory, disk drives, and other components were stored in table-sized cabinets within the computer room with each of these devices linked with cables, much like the bus in today's PCs.

Information is stored and processed inside a computer as digital information, similar in concept to Morse Code used in the telegraph network. However, instead of assigning a series of dots and dashes to each character of the alphabet, each character is signified by a combination of eight zeroes and/or ones. This is called ASCII code, which is discussed in the next chapter.

A switch can represent one or zero, and is called a binary value. Imagine a light switch. If the switch is off, so is the light. We can say this represents a zero value. Turn the switch on and the light goes on. We can say this represents a one value. Now assemble a set of eight light switches and you can represent any character on the computer keyboard by following ASCII code and setting each switch on or off to represent the character you want to transmit.

THE NUMBERING SYSTEM

You've probably heard the term "binary" used whenever anyone talks about the zeros and ones used to represent data inside a computer. Binary refers to a mathematical system used to count and perform math.

Let's take the mystery out of binary math by first reviewing our common system of mathematics, called the decimal system. Our system contains ten digits (zero through nine), which is referred to as base 10 because there are ten digits before we must carry over a value.

When we reach the ninth digit, we carry over one value, which gives us the value 10. Notice the right-most digit is zero, the digit we started with. We count sequentially and when we reach 19—notice the right-most digit is nine—we carry over another value to give us 20.

A similar process occurs within the binary system, except the binary system contains only two digits: zero and one. Counting begins with zero just like in the decimal system, but a value is carried over when the value reaches two because there isn't a digit two in the binary system.

Let's say we wanted to write the value two in decimal. We simply use the digit 2. However, we'd write 10 to represent the same value in binary. No, this is not the 10 that we know, although it resembles the value 10 in decimal.

Here's how it works. We begin counting with zero. Remember, this is binary so we must stop counting when the right-most digit reaches one, then carry over a value and reset the right digit to zero.

Don't feel embarrassed if you are confused by binary math. This baffles even computer science majors until they become used to dealing with the concept of using two digits instead of ten. However, there is a reason computer scientists settled on binary math when dealing with computers.

Computers manipulate information by performing addition and subtraction on data stored inside the computer. Remember, data is represented by a setting of eight switches and each switch can be on or off. Sometimes more than eight switches are used, but don't concern yourself with that now; for illustrative purposes, let's assume there are just eight.

Binary math lends itself to representing the state of a switch and enables standard mathematical operations to be performed on those values. You can perform the same math using binary values that can be performed using our decimal values.

Let's see if you can solve this problem. How would you determine if the letter A is the same as the letter Z? Computers need to do this kind of operation daily when determining if you entered the correct password to log onto the network. Computers recognize only numbers and not letters.

The answer lies with binary math and subtraction. Inside the computer, both the letter A and Z are represented by the settings of two sets of eight switches and each switch is called a bit, the state of which is represented as zero or one.

The computer subtracts the first bit of Z from the first bit of A. If the result is zero, then both bits are the same. If the result is not zero, then the bits are different. This same process is followed for all eight bits of each letter. If at the end of the process the result is zero, then the letters are the same; otherwise they are different.

Someone could code information into switches by manually turning the switches on and off, but this isn't practical. So scientists developed an electronic switch that can be set using electricity.

The vacuum tube was the first electronic switch. A vacuum tube resembles a light bulb and has two wires passing through it. The first wire carries the electricity throughout the computer. This is similar to the wire that powers the light in our light switch example. The second wire activates the switch.

When electricity is sent over the second wire, the vacuum tube permits electricity to flow over the first wire. This is similar to turning on the light switch. Electricity stops flowing over the first wire when electricity is removed from the second wire of the vacuum tube, which turns off the switch (Figure 1.11).

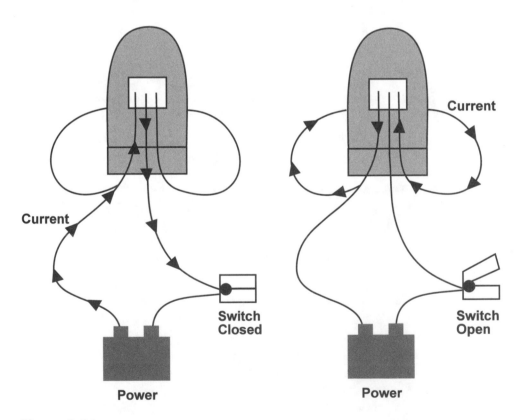

Figure 1.11
A vacuum tube acts like a switch by changing the flow of current based on the flow of a second current.

Eight vacuum tubes were required to store one character, and the number of vacuum tubes that could be linked was limited only by physical considerations. Vacuum tubes took up space, required a substantial amount of power, and generated a great deal of heat.

Bell Labs scientists overcame these limitations with the discovery of the transistor. A transistor uses basically the same concept as a vacuum tube to control the flow of electricity over a wire. However, instead of using a vacuum tube, a sandwich of solid material provided the same conductivity power as the elements of a vacuum tube. Transistors takes up much less room, use less power, and very little heat compared to a vacuum tube.

The size of electronic switches continued to drop. Transistors were replaced by integrated circuits that contain thousands of tiny transistors stored on circuitry the size of a pinhead. We know this today as a computer chip.

Tech Talk

Integrated circuit: A network of transistors connected by microscopic wires similar to a bus inside the computer. It uses the same basic concept used by mainframe computers to link together microscopic components built into circuits on the chip.

In the telephone, a unique number identifies each telephone set. Likewise, each component connected to the bus has a unique address. Using a specific address accesses information within the computer or on the integrated circuit.

Let's say a character represented by ones and zeros is stored in a specific memory location. The memory location is a set of eight electronic switches, each of which has an address on the bus. Information travels along the bus to the specific memory location where the state of the switches is changed to reflect the ones and zeros used to represent the character.

Basically, the same technique is used to receive information from a keyboard, a mouse, and a modem, and to send information to a monitor, a disk drive, a printer, or store it in memory.

The Mainframe Connection

Big clunky mainframe computers were the first computers to have electronic devices talk to each other. Mainframe components are the ancestors of components inside of today's personal computers and were large boxes of circuits housed in an environmentally controlled room. The boxes were connected by cables running beneath the floor.

Terminals were used to access the mainframe computer. At first glance, terminals connected to a mainframe appears similar to personal computer networks that currently dot the office landscape. However, there are important technical differences that make today's networks far more flexible than mainframe terminals were decades ago.

Tech Talk

Terminal: Sometimes called a dumb terminal, a terminal consisted of a monitor and a keyboard, which could be placed anywhere in the building. A cable from the terminal ran to a connector box inside the computer room to form a primitive computer network.

Although a mainframe terminal resembles a personal compuer, it lacks most of the computer's technology. The brain of a computer is the central processing unit (CPU). This is what reads information from the keyboard, stores information in memory, and processes information.

Early terminals did not have a CPU. Instead, a terminal used the mainframe's CPU in the computer room to handle all the processing. The only purpose of a terminal was to capture keystrokes from the keyboard and to display characters sent from components inside the computer room. All programs, data storage, and data processing took place inside the computer room and not inside the terminal.

Each terminal was assigned a terminal ID, which was treated as a port within the computer. This is similar to a component address on the bus within a PC. Software running on the mainframe kept track of ports, and information was received from the terminals. Once the mainframe processed the information , the results were sent to the corresponding port and back to the terminal.

Using terminals to communicate with a mainframe computer greatly broadened the accessibility to computer power throughout an office complex. Until then, requests were made to technicians in the computer room, who then used punch cards, paper tapes, keyboards, and monitors to process the requests.

Computers Talking to Computers

With the onset of the Altair, the first personal computer, companies like Apple Computer and IBM moved computing from large, custom-made rooms affordable only to major corporations, to the desktop.

It wasn't until the early 1980s that corporations began to embrace the concept of having computers on employees' desks. Personal computers still were not proven to be effective office tools and many corporate executives saw this new gizmo as an expensive calculator. At $2,000 each, it didn't seem economical to place a computer on every desk in the organization.

All this changed with two "killer" applications: spreadsheet and word processor programs. The cost-effectiveness of the computer became obvious. However, unlike a calculator and a typewriter, special equipment was required to print documents created on a personal computer. In addition to buying a computer, executives found it nec essary to buy a printer. Having a printer on every desk wasn't economical, especially since printers stay idle most of the time. Engineers seized this opportunity to link many computers to one printer. This was the birth of the computer network as we know it today.

A switch in the form of a "black box" was developed to connect cables from computers and a printer. At first, the switch was designed to share a printer among two computers. This was called an A-B switch (Figure 1.12). One computer was designated A and the other B. A dial on the switch was manually turned to the A position when computer A wanted to use the printer. Similarly, the B position was selected when computer B wanted to print.

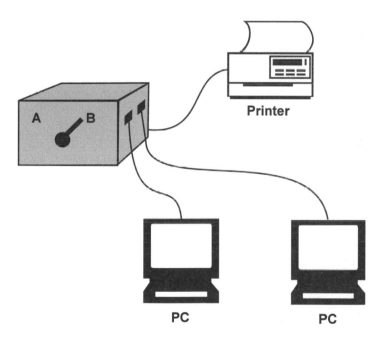

Figure 1.12
An A-B box enables two computers to share the same printer.

Sharing a printer between two computers was the forerunner of PC networks. The economy of sharing a printer became evident to the business community, which demanded more efficiency in sharing printer resources.

....

SERIAL AND PARALLEL COMMUNICATION

We take for granted printing a document from our PC, yet a complex process takes place that resembles cars moving along the highway at rush hour. Here's a look behind the scenes.

A document that is to be printed is stored in the PC's memory. When you give the order to print a document, each character of the document must travel along the bus inside the computer to the printer interface circuit, then over the printer cable to the printer, where the electronic representation of the character is turned into a printed character.

Remember, a character is stored in memory as a set of eight switches set to zeroes and ones. Therefore, these eight pieces of information must all complete the transfer from memory to the printer before the character is printed on paper.

You can think of these eight values as cars trying to travel a highway to get home. The highway inside the computer is the bus and has at least eight lanes (etched wires), one lane for each value. This means all eight cars travel the full length of the highway at the same speed and reach their destination at the same time. This is called parallel transmission. The destination in this case is the circuitry that interfaces the PC with the printer.

The printer interface circuit is like a crossroads to the printer. Among other things, the interface circuit determines if the cars continue to travel to the printer in their own lanes or merge into a single lane. The highway to the printer is the printer cable, which can have at least eight wires (one for each bit) or a single wire, which must be shared by each bit.

In the early days of PC printers, eight wires were used in the printer cable to transport each bit. This was known as a parallel cable. As transmission speeds and reliability increased, manufacturers used serial cables. A serial cable is like a single lane highway where each bit has to wait for the previous bit to be transmitted before embarking on its journey to the printer.

Although conceptually serial printing appears to be less efficient than parallel printing, technology advancements ensured the same results regardless if serial or parallel transmission was used. Serial transmission also provided economical savings for equipment manufacturers since fewer wires were necessary to create a printer cable.

Technicians created an A-B-C switch in response to this demand. The A-B-C switch enabled three computers to share a printer by turning a dial on the switch to the desired computer. Soon, manually switching among computers was replaced by circuitry that queued documents from any computer that was connected to the switch.

Tech Talk

Queuing documents: Similar to standing on line at the checkout counter. The first person in line is served first while others wait their turn. That is, the first document the switch receives is the first document printed.

As documents were sent to the switch, circuitry within the switch stored the documents in memory within the switch. Other circuitry removed documents from memory and sent them to the printer. Computer users no longer needed to manually change the switch or conflict with others who wanted to print documents at the same time. The electronic printer switch broke ground for today's printer server, which we'll discuss later in this book.

THE HIDDEN NETWORK OF DATA STORAGE ....

Storing information was limited in the early days of the personal computer. The first PCs could store information only in memory, which reset automatically when the computer was powered off. This meant all the information (programs and data) were lost and needed to be re-entered.

PCs weren't the only computers that had storage problems. Mainframe computers also lacked the capability to store information electronically when they were shut down. In the 1950s, programs and data were stored on punch cards and on paper tape by using carefully placed holes, which were translated into bits by the computer.

Magnetic tape soon became the medium of choice for storing data and programs off-line. Magnetic tape was coated with iron oxide. Bits were encoded by magnetizing the iron oxide with a powerful electronic magnet. The magnetized portions of the tape were deciphered by circuitry.

Tech Talk

Iron oxide: A chemical compound that contains elements of iron that retain a magnetic charge over long time periods.

Early PCs, such as the Radio Shack TRS-80, used a tape recorder and audiotape to store data and programs. However, this technology was suited for recording sound waves, but wasn't sufficiently developed to reliably store bits of data. Later, digital technology was used to record bits on tape.

THE DIGITAL RECORDED SIGNAL

Earlier in this chapter you learned how sound was transmitted by waves. Scientists attempted to encode digital information stored in a computer to an audiotape using analog technology, which is the same way sound is recorded. However, the circuitry interface between the PC and the tape recorder had difficulty determining if the wave represented a zero or a one.

Digital recording technology resolved this issue by reducing fluctuation in the height of the wave. That is, the wave is either a fixed height or it has no height. A flat wave clearly represented a zero and a wave of a fixed height represented a one (Figure 1.13).

Here's a way to appreciate the difference between analog and digital technology. Consider two light switches: one a toggle switch and the other a dimmer switch. A toggle switch turns the light on or off. There is no ambiguity of whether or not the light is on. This is similar to digital technology in which a one is represented when the light is on and a zero when the light is off.

Figure 1.13
A digital wave has two values: no height (considered zero) and height (considered one).

An inherent problem with both analog- and digital-tape storage was that information was stored and read sequentially. That is, if the data you wanted was stored midway on the tape, the PC had to read half the tape before reaching the data. While fast tape drives were developed, there was still need to store and retrieve data randomly.

Disk drives solved this problem. PCs used a rather large round piece of Mylar coated with iron oxide. This was called a floppy disk. The term floppy stems from the fact that the disk was pliable. Within reason, you could bend the disk without damaging the information stored on the disk.

Etched onto the disk were concentric circles on which data was stored using technology similar to that used to store information on a magnetic tape. The operating system of the computer logically divided each circle into small storage areas called sectors. Each sector could hold a specific number of bytes. Each sector was networked together with a linked list.

Tech Talk

Operating system: Consists of software that interacts with all the hardware components to receive, process, and output information.

Let's say information to be stored on the disk contained 1,024 bytes. Let's also assume that each sector can hold 512 bytes. This means two sectors are necessary to store the information. The operating system identifies vacant sectors on the disk by using the disk's file allocation table. The file allocation table, also known as the FAT table, contains the location of used and unused sectors on the disk.

Tech Talk

FAT (file allocation table): Used to manage where files are stored on a disk.

The first 512 bytes are stored in the next available sector. Let's call this sector 1. The remaining bytes are stored in the next available sector. Let's call this sector 15. Notice that these sectors are not necessarily consecutive on the disk.

Information stored on the disk is identifiable by a name called the file name and is listed in the file directory on the disk. The file name is associated with the sector that contains the first 512 bytes. This is sector 1 in our example. Sector 1 also contains the sector number of the sector that contains the next 512 bytes of the file. Therefore, sector 1 points to sector 15 in our example.

This is known as a linked list, which is used to network related information randomly on a disk. There is no need to read all the sectors sequentially to locate information (Figure 1.14).

SENDING AND RECEIVING INFORMATION AMONG COMPUTERS.....................

The technical and business community recognized the need to share information among computers. However, there were still a few hurdles that needed to be overcome before a computer network could be created.

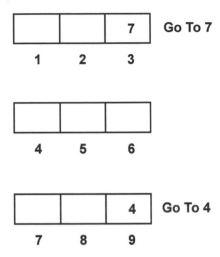

Figure 1.14
Items in a linked list identify the location of the next item on the list.

The earliest PC network linked computers and a printer through an electronic switch. This posed less of a challenge than networking computers together since information flowed in one direction: from a computer to the electronic switch.

Information in a PC network flows from a computer to any other computer on the network. The initial attempt to have computers communicate with each other was to use a modem and the telephone lines. Think of a modem as a telephone for the computer.

Each computer connected using a modem has a unique identifier known to us as a telephone number. The originator of the call dials the phone number of the remote computer using the modem to establish the connection. The remote computer's modem answers the call and follows rules called protocols to begin the transmission process.

Tech Talk
Protocol: A set of rules that determines the method that will be used to do a task, such as to send and receive information.

The protocol used to connect computers using a modem is much like the rules we use in a phone call. We greet the caller with a familiar greeting, which elicits an expected response. Through this process we also determine the way in which we communicate. For example, a conversation with a stranger will call for a more formal approach than with a friend. We'll take a closer look at protocols later in this book.

Once the connection is established, the remote computer signals that it is ready to receive information, and then waits for the information to be sent. The method in which most computers transmit information using a modem is called asynchronous communication.

Tech Talk

Asynchronous communication: Divides information into pieces and transmits each piece separately to the remote computer. The remote computer acknowledges each piece before the next piece is sent. The pieces are reassembled at the destination.

Another way to look at asynchronous communication is to imagine the technology used in walkie-talkies. The full message is broken into short sentences. A person speaks usually for a few seconds before pausing and waiting for the other person to acknowledge what has been said. Once acknowledged, the next few sentences of the message are transmitted.

Transmitting pieces of information over time rather than sending the entire information provides efficiency along the telephone network and reduces the likelihood of extended delays caused by miscommunication.

Let's say a 1,000-word document is transmitted to a remote computer using a modem. Instead of sending the document in several pieces, the whole document is sent as one piece. The remote computer, however, doesn't check the accuracy of the communication until the piece is received. If one character of the document is inaccurately received, then the entire document must be resent.

When the document is sent in pieces, only the piece that is received inaccurately is resent, thereby reducing the overall transmission time and freeing the telephone network to transmit information from other callers.

Linking computers by modems opened great possibilities for exchanging information between computers located across the hall or around the world. Yet a modem link required computers to be directly connected to the public telephone network. This was an expensive proposition for large organizations that had their own internal telephone network, called a Private Branch Exchange (PBX).

Tech Talk

Private Branch Exchange: A subnetwork of the telephone system that is privately owned by an organization. As mentioned previously in this chapter, the public telephone network is divided into smaller subnetworks called an exchange. Organizations save considerable money by having a private exchange that is linked to the telephone network.

Organizations had to purchase their own PBX equipment and in the early days of PCs, this was not compatible with modems. An organization that wanted to link computers had to buy regular telephone lines for each computer.

The Second Network

Demand drives development of technology, and that was the case with PC networks. Connecting computers using modems was cost-effective for linking remote computers, such as your home computer to your office computer. However, there needed to be a better way to communicate among computers within the same office.

Experience gained from the first networked computers used to share a printer combined with new technology provided a way to link computers without using modems. Instead, technicians devised a way to share information among computers by joining them with a cable.

This next stage in the evolution of a PC network enabled computers to store to and retrieve files from a central computer called a file server.

Tech Talk
File server: A dedicated computer on a computer network that is used to store files that are shared among computers connected to the network.

The same basic technology used to save to and retrieve information from a disk within a computer is used to share files using a file server. However, technicians had to address new issues, such as:

- How to link computers and the file server
- How to have computers built by various manufacturers access the file server
- How to avoid communications conflicts if two computers attempted to access the file server at the same time

Tech Talk
Contention: When two or more computers attempt to access a network resource at the same time.

New technology had to be developed to meet these challenges. Technicians focused on three components: a network circuit board, cabling, and a network operating system (Figure 1.15).

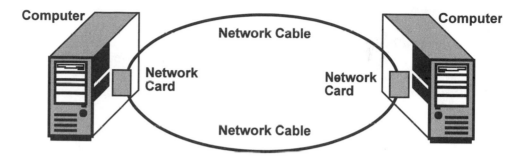

Figure 1.15
The networking system uses cable to connect to each computer's
network card.

A network circuit board called a network card provided the extension of the bus inside the computer to the network. Think of the network card like the on and off ramp from the local streets to the highway.

Cabling is the electronic highway connecting computers with the file server and the early PC networks used the same type of cable that connects your telephone to the telephone network. This is called twisted pair, which you'll learn more about later in this book.

Software was created to control the flow of information over the network. This is called the network operating system. The network operating system functions similarly to the operating system inside your computer (i.e., Windows™) in that the operating system gives life to the circuits and cables.

The network operating system was divided into two components. There was software on each computer that handled communications between the network and the computers and software on the file server that controlled the operation of the network.

The forerunner of today's computer networks lacked many of the features that we find common place today, such as e-mail. The network's sole purpose was to become a shared hard disk. Network software on the computer made the file server appear as another disk drive. For example, the local floppy drive was designated as drive A. The local hard disk was drive C. The network file server might be designated drive D. The user used the letter of the drive to access the file server just as he would access the local floppy and hard disk drives.

Behind the Scenes

Much was taking place behind the scenes. The personal compouter operating system, which was DOS or Applesoft in those days, had to recognize that the D drive was really a call to invoke the network software on the computer. Once invoked, the network software used the network card to begin communications with the network software on the file server.

A protocol was followed much like a protocol used to have two computers communicate using modems and the telephone network. In a general sense, here is what takes place when a user selects drive D, the network file server. The PC operating system sends a signal within the computer to wake up the network software. The message is simple: "Get up. It's your turn to do some work for a change."

The network software on the PC takes over and sends a message to the file server network software asking the file server to send the PC a copy of file directory, which lists files and subdirectories. These are better known today as folders.

Network software on the file server is always listening for requests from any PC on the network as long as the file server is powered up. The file server must be prepared to respond to such requests as:

- Send a copy of a file to a PC.

- Save a file from a PC.

- Delete a file.

- Rename a file.

- Create and remove a subdirectory.

- Copy a file to another subdirectory on the file server.

These are meager requests by today's standards, but they were major achievements in the early days of PC networks. When the network software on the file server receives a request for a file, the file is sent along the network to the PC that requested the file. Network software on the PC listens for the response from the file server.

There are a number of responses that can be sent, some of which include a message saying the file is not found; here is the file; and an acknowledgement that a request such as to delete a file has been successfully carried out.

The response from the network operating system is translated by the PC-side network software into a message that is understood by the PC's operating system. The PC's operating system then displays a corresponding message on the screen.

Let's return to the initial request to display the file server's directory on the PC screen (Figure 1.16). Typically, a person selects the network driver, which we'll call the E: drive. This is the cue to request the file server's directory, a copy of which is sent over the network and displayed on the screen. Any file commands, such as to copy or delete a file, that are prefaced by E: causes the command in the form of a request to be sent to the file servers.

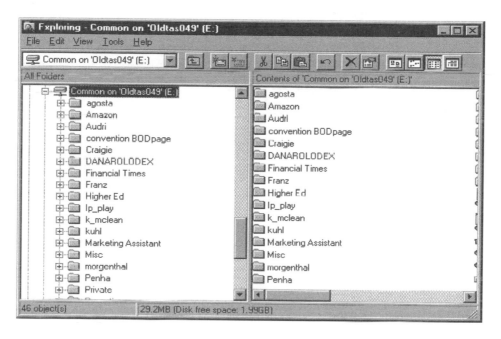

Figure 1.16
The file server's directory on the PC screen.

The network operating system is able to avoid misdirecting requests and files in much the same way as telephone calls are routed to the proper telephone. That is, each ·computer on the network, including the file server, has a unique network address. This is like their telephone number.

Unique addresses were assigned in the early PC networks by making minor adjustments to the network card in each computer. Every request and response transmitted over the network carried two network addresses. One was the address of the PC that made the request and the other the destination address. A combination of the circuitry in the network card and the network software on each PC and file server was used to read the addresses in the request and response.

The Internet

The U.S. Department of Defense and associated research universities and contractors had a need to share information over long distances rather than to use telephones or the U.S. Postal Service. Since the information they wanted to share was stored inside computers, an idea was put forward to link these computers. We know this today as the Internet.

By now you realize the Internet is not owned by anyone, but instead is a cooperative effort by many organizations to share access to their computers with others. What started out purely as a communications vehicle to exchange information about defense-related research has blossomed into a world community.

Behind the concept of the Internet is a careful organization of computers. As with other networks explored in this chapter, each computer on the network is assigned a unique address called an IP address. IP stands for Internet Protocol, which will be discussed later in this book. The electronic highway that connects these computers is a segment of the telephone network. You can consider the IP address to be the special telephone number for the distant computer, commonly referred to as a remote computer.

The remote computer is called by using telnet, which is a program that calls the remote computer over the Internet. A caller is able to interact with the remote computer by using commands recognized by the telnet program. For example, the command Open followed by the remote computer's IP address initiates the call.

Tech Talk

telnet: A program used to connect a computer to a remote computer.

Not everyone can gain access to a remote computer even if an IP address is known. This is similar to calling your boss only to have the telephone answered by her assistant. The call is answered, but you must convince her assistant that your boss should speak with you.

The telnet program on the Internet calls the remote computer, but the remote computer presents you with a prompt, which is a kind of greeting. The prompt asks you for your ID and password.

The ID and password is compared with information in the password file stored on the remote computer. If there isn't a match, you are typically given two additional attempts to submit the correct information before the remote computer disconnects the call.

A match will grant you limited or unlimited access to the computer, depending on the permissions associated with your ID. You may be limited to certain files and directories on the computer or have the freedom to roam around the entire computer. We'll explore more about permissions later in this book.

There was a lack of continuity among computers on the early Internet. After a successful log-in, a user might be presented with a menu of options or an operating system prompt. This is similar to opening an MS-DOS Prompt window in Windows, in which the prompt waits for you to enter the proper command.

Tech Talk

Log-in: The process by which a remote computer or network operating system grants or rejects access to resources.
FTP (File Transfer Protocol): A program that uses the file transfer protocol to transfer files to and from computers over a network.

Files on a remote computer can be shared with other computers by using another program called FTP, which is File Transfer Protocol. The FTP program enables someone to connect and log-in to a remote computer, then use FTP commands to copy a file from the remote computer to the person's local computer. The FTP program, however, limits activities to changing directories on the remote computer and copying or deleting files. For example, the FTP `Put` command copies a file from the local computer to the remote computer and the FTP `Get` command reverses this process.

The telnet and FTP programs gave the user the feeling that the remote computer was her computer. That is, she could run and interact with programs on the remote computer just as if she was sitting in front of her local computer.

The freedom to share information by accessing remote computers on the Internet drew the attention of corporations and universities that were not associated with the U.S. Department of Defense.

As the Internet grew, so did the development of Internet programs. Programs were developed to meet new demands of Internet users, which included electronic mail and Gofer, which is a program that searched computers on the Internet for search criteria a user entered.

The World Wide Web

The Internet joined many computers throughout the world, but something was missing: the ease with which to locate and access information on those computers. Although programs such as telnet and FTP opened a remote computer to the world, the organization that maintained the computer had the freedom to organize the computer any way they deemed fit.

There was a need for a uniform presentation of information on all Internet computers. Tim Berners-Lee filled this need by creating the World Wide Web (WWW).

There is a difference between the Internet and the World Wide Web. In general, we can say the Internet provides the raw means to link computers, and the World Wide Web is a standardized way of accessing content on those computers.

When someone connects to a computer through the Web, they are presented with a page called a home page without having to log on to the computer. The early home pages contained textual information only. There were no pictures or animation. Text appeared in two forms: standard text similar to text created using a word processor, and underlined text called hypertext.

Early hypertext was like a door that opened another page, which is called a hyperlink. When a person selected hypertext, the computer displayed a different page on the screen. This is a common activity today for anyone who uses the Web, but this was a revolutionary concept when the Web was introduced to the Internet.

Hypertext enabled information to be organized in a hierarchical arrangement similar to an organization of a book in which the beginning chapter generalized information that is covered in more detail in later chapters. However, books use indexes and reference marks (i.e., "see page 43 for more information") to show the reader where to find more detailed information about a topic.

No reference is made when using hypertext. Instead, the link to the additional information is encoded in the hypertext. That is, hypertext is smart enough to know the location of the referenced material and to display the material when the hypertext is selected.

The concept of hypertext revolutionized the way information was used on the Internet. You no longer needed to memorize commands to navigate inside a remote computer. Instead, all you needed was a program capable of reading a hypertext document. This program is called a browser.

A hypertext document is created using a language called HyperText Markup Language (HTML). HTML uses tags to identify how standard text is to be displayed. A tag contains instructions that a browser understands. Embedded within the tag is text and hyperlinks. Just as the Internet networks computers, HTML is used to network documents.

The Internet and the World Wide Web lived quietly out of the public eye until the 1990s, when entrepreneurs began to commercialize the Web into the information and electronic commerce services that we know today. Many organizations have adopted Internet technology to run their networks, which are called Intranets.

SUMMARY ....

We take for granted the ease with which we transmit information using a computer. Our thoughts can travel to the ends of the earth in the fraction of a second that it takes to click a mouse button. Yet this marvel of the 20th century has deep technological roots dating back 500 years.

Early in the first millennium, mathematicians devised the binary numbering system that became the foundation of modern computer networks. The discovery of electricity, electromagnetism, and cabling formed the first primitive communications network called the telegraph.

The study of waves and the discovery of devices to convert one wave form into another, such as sound to electrical waves, brought networks into the home in the form of the telephone.

Further studies in waves and the discovery of the electromagnetic spectrum replaced cables with airwaves and transmitted sound and pictures using radio and television waves. Broadcast stations joined together and shared radio and television programming through radio and television networks, which used a combination of cable and the airwaves to transmit their signal.

Computer networks use technology perfected by the telegraph, telephone, radio, and television networks to transmit information in a digital format using binary math to process the information. Information is composed of alphabetical characters and symbols that are encoded into eight switches by using the ASCII code.

The setting of each switch is represented by a zero or a one, which is transmitted to computers devices such as the CPU, memory, disk and tape drives, a printer, and a monitor. These components were large during the early days of the mainframe computer and were linked by cables to form a network of computer devices.

PCs required the same components, but the size of these devices was greatly reduced to fit on a large circuit board within the PC cabinet. Instead of using a cable, these devices were connected using wires etched into the circuit board.

Demand to share resources among PCs grew in the late 1990s. This brought about the forerunner of the first PC network in which two or more PCs shared the same printer. The small printer network showed that information could be shared among computer devices, and an all-out effort was made to devise a way for PCs to share information.

The early solution came with the development of the modem, which linked two PCs using the public telephone network. Information was easily exchanged between computers, but the modem link was costly since each PC required a private telephone number.

The business community demanded that a mechanism be developed that would enable a group of PCs to share information over the same cable without the use of the public telephone network. The PC network was born and met this demand. The early PC network linked PCs, one of which was a file server. The file server acted as a depository for files that could be shared among PCs on the network. This became the forerunner of today's PC networks.

In the next chapter you'll learn the basic concept needed to understand how networks operate.

Summary Questions

1. How does Morse Code used in the telegraph network compare with the ASCII code used in PC networks?

2. How is digital information encoded in a wave?

3. What is the difference between parallel and serial transmission?

4. Describe the sequence of events that occur when a PC connects to a remote PC using a modem connection.

5. What is the difference between binary- and decimal-based numbers?

6. Explain the difference between the Internet and an Intranet.

7. What is the difference between the Internet and the World Wide Web?

8. How does hypertext create a network of documents?

9. What are the limitations of a file server network?

10. What are the limitations of the original printer network?

2 Networks: Basic Concepts

In this chapter...

When you write an e-mail, characters that you enter into the keyboard are convert-ed into zeroes and ones, which are the only characters that a computer understands. The e-mail is placed in an electronic envelope and shipped over a network. After the e-mail reaches its destination, the electronic envelope is opened and the zeroes and ones are converted back into the message that you typed.

This process might seem imposing, but the concept is easy to understand and is explained in this chapter. In this chapter you'll learn:

- the difference between analog and digital technology

- the concept of bits and bytes

- how your thoughts are converted to bits

- how your thoughts are transmitted over a network

- about transmission speeds

REALITY CHECK ....

Computers do little more than perform addition and subtraction, which you and I can do using the time-tested method adopted by the corner grocer; that is, by using a pen-cil and a brown paper bag—the grocer's calculator. However, computers perform these calculations a million times faster than us and would leave you and me in the dust in a head-to-head competition.

What seems amazing is how scientists and technicians are able to use basic arithmetic to manipulate data and send it around the globe in a fraction of a second.

Here's the challenge. Using only numbers, addition, and subtraction, devise a way to capture and store words and numbers, then send this information to a remote computer. Impossible, you're thinking. My friends thought long and hard and still ha-ven't arrived at an answer. Yet, we know there is a way to combine these three simple elements into an elaborate scheme to process information.

We'll spend the next few pages demystifying this complex system of electronics and show you how scientists are able to use numbers, addition, and subtraction to create a computer network.

ANALOG AND DIGITAL....................................

Analog. Digital. By now these terms sound as familiar to you as floppy disk and CD. By reading advertisements for stereos, you probably have the impression that digital is much better than analog. But do you know why this is true?

Digital technology is the foundation of every computer. However, computer networks use both analog and digital technologies to transmit and receive information over a network. These technologies are similar in that information is encoded into a signal, but they differ in the way information is represented.

Tech Talk

**Analog technology: Uses a variation of values to store information.
Digital technically: Uses one of two values to store information.**

The best way to see the difference between analog and digital technology is to picture electricity. We tend to imagine electricity as something invisible that flows over wires. This is true; however, by passing electricity through a device called an oscilloscope, we can see a presentation of the electrical wave.

Tech Talk

An oscilloscope: Similar to a computer monitor in that an electron gun fires electrons at the back of a picture tube. The inside of the picture tube is coated with material that glows when struck by an electron. This creates an image on the screen. The image can be characters and pictures as in the case of a computer monitor and television. However, the oscilloscope uses the same technology to depict an electrical wave.

Electricity flows over wires as long as the wire isn't broken. The flow is controlled by breaking the wire with a switch, such as a light switch, which we learned in our school days. You can see this effect by using an oscilloscope. The line takes on a shape when electricity flows. The actual shape is dependent on the amount of electricity that flows over the wire. A flat line is displayed when electricity doesn't flow (Figure 2.1). This is similar to the image on a heart monitor. Most of us have seen medical television shows that show the heart monitor flatline when a patient dies.

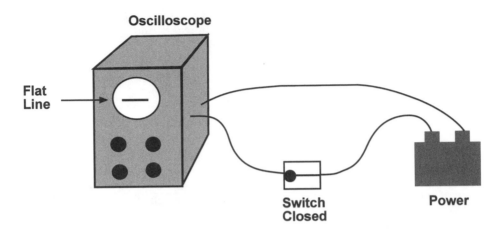

Figure 2.1
A flat line appears on an oscilloscope when no current flows in the circuit.

Let's say a dimmer switch is used to control the flow. The amount of electricity fluctuates depending on the turning of the dimmer switch. This is represented on an oscilloscope as a fluctuating line. The height of the line reflects the amount of electricity that is passing over the wire. Since the amount varies by turning the dimmer switch, a wave forms on the oscilloscope (Figure 2.2).

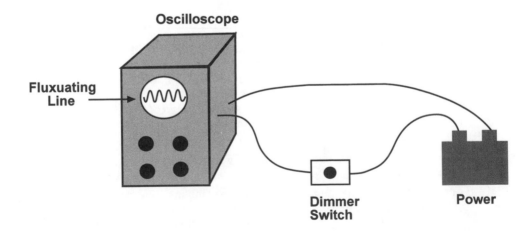

Figure 2.2
Rotating a dimmer switch fluctuates the current and causes a wave to appear on the oscilloscope.

Digital technology can also be pictured using electricity and an oscilloscope. Let's say you use a toggle light switch to control electricity. Unlike a dimmer switch, a toggle light switch enables the full amount of electricity or no electricity to flow.

As with the dimmer switch example, a flat line is displayed on the oscilloscope when the toggle switch is open. However, the line jumps to the full height when the toggle switch is closed. A square wave forms on the oscilloscope when the toggle switch is opened and closed quickly (Figure 2.3).

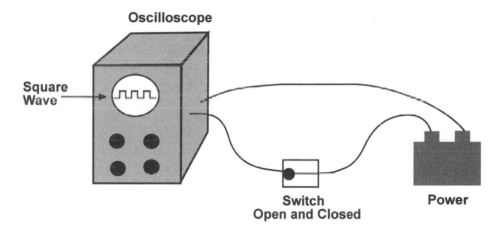

Figure 2.3
Opening and closing a toggle switch in a circuit causes a square wave to appear on the oscilloscope.

Why is digital technology considered by many to be superior to analog technology? The answer lies with the signal's clarity. Both analog and digital technologies are used to transmit information and both use circuitry to encode and decode information onto the signal. However, analog technology introduces ambiguity into the communication.

Tech Talk

**A signal: the transmission of electrical waves that carries information.
Encode: a method used to translate our words into a form that can be carried by a signal.
Decode: a method used to translate information carried on a signal back to our words.**

An analog signal, such as those used to broadcast a radio program, encodes information by varying the value of the signal, as discussed in the previous chapter. The receiver must be able to distinguish these values to properly decode the information carried by the signal. However, a receiver could become confused if the variation of the value conflicts with signals sent by other transmitters. You've likely noticed this when your telephone—especially cordless phone—picks up a signal from a radio station.

In contrast, a digital signal has only two values to encode and decode. That is, the signal is either at the maximum height or it is not. There is a lesser chance that the receiver will misinterpret the message with a digital signal than by using analog technology.

Bits and Bytes

Digital technology provides a way to signal one of two values. For example, a light is either on or off. However, by itself this is useless unless someone assigns a meaning to each value.

Let's say a friend is coming to visit but she doesn't know which house is yours. Both of you agree that you'll turn on the light in front of your house. You have encoded a message—"This is my house"—by turning the light on, and your friend can decode the message because you both agreed on the encryption method.

Tech Talk
Encryption method: a way of encoding information.

Engineers obviously don't use light switches inside a computer. Instead, submicroscopic electronic switches, called transistors, are used to control the flow of electricity in much the same way the toggle switch is used to control the light. You recognize electronic switches as chips found on the circuit board inside your computer. Actually, there are millions of these switches contained on one chip.

Tech Talk
Transistor: a sandwich of two elements that contains two circuits. If electricity flows through the first circuit, then no electricity flows through the second. If electricity does not flow through the first circuit, then electricity does flow through the second (Figure 2.4). Chip technology reduced the size of a transistor from a small, bug-like device to a submicroscopic piece etched into a chip.

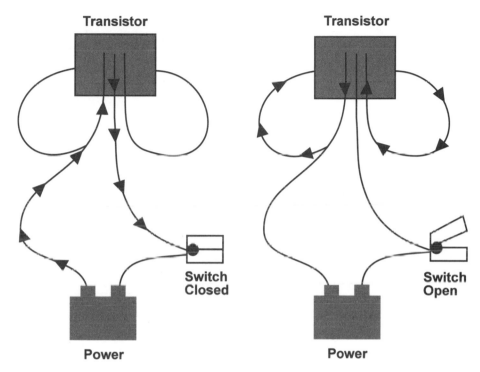

Figure 2.4
A transistor controls the flow of current in a circuit by the flow of another
current on another circuit.

Each electronic switch is activated by a flow of electricity on the circuit board,
which is controlled by other electronic switches. To clarify, imagine a maze of these
switches. The setting of one switch depends on the settings of one of many switches.

Engineers applied the binary numbering system as a way to assign a meaning to
the settings of each switch: on or off (1 or 0, respectively). Figure 2.5 illustrates the
basics of the binary numbering system.

Tech Talk

**A number system: defines the way in which we count. We use the
decimal system to count. This is called a base 10 system because there
are 10 digits—zero through nine. Once we exceed the last digit, we
carry over one value one place and begin counting from zero. So after
nine, a one is placed in the next position and we begin over with zero in
the first position. You and I recognize this as the number 10.**

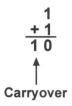

Carryover

Figure 2.5
Adding two binary ones carries over one value, similar to adding a decimal one to a nine.

CONVERT FROM DECIMAL TO BINARY THE EASY WAY

Understanding numbering systems confuses even freshmen computer science majors. However, if you're intrigued by numbering systems, use the calculator supplied by Windows to explore common numberings systems. Follow these steps:

1. Select the Start button, then choose Programs, then Accessories.

2. Choose Calculator. The calculator appears in standard view, so you'll need to change the view to scientific. Select View from the menu bar, then Scientific. You'll notice that the calculator displays more buttons.

3. You'll see a set of radio buttons beginning with Hex. These represent various kinds of numbering systems. Hex is hexadecimal, which has 16 digits. Dec is decimal, which is the default selection. Oct is octal, which has eight digits. Bin is binary.

4. Enter 2 on the calculator. The number 2 appears as a decimal value on the calculator.

5. Click Bin and you'll notice that the decimal value 2 is automatically converted to the binary value of 2, which appears as the number 10.

Besides being a convenient way to represent the state of a switch, the binary numbering system also provides a mechanism to manipulate the settings. That is, binary values can be added and subtracted similarly to how we perform math using decimal values. Binary numbers can be used to perform any mathematical and logical operations.

Tech Talk

A logical operation: a method used to compare two settings and answers such questions as, "Do switch A and switch B have the same settings?" You see this technique used when someone tries to find your information inside a computer by searching for your Social Security Number.

Freshmen computer science majors are commonly asked "How could you determine if the settings of two switches are the same if you could only use addition or subtraction?" Sounds like a tough brainteaser, but the answer is simple: You subtract the values.

Here's how it works. Let's say switch A is on and switch B is off. Using the binary numbering system, we can restate this by saying switch A has a value of one and switch B a value of zero. We can perform arithmetic using binary numbers.

If we subtract the value of both switches and the result is zero, then the switches have the same settings. If the result is not zero, then the switches have different settings. Electrical engineers devised circuitry inside the computer to perform the math.

You can imagine the power that logical operations have on computing. For example, subtraction enables the computer to make a decision. Simply said, if switch A and switch B have the same settings, then execute instruction X; otherwise, execute instruction Y.

Tech Talk

An instruction: a series of commands written in a programming language that is executed in sequence, typically in the form of a computer program.
A programming language: consists of a set of words and symbols that can be translated into machine language, which a computer can understand.

Each switch is assigned an address that uniquely identifies its location inside the computer. This is similar to a house address. Circuitry within the computer is able to locate and turn any switch on or off within a fraction of a second.

Let's take a look behind the scenes and see the instructions that are necessary to determine if the values of two switches are the same. Instructions are contained in a program, but for this example we'll write the program using English rather than a fancy programming language. Assume that switch A is assigned address zero and switch B is assigned address one. Here is the program that determines if the setting of both switches is the same (Figure 2.6).

1. **Go to address 0**
2. **Read the value of address 0**
3. **Go to address 1**
4. **Read the value of address 1**
5. **Subtract the value of address 0 and address 1**
6. **If the result is 0, then display, "the settings are the same"**
7. **If the result is not 0, then display, "the settings are not the same"**

Figure 2.6
Instructions compare the value of two switches.

Grouping Switches

The state of a switch can represent two pieces of information: one when a switch is on and the other when it is off. We can store two numbers in a switch using binary numbers. That is, using a 0 and a 1.

Obviously, this is limiting. However, by logically combining two switches, we can store four numbers: 0 and 1 for each switch. Grouping three switches enables us to store eight numbers and referencing eight switches together increases the value that can be stored to 256.

The term "logically grouping switches" might seem baffling at first because electronic switches inside a computer are tangible. Although you're unable to see the switches, millions of them are etched into computer chips connected to the motherboard of a computer. This seems more like a physical grouping than a logical one.

Imagine a series of eight light bulbs and switches. An open switch (light is off) is a binary 0 and a closed switch (light is on) is a binary 1. If you look at one of the bulbs and it is on, you assume a binary value of 1.

Now imagine looking at two bulbs, both of which are on. This time, you assume a binary value of 11 (not eleven, but one one), which is the maximum value that can be stored in two light bulbs. Physically there are two light bulbs, but logically we are relating them together as a set.

Likewise, electronic switches are physically inside a computer, but a computer program logically looks at two or more of them to create a set. Engineers call each switch a bit and a group of eight bits is a byte. A byte can represent a value of 256 and two bytes a value of 65,536.

Convert Your Thoughts to Bits

One byte is sufficient to represent any whole number from 0 to 255. This means a computer could add 5 and 10 to arrive at a sum of 15. However, adding 1 to 255 causes a problem. The result is 256, which is beyond the values that a byte can represent.

Another problem arises when a calculation involves negative numbers. And we cannot ignore the problem posed by fractional numbers, numbers to the right of the decimal. Neither negative numbers nor partial numbers can be represented in a byte that can hold a maximum of 256 whole numbers.

Engineers were faced with three problems:

1. How to represent whole numbers larger than 255
2. How to represent negative whole numbers
3. How to represent fractional numbers

The first problem is easily resolved by grouping more than one byte together to represent the number. Negative numbers posed another challenge. Somehow engineers needed to represent the sign of the number and the number itself within a byte.

The solution is to make one bit of the byte represent the sign and use the seven remaining bits to represent the number. This enables 127 positive and 126 negative numbers to be represented by a byte. Combining bytes can represent larger and smaller (negative) numbers.

Finally, we use a decimal point or a comma, depending on local convention, to represent fractional numbers. Engineers solved this problem by changing the meaning of other bits to indicate the position of the decimal point. One group of bits represents a number and another group of bits indicates the position of the decimal within the number.

Let's say we want to use the number 123.45. One set of bits represents 12345. Notice there isn't a decimal point. Another set of bits represents two, which implies the decimal is two places from the right.

Before a program manipulates values (i.e., adds or subtracts), it determines if each value is an unsigned number, signed number, or contains a fraction. This ensures that the results are calculated properly and represented in memory.

ASCII

If all our communication dealt in numbers, encoding numerical meaning to switches within the computer would suffice. However, we use words and numbers in our communication, so engineers needed to devise a way to represent all of these characters on the keyboard—and some not shown on the keyboard—into switches inside the computer.

A new standard called ASCII (Figure 2.7) was created to meet this challenge. As discussed briefly in the previous chapter, each character is assigned a value from 0 to 255, which enables a byte to be used to represent 256 characters.

S **= 0101 0011**
M **= 0100 1101**
I **= 0100 1001**
T **= 0101 0100**
H **= 0100 1000**

Figure 2.7
The ASCII code translates characters to bytes.

The computer operating system translates each keystroke from the keyboard into the corresponding settings of switches in a byte. The operating system also interprets these switch settings into characters, which are displayed on the screen.

HIDDEN CHARACTERS

The ASCII code assigns characters that appear on the keyboard (called printable characters) and some that do not (called nonprintable characters) to 1 of the 256 values represented by a byte. These are sometimes called hidden or nonprintable characters because they don't appear on the keyboard, in text displayed on the screen, or printed on paper. Hidden characters are used to represent the end of a line character; the carriage feed character, and a tab character, among others.

Text entered using a word processor seems to wrap around lines on the screen until we press the Enter key, which causes the cursor to jump to the next line. Each character entered from the keyboard is encoded into an electronic switch in memory. Word wrap is performed by the word processor and has nothing to do with bytes. Before displaying the character on the screen, the word processor performs a calculation that determines if there is room on the line. If not, the cursor is moved to the beginning of the next line. This is called a soft line-feed and carriage-return because these characters are not stored in memory.

However, two characters are placed into memory when the Enter key is pressed. These characters are called the line-feed character and the carriage-return character, and they are referred to as hard line-feed and carriage-return because these characters become part of the text.

The concept of line-feed and carriage-return originates from typewriters and days of the Teletype. A Teletype was the forerunner of the telegraph machine. Instead of sending dots and dashes like the telegraph (see Chapter 1), signals were sent along the telegraph wires to cause a keyboard character to be printed on a remote Teletype machine, which was similar to a typewriter.

Among other signals, there was a signal to move the printer down to the next line (line-feed) and another signal to move the printer to the beginning of the next line (carriage-return).

The tab character too is an invisible character held over from the Teletype days. A tab character implied that the typist wanted to begin the next character a standard number of characters in from the beginning of the line of text. However, the tab character didn't explicitly indicate the number of characters to indent. Instead, the Teletype (or today the program) reading the text determined the actual tab position.

Now most word processors use their own hidden characters to format text. These are called format characters, which are not necessarily identified by the ASCII code. Some ASCII characters are used to send a special code to devices, such as a printer, to turn on and off features, such as font. These are called controlled characters.

TRANSMITTING YOUR THOUGHTS ....

As we write a message using a word processing program, our keystrokes are converted by the operating system into switch settings in memory, which are echoed onto the computer monitor.

Switch settings can be saved to a disk and stored in a file (see Chapter 1), then reloaded back into memory anytime we need to access the information. The same characters can be sent over a cable to a distant computer.

Both digital and analog technology is used to move a signal from one computer to another. Each bit that represents information is encoded into an electrical signal generated by a network card located inside a computer. You'll learn more about the other activities a network card performs later in this book.

Tech Talk

The network card: consists of circuitry that, among other things, takes information from memory and encodes it into a signal that is transmitted over the network cable.

There are two methods used to transmit the network signal. These are baseband and broadband. The best way to understand these terms is to envision a highway. A single-lane highway enables one car at a time to travel in the same direction. This is similar to baseband technology. However, a multi-lane highway enables more than one car to travel at the same time. This is similar to broadband technology.

Tech Talk

Baseband technology: one bit at a time is transmitted on a digital signal.
Broadband technology: multiple bits are transmitted at the same time on an analog signal.

Baseband transmission uses digital technology to distribute information. As discussed previously in this chapter, the signal is either there or it isn't in a digitally encoded signal, and it appears as a square wave on an oscilloscope.

There are two disadvantages of baseband transmission. First, a bit of information at a time can be transmitted over the cable, which could affect the time it takes to transmit information. There are many variables involved with transmission speed other than the kind of transmission technology selected for communication. You'll learn more about these factors later in this book.

The other problem is the distance over which a baseband signal can travel. Baseband technology transmits a shorter distance than broadband technology and must use repeaters to amplify the signal.

Tech Talk

Repeater: a device that receives a network signal, then retransmits the signal giving it a boost in power.

Broadband uses analog technology that is digitally encoded with information. Information is encoded into analog technology in the form of a sine wave. A sine wave begins on the baseline then moves to a height determined by the electronic power used to transmit the wave. As the power fluctuates, the sine wave returns to the baseline, then continues to a height below the baseline (Figure 2.8).

Figure 2.8
A sine wave travels above and below a baseline.

A common way to encode a bit onto a sine wave is to adjust the fluctuation in the transmission signal. Power is measured in voltage or micro-voltage depending on the size of the circuit. For example, a +5 voltage, which is the height of the wave above the baseline, might represent a binary 1, and a –5 voltage, which is the height of the wave below the baseline, might represent a binary 0.

Broadband technology enables multiple signals to flow over the network at the same time and for a greater distance than baseband technology. Each signal is transmitted on its own frequency, called a channel, so as not to interfere with other signals. This is similar to how radio and television signals are broadcast (see Chapter 1).

Tech Talk

A frequency: the number of complete sine waves that occur within a second.
A complete sine wave: a wave that has flowed from the baseline through its positive and negative heights, then returns to the baseline.

INTERFERENCE

You've probably experienced the problem of a stray radio signal interfering with your favorite radio station. This is frustrating, to say the least, and there is little you could do to remedy the situation. The same phenomenon occurs with broadband technology.

Like a radio receiver, the network card is also a receiver that is designed to receive a specific signal. The network cable can pick up stray signals and transmit them to network cards across the network, which can disrupt the success of the transmission.

As you'll see later in this book, precautions are taken to insulate the network cable from stray signals. Furthermore, steps are taken to ensure that signals purposely transmitted over the network use frequencies different enough from other signals to avoid interference.

Measuring Transmission Speed

In the days before the telegraph, sending a message from one U.S. coast to the other required a week or so of riding by a series of pony express riders. The speed of transmitting the message was measured in days, which was acceptable until the telegraph became popular. Telegraph messages were received minutes after they were sent. The coded message actually arrived within seconds, but the telegraph operator had to decipher the Morse Code.

Today, even seconds seem too long to wait to receive a message, because we judge acceptability of communication by our experience and compare all forms of communication to the fastest form that we know, which, for most of us, could be surfing cable television.

I was once preparing for a television appearance with an interviewer, who said that we had about four minutes on the air. She pointed out that we needed to change the slant on the topic almost every 5 to 10 seconds if we were to attract the most people. Apparently, television producers found that 5 to 10 seconds is the length of a viewer's attention span before he or she clicks to another channel.

Most of us inadvertently apply the cable television expectation to a computer network. That is, a response more than about 10 seconds creates frustration. However, there isn't another channel to switch to, so we tend to speak in unpleasant terms to the computer.

Network engineers determined two critical factors that influence information transmission. These are the size of the message being transmitted and the number of communication channels that can be used to transmit the information.

Tech Talk
Communications channel: a pathway used to transmit information.

The size of the message is one of the critical factors in transmission. For example, the amount of pages that could be sent by pony express is limited by the space available in the mail pouch. By comparison, only a few words were transmitted by the telegraph because of the labor-intensive process needed to translate and decipher the telegraph signal.

The size of the message is also a factor in transmitting information over a computer network. The first computer networks were expected to transmit characters. Today's networks are expected to send and receive sound, pictures, and animation at the same speed as our words are transmitted. However, sound and graphics require more bits to be transmitted than words.

Engineers devised a method to reduce the number of bits that are necessary to represent information transmitted over a network. This technique is called compression.

Tech Talk

Compression: a technique for reducing the number of bits to represent information.

There are many compression techniques used—too many to list here. However, we'll explore one of the first compression techniques to illustrate the concept. The objective of a compression technique is to shrink the number of bits that need to be sent over the network by removing repeating bits and indicating the number of times the bit is repeated. Instead of encoding five binary 1 values, the compression method encodes that the binary 1 value is repeated five times. The destination computer then decodes the information and expands the message back to its original number of bits.

The speed at which bits are transmitted is measured in a baud rate. You probably heard the term baud rate used in reference to modems. There are a number of standard baud rates; the most common today is 56 KB, which is 56,000 bits per second.

There are two common misconceptions about baud rate. The first is that the baud rate identifies the number of characters that can be transmitted per second. You could divide 56,000 by eight and estimate that 7,000 characters are sent per second. This seems a logical conclusion because eight bits represent a character; however, bits that represent those characters are compressed. Therefore, more than 7,000 characters are transmitted each second.

Tech Talk

Baud rate: the number of bits that can be transmitted per second.

The other misconception is that the transmission speed is always at the highest speed available. That is, a 56 KB modem always transmits 56,000 bits per second. This is not true. When a modem dials another modem, communication software at both modems negotiates and agrees on the speed of the communication. Modems automatically adjust to the highest common speed, which is the highest baud rate of the slower of the two modems.

Let's say that you use a 56 KB modem, but the remote computer uses a 9.6 KB modem. Your modem can slow itself down to 9.6 KB. However, the 9.6 KB modem, which is likely to be an older modem, cannot increase its speed beyond its maximum.

The other critical factor affecting transmission is the number of communication channels available to transmit a message. For example, a modem uses a telephone line, which is a single communication channel. That is, one bit at a time is transmitted.

The number of communication channels available for transmission is referred to as a network's bandwidth. Networks with larger bandwidth can transmit more bits at the same time across the network. The size of the bandwidth is limited by various hardware components that comprise a network, which are discussed later in this book.

Tech Talk

Bandwidth: the number of communication channels available to transmit information across the network.

Sending and Receiving Information Over a Network

Moving information from inside the computer and across a network is a complex operation, especially when you consider the obstacles. Engineers needed to design a process that followed strict rules yet remained flexible to work with various applications and on different kinds of hardware, such as computers, routers, and other network devices (these are discussed later in this book).

And to further complicate the situation, engineers needed to make each process independent, yet able to communicate with each other. This ensured that network components could be enhanced without re-engineering other components.

Sending information across a network begins when an application running on a computer makes a request for a network resource, such as a file server used to store a file. Practically any application, such as a word processor, can make such a request.

Tech Talk

A network resource: any device or file available on a network. This includes file server, printers, modems, and other such devices.

Network software that runs on a computer makes network resources appear as if they are local to the computer. For example, a file server might appear as the I drive similar to how the local C drive appears.

A request for a network resource must be translated into a format that is recognized by the network operating system. Let's say that you want to save a word processing document to the file server. You select File/Save As from the menu bar, then choose the letter of the drive.

Your request causes network software on your computer to change the format of the document from a word processing document to a format required by the network operating system to send the document to the file server. During this process, the documents might be compressed (see "Measuring Transmission Speed" on page 58) and encrypted for security concerns.

Next, a session must be established with the network. You can think of a session as the process of initiating the conversation and determining whether or not your computer has security rights to access the network resource. Assuming you pass security clearance, then your document is placed within one or multiple packets.

Tech Talk

A packet: an electronic envelope that contains the address of the destination network resource, the address of the computer making the request, and either all or a piece of the request along with information that controls the packet.

LOGICAL AND PHYSICAL ADDRESSES

Every computer and resource on a network is identified by two addresses similar to addresses you and I use to identify the location of a friend's house. These addresses are called the logical and physical addresses.

Let's say my wife asks me to stop by our friend Bob's house on the way home to pick up a package. All I need to know is that it's Bob's house because I already know how to get there. So in this example, "Bob's house" is the logical address, which is a name we'd recognized that relates to a real address.

However, I might ask my father-in-law to pick up the package. He doesn't know where Bob lives, so I give him the address: 121 Maple Street. This is the physical address of Bob's house.

Every device on a network is assigned a physical address, which is encoded in the network interface card (sometimes referred to as the network card). This is the circuitry that physically connects a device to the network.

As you will see later in this book, many networks enable the network administrator (the technician who runs the network) to assign logical addresses to a device. For example, a network printer might be identified as "NetPrinter 1."

A file contains both the logical and physical addresses. If a request contains a logical address, network software searches the file for the logical address, then assigns the corresponding physical address to the packet that contains the request.

Let's say you want to save a memo that contains 2,560 characters. Engineers could send all of these characters plus the address and control characters to one packet, then transmit the packet across the network. However, unnecessary delays could occur if an error is detected in the transmission, in which case the packet must be retransmitted.

This is like having a busload of friends going on vacation and the bus driver leaves someone standing at the bus station. Everyone on the bus must return to pick up the missing person.

A much better approach for the friends is to divide into several cars. That way, if someone is left behind, only one carload of friends has to return to pick up the person. The others can continue toward their destination. This is basically the technique used to transmit the memo over the network.

Instead of stuffing the entire memo into a single packet, engineers developed software that divides a document into smaller packets. In our example, five packets of 512 characters can be used to transport the memo. If an error is detected, only the packet that contains the error is retransmitted.

There is information other than the characters of the document stored in every packet. There is the destination address, the originator's address, sequencing information, and error detection information (Figure 2.9).

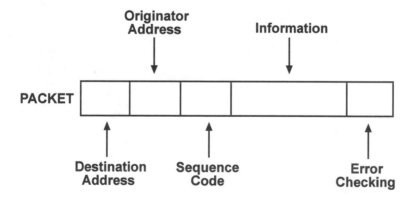

Figure 2.9
A packet is an electronic envelope containing data and information needed to send the packet to its destination.

Every pack contains the physical address of the network resource (i.e., file server) that is to receive the information and the physical address of the network resource (i.e., computer) that sent the packet. This enables both resources to communicate with each other during the transmission process.

Since the information that is being transmitted is divided into more than one packet, engineers devised a way to track the order of the packet. This is referred to sequencing.

Tech Talk
Sequencing: a method that tracks the order of packets.

Every packet has a sequencing number that enables the destination resource to reassemble information contained in the packets. You can think of this as numbering every car in the caravan of friends headed for vacation so that every car can be accounted for when they reach their destination.

Error checking is critical to successful network transmission. Although we tend to assume messages are transmitted reliably, this can be deceiving because we only see the results of successful transmissions. Retransmissions of packets are hidden from us.

Tech Talk
Retransmission: the process of resending a packet because the destination network resource suspects the data within it is corrupted.
Cyclic Redundancy Check (CRC): used to determine whether errors occurred in transmission.

Engineers came up with a method to have network software determine the likelihood that an error occurred in transmission. This method is called Cyclic Redundancy Check (CRC). The name might sound imposing, but the concept is easy to understand.

Remember that packets contain only binary values that are encoded into an electronic signal. Therefore, a packet contains a series of zeros and ones. It would be nice if network software could read the words in our information to determine if it was transmitted in its entirety, but that's not the case.

The next best thing is to perform a calculation using the binary values contained in the packet, then store the result in the packet. Software on the destination resource performs the same calculation and compares the result with the result stored in the packet. If the results are the same, an assumption is made that the information was received intact. If the results are different, then an error is suspected and a request is made to retransmit the packet.

When packets are received successfully, the process reverses. Address and control information are stripped from each packet and pieces of information are reassembled into the complete document. The document is then expanded if it was compressed and deciphered if it was encrypted. The original format of the document is restored and the document is ready to be read (i.e., by the word processor).

Open Systems Interconnect Reference (OSI) Model

Technology used for computer networks has always changed as new and improved methods for transmitting information are developed. The problem confronting network engineers was how to create a framework for network communication without imposing rules that would hinder the growth of network technology.

The solution to this problem was to create a set of rules that divided network communication into several processes, then determine the protocols (rules) that govern how each process communicates with other processes. This set of rules was developed in 1977 by the International Standards Organization and is called the Open Systems Interconnect (OSI) Reference Model. At the same time, the Institute of Electrical and Electronics Engineers (IEEE) was developing standards for the network interface card and the physical connection. Their efforts resulted in Project 802, which enhanced the OSI Reference Model.

OSI divided network communications processes into seven components called layers. Every layer consists of protocols for communicating with the preceding and succeeding layer. That is, layer four knows the rules for communicating with layers three and five.

Software and hardware manufacturers are able to create new and improved network components without fear of being incompatible with existing networks. As long as the new component is able to read and send information using existing protocols, the new component will be compatible with existing network components.

Each OSI layer corresponds to steps in the network transmission process.

Layer one is called the physical layer and is responsible for translating bits into signals that are transmitted over the network. This layer also converts incoming signals into bits. The physical layer is used in conjunction with repeaters, hubs, connectors, network cards, transceivers, and cables, (which are explored later in this book), and determines the signaling method (i.e., baseband or broadband).

Layer two is called the data link layer, which sends bits to the physical layer and receives incoming bits from it. The data link layer groups data into frames. A frame is a form of packet. This layer ungroups data from a frame received from another network resource. It also handles error control and assigns the physical addresses of both the destination and originator resource and works in conjunction with a bridge, which is presented in later chapters.

IEEE's Project 802, which is discussed in more detail later in this book, created two sublayers beneath the data link layer. These are the logical link control sublayer, which is responsible for maintaining the link between two computers when they send data, and the Media Access Control sublayer (MAC), which allows the computers to take turns sending data on the network.

Layer three is the network layer and is responsible for defining the logical addresses of the destination and originator resource. The network layer works with routers, which you'll learn more about later.

Layer four is called the transport layer, which is responsible for creating and sequencing packets, acknowledging the receipt of packets, and handling retransmissions.

Layer five is the session layer. It opens and maintains a connection between the destination and originator resources and handles security issues for the communication.

Layer six is called the presentation layer. The presentation layer reformats data into the form required by the network and the application layer. It also handles data compression and encryption.

Layer seven is called the application layer, which handles the interface between applications running on the computer and the network.

The Working OSI Model

There is a practical side to the OSI Model. Computers that are connected to a network require communication software called a protocol stack, also known as a protocol suite. You can think of a protocol stack as seven programs, each of which handles an aspect of network communications. Each of these programs conforms to one of the seven OSI Model layers.

There are a number of different protocol stacks. These are the ISP/OSI protocol stack, TCP/IP (also know as the Internet protocol suite), Novell NetWare®, IBM's System Network Architecture (SNA), Microsoft's NetBEUI, and Apple's AppleTalk. Each of these is discussed in more detail later in this book.

Computers linked to the network must use the same protocol stack or they won't be able to understand each other. However, many computers today can run multiple protocol stacks at the same time.

Let's say you want to send an e-mail. You enter the e-mail into a program, such as Microsoft Outlook, which is called an application (see Table 2.1). Programmers who developed the e-mail program used special software called an application programming interface to send your e-mail to the applications layer of the protocol stack that is running on the computer.

Table 2.1   *Transmitting using the OSI Model*

Sending Layer	Action	Receiving Layer	Action
7. Application	Translate from application's format into an intermediary format	7. Application	Translates from the intermediary format into the application's format
6. Presentation	Encrypted Compressed	6. Presentation	Deciphered Expanded
5. Session	Begins session Verifies network permissions Inserts checkpoints Terminates session	5. Session	Removes checkpoints
4. Transport	Creates packets	4. Transport	Tracks packets Requests retransmission of packets Unpacks packets
3. Network	Converts the logical address to the physical address Determines the best route over the network to use to reach the destination	3. Network	Strips away addresses
2. Data Link	Places packets in network frames Sets the CRC Resends frames	2. Data Link	Determines if frame is addressed to that computer Determines if transmission errors occur Acknowledges receipt of frames Strips away the frame and CRC
1. Physical	Transmits frame	1. Physical	Receives frame

The application layer sends the e-mail to the presentation layer, where it is translated from the format your e-mail program understands to an intermediary, standard format. It is here that your e-mail is also encrypted and reduced in size using a technique called compression. This is the final format required to send the e-mail over the network.

When the e-mail is received, the presentation layer expands and deciphers it, returning the e-mail to the intermediary format. The application layer than translates the e-mail from the intermediary formation back to the format required by the e-mail program.

When sending an e-mail, the presentation layer sends the rearranged e-mail to the sessions layer. The sessions layer opens a session with the network and makes sure that you have permission to use the network.

Even the shortest e-mail is too long to be transmitted all at once over the network. Therefore, the protocol stack divides the e-mail into small pieces, called packets. However, before this happens the sessions layer inserts checkpoints into the e-mail. A checkpoint is like a number assigned to pieces of the e-mail.

Whenever the destination computer doesn't receive a piece of the e-mail correctly, a request is made to the sending computer to re-send the corrupted piece using the checkpoint to identify the piece. Later in this book you'll learn more about packets and how they are transmitted. Once transmission is completed, the sessions layer terminates the session.

The session layer passes your e-mail to the transport layer where it is divided into packets before being sent to the network layer. When the e-mail is received, the transport layer keeps track of the packets and requests any missing packets. Once all the packets are received, the transport layer unpacks information, reassembles the e-mail and passes the e-mail to the session layer, where the checkpoints are removed.

The transport layer sends packets that contain pieces of your e-mail to the network layer. The network layer places the destination and sender's address on the e-mail. This is where the logical address you entered into the e-mail is converted to the physical address.

The network layer is also where the best route over the network to the destination address is determined and the frame is modified accordingly. The network layer knows the fastest route based on network traffic, priority, and other technical factors.

The network layer passes the addressed packets to the data link layer, where packets are placed in a network frame, which is a slightly larger packet that contains error checking data. This is where the CRC is calculated and placed into the e-mail.

The transport layer is also the place in the protocol stack where acknowledgements of frames are sent and received between computers. If a frame is not acknowledged, it is re-sent over the network. The transport layer looks at all frames sent across the network and determines if a frame is addressed to its computer. If so, then the transport layer accepts the frame, otherwise the frame is ignored.

The data link layer sends the frame containing a piece of the e-mail to the physical layer where the frame is then sent over the network. The physical layer determines the physical media (i.e., cables) used to connect to the network and converts the e-mail into electrical signals.

SUMMARY ....

Information is transmitted over a computer network using both analog and digital technology. Analog technology involves a variation of values used to represent information. In contrast, digital technology uses two values.

A binary value is used to represent the value of a switch inside your computer. The switch consists of a sandwich of material that acts like a toggle switch and is controlled by other switches. The value 0 is assigned to the switch when it is open (e.g., light is off) and the value 1 when it is closed (e.g., light is on).

Each switch is considered a piece of information, called a bit. One bit is used to store one of two numeric values—0 or 1. This is limiting since a computer is required to store larger and smaller numbers. Engineers group bits together as a way to expand the amount of values that can be stored inside a computer. Typically, eight bits are grouped together and called a byte.

A byte can store any of 256 numbers from 0 to 255. However, positive and negative numbers from a −126 to 127 can be stored in a byte if one bit is used to represent the sign. Increasing the group size accommodates very large and small whole numbers. For example, two bytes can represent a whole number as large as 65,535. Decimal values are represented by storing the whole number and the position of the decimal within the whole number.

Each character entered into the keyboard is assigned a numeric value between 0 and 255 called an ASCII value, which is stored as a byte inside the computer. Characters and numbers that make up a message are joined with control information and sent over the network using either baseband or broadband technology.

Baseband technology transmits one bit at a time using a digital signal. This is similar to a single-lane highway. Broadband technology can transmit multiple bits at a time using an analog signal. This is similar to a multi-lane highway. Each bit travels at a unique frequency, which prevents multiple signals from interfering with each other. This is similar to radio and television broadcasts.

Transmission speed is measured as baud rate, which is the number of bits transmitted per second. There isn't a direct correlation between the size of the document transmitted and the baud rate because the document is reduced in size—called data compression—before transmission begins.

Engineers divide the transmission standards into seven steps called layers, which are based on specifications set forth in the OSI Model. This enables component manufacturers to improve upon existing designs without concern that the new component will be incompatible with existing network components.

Documents are divided into smaller units called packets. A packet is like an electronic envelope that contains the address of the designation device and the originator device as well as control data that ensures that packets are received correctly. The destination device opens packets and the information is reassembled.

Summary Questions

1. Name each layer in the OSI model.

2. How is digital data encoded in an analog signal?

3. How many bytes are used to represent the positive whole number 66,000?

4. How does data compression work?

5. What is the difference between a logical and a physical address?

6. How does a destination device know that a packet was received without errors?

7. How is information reassembled from packets?

8. How do two devices determine which baud rate to use for communication?

9. How does a stray signal interfere with network transmission?

10. How are hidden characters used in a document?

PUTTING IT ALL TOGETHER ....

Sending an e-mail is a rather simple task for you and me. However, a lot of science takes place behind the scenes as your computer and a communications software translates your words into an electronic signal and sends the e-mail over cables to its destination.

The program you use to write your e-mail ultimately passes your e-mail to communication software to begin its journey. Communication software, called a protocol suite, consists of seven components, each of which follow rules, called layers, established by the OSI Model. Every component knows how to communicate with the program before and after it in the communications process.

Your e-mail program passes your e-mail to the applications layer, which converts the e-mail from the format of the e-mail program to a standard intermediary format that can be used throughout the communication process.

The application layer passes your e-mail—now in the standard intermediary format—to the presentation layer, where the e-mail is encrypted and compressed before it is passed to the session layer.

The session layer begins the session with the destination computer, verifying that you have permission to access the network, and inserts checkpoints into your e-mail. Checkpoints are markers the network uses to identify pieces of your e-mail. Once the e-mail is transmitted, the session layer terminates the session.

The transport layer receives the e-mail from the session layer and divides it into pieces. It places the pieces into electronic envelopes called packets. Sending packets containing small amounts of information is more efficient than sending the entire e-mail in one large packet because this gives other computers the opportunity to use the network.

The network layer takes packets containing the e-mail from the transport layer and places the destination address in each packet. Then it determines the best route to use when sending the pack across the network.

Packets are sent from the network layer to the data link layer, where packets are placed into a frame, which is a format the network needs to transmit the packet. The data link layer also inserts the Cyclic Redundancy Check, which is used to determine if errors occur in transmission. Now your e-mail is ready to be transmitted. The physical layer receives the prepared frame from the data link layer, converts the e-mail into an electronic signal, and sends it over the network.

The e-mail is represented inside the computer as a unique series of bits, which is a binary digit that we recognize as a 0 or a 1. Each character in the e-mail is identified according to the ASCII code by eight bits, called a byte.

Each bit of your e-mail is encoded onto an electrical wave that flows over the network cables. An electronic wave is similar to a wave that results from tossing a rock in a still pond. A wave rises then returns to its starting point. The highest point the wave reaches over its starting point is called the height of the wave. The number of waves occurring within a second is called the wave's frequency.

A bit is encoded onto the wave by representing the value of the bit by the height of the wave. For example, we can say that a wave at its maximum height is equivalent to a 1, and a wave at its minimum height is equivalent to a 0.

By changing the voltage applied to the electricity over the network cable we can alter the height of the wave and therefore encode the electrical signal with the 0s and 1s that represent your e-mail. For example, a high voltage causes the wave to reach its height and this can be considered a 1. A lower voltage causes the wave to fall to its minimum height and this can be considered a 0.

There can be more than one signal used to transmit e-mail and other information over a network. Each signal is defined by a unique frequency much like radio stations, each of which has its own frequency.

The electromagnetic spectrum is a chart that groups frequencies that have similar characteristics. You recognize these categories as sound waves, radio waves, microwaves, infrared waves, and light waves, among others. Within these groups is a band of frequencies. Regardless of the category, bits are encoded in each wave the same way.

When a signal representing your e-mail is received by the destination address, the physical layer translates the signal into bits and passes it to the data link layer. The data link layer checks the CRC to determine if there were any errors in transmission. If there were errors, the data link layer sends a message to the physical layer to request the frame be resent.

Once the frame is received in good condition, the data link layer sends an acknowledgement to the sender, then strips away the frame, leaving only the packet that contains the piece of your e-mail. The packet is handed to the network layer, where the address information is stripped away from the packet.

The network layer turns the packet over to the transport layer, which removes the piece of e-mail from the packet and reassembles packets into your complete e-mail. Once this process is completed, the e-mail is passed to the session layer, where the checkpoints are removed from it.

The presentation layer receives the e-mail next and it expands the compressed e-mail. Then it deciphers it before giving the e-mail to the application layer. The application layer converts the e-mail from the intermediary format into the format required by the e-mail program.

Part 2

The Connection

I always see commercials on television, especially during the Super Bowl, that try to convey the latest network technology in 30 seconds or less. Of course, this is impossible because as you'll soon discover, networks are complex mixtures of special computers, cables, and software that make it all work together.

Networks are built from cables, such as those that connect your computer to the telephone lines, and modems that act like your computer's telephone. Networks also use components that you and I don't see because they are kept locked away in a closet. I'll unlock the closet for you in this part of the book, point out each device and tell you how it works, and then I'll show you how they connect to form the backbone of the network.

When I hear the term "network" mentioned around the office, I immediately think of the network local to my office, called a local area network. However, networks can extend beyond the walls of the office and reach great distances. These networks are called wide area networks, and I'll give you an e-mail view of a wide area network in this part so you can show off at your next meeting with your systems staff.

Heed this warning: Hold on to your seat when our journey begins because we'll be traveling over wide area network cables, leaping into the sky using mobile communication, and then entering out-of-this-world satellite technology.

Your network tour won't be complete without an inside look at the widest area network, the Internet. Did you ever wonder what happens after you request your favorite Web page? You can stop wondering after you finish reading this part, because you'll be able to tell your friends how the Internet works. And you'll also learn how Intranets and Extranets work.

Chapter 3 begins your journey with a look at each network device. From there you'll move on to Chapter 4, where we connect those devices. In Chapter 5, you learn how the network's superstructure is stretched to cover a wide area.

Chapter 6 gives you a down-and-dirty look at the Internet and its offspring—Intranets and Extranets. Your adventure comes to an end in Chapter 7, where you explore client/server technology and learn how you can share files, printers, and data with others on the network.

3 Networks: Parts and Pieces

In this chapter...

Your e-mail leaves the network wire that runs from your computer to the socket in the wall. From there you probably have no idea what happens next except that within a fraction of a second you know the e-mail is delivered to your colleague's electronic mailbox.

In this chapter you'll be taken down the long, winding road of the network and follow along as your e-mail moves through various network components on its way to its destination. You'll learn about:

- interrupts
- network cards
- network media
- transmitting a signal over a cable
- transmitting a signal over the airwaves
- repeaters
- hubs
- switches
- bridges
- routers
- brouters
- gateways

REALITY CHECK ....

Sending an e-mail over a network is similar to mailing a letter except that your e-mail is delivered much faster than the postal carrier delivers the mail. The e-mail has a destination address like a regular letter, except the e-mail address identifies a computer rather than a building.

The layout of a network resembles a town in which each building is a computer or other network device, and streets are the network cables. At the center of town is a post office that receives all e-mail sent from everyone in town.

The post office sorts each letter to determine if the letter is destined for a building in this town or a building in a different town. Letters are then redistributed according to their address. Something just like a post office exists on a network and is called a router.

A router sorts through e-mail and other information sent across the network and determines if the e-mail is for a computer on the network or a computer on a different network. The e-mail is then shipped to either the destination computer or to a router on the other network, much the same way as your town's post office sends letters addressed to a building in a neighboring town by forwarding the letter to that town's post office.

A router is just one of many network devices used to send e-mail and other information to various computers on a network. You'll learn about each of these and how they operate later in this chapter.

INTERRUPTS ....

Looking at the jumble of chips and other tiny components that dot the landscape inside the computer, it's hard to imagine how the words you type are able to flow from the keyboard to the screen, and then out over the network.

In early chapters, you learned that this isn't a magical process, but a carefully designed organization of switches etched into chips where information is stored and processed using math.

Information destined for transmission over a network flows from chip to chip through what appears as a maze of etched wires on the motherboard of a computer. The journey begins when your turn on your computer, which is called booting it.

Software called the basic input output system (BIOS), which is housed in a special chip, copies the operating system software from the hard disk into random access memory (RAM). The operating system preps the computer by examining various hardware components, loading additional software for startup, such as the Windows desktop, then waits for your first command.

Tech Talk

The Operating system: a group of programs that makes a computer or network function.

Interrupt: a signal to the central processing unit (CPU) of the computer telling it to stop processing temporarily and to begin a different process.

Commands are entered using a keyboard or a mouse. Keystrokes entered on the keyboard are temporarily stored in memory, called the keyboard buffer, until the Enter key is pressed. The Enter key sends a special signal, called an interrupt, to the central processing unit (CPU). The interrupt signal tells the CPU to stop whatever it is doing and run a particular program within the operating system.

Tech Talk

A program: a specific set of tasks that are performed in a particular order to achieve a desired result.

For example, imagine that you're watching television and your doorbell rings. We tend to perform the same tasks whenever the doorbell rings. Once you've completed the task—answering the door—you return to watching television.

Another interrupt—we'll call it interrupt two—occurs when the telephone rings. This too causes you to stop whatever you are doing and answer the telephone.

The procedures for you to respond to interrupts are learned through experience and stored in your brain. Procedures for the operating system to respond to interrupts are created by programmers and stored in computer memory as part of the operating system.

A lookup table, also stored in memory, associates the interrupt with the memory address of the program that is designed to handle the interrupt. This table is called the interrupt table. Here's how this works when you press the Enter key (Figure 3.1).

An interrupt is a signal sent to the CPU, which finds the corresponding interrupt number in the interrupt table and then retrieves the memory address of the program. The CPU goes to that memory address and begins running the program.

In this case, the program reads information stored in the keyboard buffer, then determines if the information contains commands. If it does, then those commands are processed. If it doesn't, then an error message is displayed letting you know that you entered an unknown command. Once the program finishes, the CPU returns to whatever it was doing before it received the interrupt.

Some interrupts can be ignored temporarily until the CPU completes the current task. This is like ignoring the ringing telephone until you hear the referee's call during a football game. Responding to the telephone is important, but not as important to you as what you are currently doing. Other interrupts must be responded to immediately, such as hearing a police siren outside your house.

Interrupts play a crucial role in receiving information over a network because your computer must listen continually to the network signal for messages addressed to it. Once a message is received, an interrupt is sent so the information can be processed.

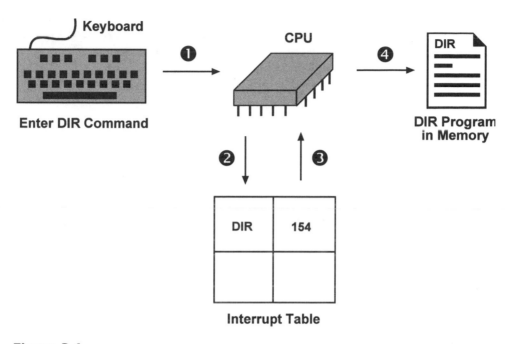

Figure 3.1
Entering the command DIR (❶) causes the operating system to locate the
memory address containing the DIR program (❷), then retrieve the address
(❸), and execute the program (❹).

NETWORK CARDS ··

The device inside your computer that listens continually to the network is called the
network interface card (NIC), or simply the network card. The network card as integral a part of the computer as if it was built into the motherboard.

Engineers designed PCs for expandability. That is, they realized that technology
evolves. Rather than redesign circuitry inside the computer each time someone devised
a new device, they developed a way to add and remove circuitry directly from the motherboard. They did this by creating expansion slots. PCs contains expansion slots inside
the computer and laptops use a PCI slot located on the side of the laptop computer.

Tech Talk

**An expansion slot: a socket that connects an add-on circuit board to the
etched wires on the motherboard. This makes it possible for information
to flow back and forth between the add-on circuit board and the
motherboard.**

The network card is an add-on circuit board that slips into an expansion slot and handles communications between the network cable and the computer. Each expansion slot is assigned an address on the computer's bus.

Each network card is assigned a unique network address. This is similar to a house number on your street. Engineers are able to avoid assigning conflicting networks addresses by having a block of network addresses assigned to each network card manufacturer. Manufacturers then assign a unique address within their block of addresses to each network card they manufacture. These addresses are stored inside a chip on the network card.

Tech Talk

A bus: is similar to a multi-lane highway that is etched into the motherboard over which instructions and data flow to and from components. There are at least three types of buses in a computer: one processes instructions, another data, and the third interrupts.

....

INSTRUCTIONS VS. DATA

An instruction is information that tells the CPU to do a task, and data is information that is manipulated by an instruction. Let's say the number 300 is stored at memory location 1, and the number 40 is stored at memory location 5. We want the computer to add these numbers and place the sum at memory location 7.

Here are the instructions necessary to complete this objective:

a. Retrieve the value from address 1.

b. Retrieve the value from address 5.

c. Add the value from address 1 and address 5.

d. Store the sum in address 7.

However, the data are:

a. 300

b. 40

c. 340

The role of a network card is to facilitate communication between devices on a network, such as between a workstation and a file server. The process begins when network cards in both devices determine how to communicate with each other. This is called handshaking (Figure 3.2). Instructions for handshaking are contained in a chip located on each network card. The chip contains software called firmware that manages the handshaking process. Firmware on a network card follows the data link layer standard of the OSI Model (see Chapter 2).

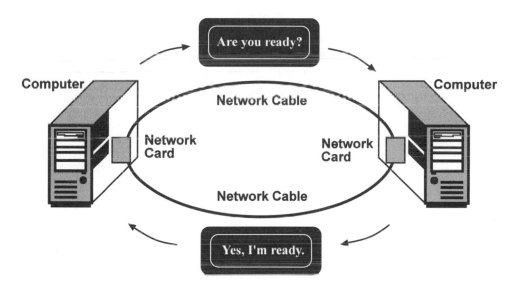

Figure 3.2
Handshaking is a process where a computer asks if the other computer is ready to receive data, and the other computer then replies.

Tech Talk
Handshaking: the process in which each network card determines the data size that can be transmitted, transmission timing, data confirmation, and data transmission rate.

Handshaking can be different for each network card—even for cards produced by the same manufacturer. For example, an older version of a network card may lack features found in a new version. However, newer versions are frequently backward compatible. That is to say the newer card contains both older and newer features and therefore can automatically use an older feature to communicate with an older network card.

Settling on the data size before communications begins is a critical part; otherwise, data could be lost. If data size isn't agreed upon, then there will be memory overflow. Simply put, there is no room to store new incoming data.

Tech Talk

Data size: determined by the amount of data that the destination network card can store in memory before the destination computer processes the data.

This is like those days you rushed home to tell your folks about how you scored the winning goal in your school soccer game. You probably burst into the room recounting every moment of the game without taking a breath. No one understood you because you were talking faster than they could listen and process what you were saying. You were told to slow down and start over. You and your parents informally agreed on a "data size" that was acceptable to all of you.

The timing factor is also a critical component of network communications since it determines the time that will elapse between each transmission. This is typically the time that is necessary for the destination network card to process the previous data.

After data is transmitted, the network card that originated the transmission waits for a confirmation that the data was received without errors. However, this can be an endless wait if the destination network card malfunctions and is unable to send the confirmation message back to the originating network card.

Engineers anticipated this problem and made a confirmation factor part of the handshaking process. The confirmation factor sets the time delay before the destination network card will transmit a confirmation message. An error is suspected if the confirmation isn't received by this deadline.

The transmission rate is the speed at which communications will occur. The agreed upon rate is the highest common rate that is possible for both the destination and origination network cards.

Choosing a Network Card

There are three factors that determine which network card is suited for a network device (i.e., computer). They are the kind of network device, the type of network, and performance. Fortunately for most of us, technicians make this choice for us.

By now you realize that a network device is any device that connects directly to the network, which is typically a computer or a server. These devices are further defined by the bus (see "Network Cards" on page 79) used to transport data and instructions inside the device. There are three commonly used buses: ISA, EISA, and PCI. Each bus type requires a specific kind of network card.

There are a variety of types of networks, which are discussed later in this book, and each has specifications that must be met by the network card. For example, a network card designed for a fiber optic network cannot be used to link a network device to a coaxial cable network. This is like trying to install a Ford fuel injection system on a Chevy. They just don't fit.

You can also think of a network card like a toll stop on a highway. Every car exiting the highway must stop and be processed. Cars begin to backup if the toll stop cannot keep pace with incoming traffic. Before long a bottleneck occurs.

The same is true on a computer network. Any network device that cannot process data at the same speed as other devices on the network will slow down network traffic. This is also called a bottleneck. Therefore, a network card is selected based on its capability to keep up with the rest of the devices on the network. There are two factors that influence the efficiency at which a network card can receive and process data. They are the use of memory and the use of the CPU.

Tech Talk

Bottleneck: the slowdown of packet transmission over a network.

Ideally, data received by the network card is immediately passed along to communications software on the network device, where packets are stripped down and data is reassembled into information. No bottleneck occurs if the communications software keeps pace with incoming data.

This rarely happens in the real world because the efficiency of the communications software depends on other factors, such as the processing capabilities of the network device and other software running on the device while transmission is occurring.

Engineers increase the throughput of data communications by storing incoming data in memory rather than passing it directly to the communications software.

Tech Talk

Throughput: a measurement of how many bits can be completely processed within one second.

Memory used to temporarily store incoming data is called a buffer or a cache. You can think of it as a mailbox. For example, a mail carrier can ring your doorbell, then wait to give you your mail. This is similar to a network card passing data directly to the communications software. However, this doesn't happen; otherwise, no one would receive mail. Instead, the mail carrier drops your mail in the mailbox, which is like a buffer or a cache.

Memory must be allocated for use by the network card and the size of the allotted memory must be determined before the network card is ready to receive data. That is, someone must designate the box that will serve as the mailbox and decide the size of the box.

There are three areas in which memory can be reserved for use by the network card. These are memory on the network device exclusive to the network card, called direct memory access (DMA); shared memory between the network device and the network card; and memory located on the network card, called RAM buffering.

Tech Talk

Direct memory access: the capability of the network card to directly use the network device's memory.
RAM buffering: a network card that contains its own memory that is used to temporarily store incoming packets.

In addition to having sufficient memory to store incoming data, engineers are also concerned about how the data is processed. The CPU is the component of the network device that processes incoming data by following instructions given by the communications software. Typically, data is moved from the buffer to another area of memory for processing, which doesn't seem time consuming but this is time that slows down throughput.

Another hindrance to throughput is the availability of the CPU to process incoming data. Although the destination and origination network cards are synchronized to communicate with each other, the CPU in the destination computer might be running other programs during transmission. For example, you might be using your word processor at the same time as you receive e-mail. The problem is that the CPU cannot do two things at once.

Engineers devised two schemes to reduce the delay of moving data in memory and the contention for the CPU to process that data. The first is to make memory on the network card used to store incoming data available to the network device's CPU. This eliminates the need to move data from a buffer to memory that the CPU uses to process the data.

The other scheme is to incorporate a CPU into the network card. This gives the network card the hardware necessary to process incoming data without having to rely on the CPU in the network device. This is called bus mastering.

Configuring a Network Card

Networks always remind me of the plumbing in my house because the concept is easy to understand, but there are fine details that exist just to trip you up. One of those details is that network cards must be fine-tuned before they'll work properly. This fine-tuning is called configuring the network card.

There are four features that must be configured. These are the base memory address, the base I/O port address, the IRQ number, and the transceiver type. Fortunately for most of us, technicians configure our network card before we connect to the network. Although you don't need to configure the card yourself, it is worthwhile to understand what needs to be configured.

Whenever memory is being reserved for an application, the operating system requires two pieces of information. These are the address of the first byte of memory to be used and the size of memory that is to be reserved. The address of the first byte of memory is called the base memory address and the operating system sequentially reserves the necessary memory.

Let's say 16,000 bytes are necessary to store incoming data. This is the buffer or cache size. The technician could designate base memory address as address 10; therefore, the last byte in the buffer is at address 16,0010.

In general, we can say that the more memory in the buffer, the better the throughput of data from the network. While this is true, there is another factor that technicians consider, which is the availability of memory for other applications running on the network device.

Network devices have a limited amount of memory that is shared among all applications running on the device. If one application, such as network operations, takes a larger share of available memory, then performance of other applications might be impaired.

Determining how much memory to set aside for the network card is a balancing act. Typically, the technician sets the size at the maximum value. This size might be reduced if the performance of other applications running on the network device becomes intolerable.

The base I/O port address is the address that identifies the location of the network card to the network device's operating system. This is like the house number of the network card on the bus inside the network device and is used to send and receive data between the network card and the network device.

The IRQ number is the number assigned to the interrupt line used to tell the CPU that data is received and needs to be processed (see "Interrupts" on page 77). Typically, there are 16 interrupt lines etched into the interrupt bus on the motherboard.

An interrupt line works like our senses. Our brain picks up uninteresting information from our eyes, nose, ears, skin, and taste buds. These are similar to interrupt lines inside the computer. However, when the nose smells something unusual, a signal is sent to the brain to react to the smell.

Every hardware device, such as the keyboard and printer port, is assigned an interrupt line. Only one device should be assigned to an interrupt line, although nothing prevents two or more devices from using the same line. If two devices use the same interrupt line, then chances are good that the network device will freeze because it doesn't know how to process the interrupt signal.

Let's say the network card and the printer both use the same interrupt line to communicate with the CPU. However, the CPU thinks the line is used only by the printer. When the CPU receives a signal from the network card, it sends a return signal destined for the printer. This of course confuses the network card.

The remaining part that a technician configures is the type of transceiver the network card uses. Many network cards have a built-in transceiver and others use an external transceiver that connects between the network card and the network cable. Still other network cards are designed to use both an internal and external transceiver.

Tech Talk

A transceiver: a component of the network card that sends and receives signals over the network.

NETWORK MEDIA ....

Let's continue to follow the flow of data from your computer through the network card and out onto the network with a look at the network media. The network media is the general term coined to identify the pavement of the electronic highway. Concrete, asphalt, stones, and dirt are used as the roadbed for our cars. Similarly, cables and other electronic means are used to send our messages electronically.

There are eight kinds of network media, better known as cables, used to connect together network devices. These are unshielded twisted pair, shielded twisted pair, thick coaxial, thin coaxial, fiber optic, infrared, radio, and microwave. These terms sound a bit technical, but like most of the concepts and devices that comprise a network, you probably will pick up the jargon quickly.

Engineers employ one or a combination of network media based on the network's requirement and the network media's characteristics. There are five characteristics that are used to select the network media for a network design. Table 3.1 contains a list of these characteristics for each network media. These media are:

- the maximum distance a signal can travel across the network media before the signal must be amplified and retransmitted
- the amount of bits that can be successfully transmitted per second
- the amount of electromagnetic interference picked up by the network media
- transmission security concerns over emissions
- cost

Tech Talk

Electromagnetic interference (EMI): is a stray signal that is generated by other devices, such as fluorescent lights and power cables.
Emissions: leaks of the signal transmitted over the network media that an intruder can detect. Some network media have a tendency to leak the signal to the area surrounding the media (i.e., cable), which provides an opportunity for a technician using the proper electronic device to eavesdrop on the transmission.

Table 3.1 Characteristics of Network Media

Media	Maximum Distance	Transmission Speed	Electromagnetic Interference	Transmission Security	Cost
Unshielded Twisted Pair	100 meters	10–100 MBPS	Medium	Medium	Low
Shielded Twisted Pair	100 meters	15 MBPS	Low	Low	Medium
Thick Coaxial	500 meters	10 MBPS	Low	Low	Medium
Thin Coaxial	185 meters	10 MBPS	Low	Low	Medium
Fiber optic	10+kilometers	100 MBPS– 2 GBPS	None	None	High
Infrared	Varies	1–16 MBPS	None	Low	Medium-High
Radio	25 meters – 1 kilometer	1–10 MBPS	High	High	High
Microwave	global	10 MBPS	Medium	Medium	High

The maximum distance of a network medium can be confusing for anyone who is not involved in designing a network. Distance is measured from transmitter to receiver. Let's say that you want to connect your computer to a computer down the hall. Intuitively you might pace the distance through the corridors to determine the length of cable. However, this isn't the actual distance between the computers.

Tech Talk
MBPS: million bits per second
GBPS: giga bits per second

As you'll see in later chapters, the network cable leaves your computer and travels through floors, walls, and ceilings to a communications closet located on your floor (Figure 3.3). That is, the end of the network wires from all the computers on your floor converge in the communications closet.

Therefore, the length of the network media must include the full path (i.e., through the walls) from your computer to the communications closet. Typically, the signal in the closet is regenerated to send it to other areas of the network.

Tech Talk
A communications closet: a room where all the network connection terminates

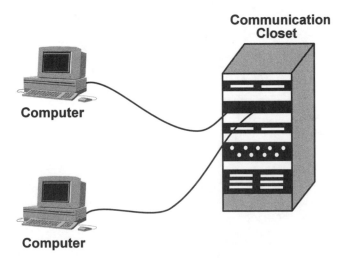

Figure 3.3
Cables from network devices lead to a communications closet located on each floor of an office building.

TRANSMITTING A SIGNAL OVER A CABLE ....

The transmitter component on the network card converts the bits that comprise the packet into an electronic signal, as discussed in Chapter 2. If we could use a powerful microscope, we would see the signal as a vibration of molecules of material used in the network media. For example, these would be molecules of copper if a coaxial cable were used.

The vibration occurs at a specific number of vibrations per second, called the signal's frequency. This is like moving a stick up and down in a still pond. For each up and down motion a wave is generated. Water molecules instead of copper vibrate in synchronization with the movement of the stick in the pond.

The energy exerted to move the stick supplies the power to move the wave across the pond. The more energy used, the greater the distance the wave travels. The same principle is used in an electronic signal except electrical power is the force behind the network signal.

Some basic science comes into play in terms of how much energy is required to transmit the signal. We'll let the engineers use math to calculate the amount and we'll concentrate on understanding the concept.

Sir Isaac Newton defined the problem concisely in his Laws of Motion, particularly when he said that a resting body tends to want to remain at rest and a body in motion tends to want to remain in motion.

The body that we're concerned with consists of the molecules that must be set into motion to transmit the signal to the other end of the network media. A molecule at rest resists the push to be placed into motion.

Each network media has a similar resistance, which is called impedance and is measured in ohms. The only way to overcome the resistance is to increase the power used to generate the signal. However, there is a limit to the amount of power that can be used.

Tech Talk
Impedance: the measurement in ohms of the resistance of a molecule to being placed in motion.
Voltage: the measurement of power used to transmit a signal.

Network transmitters are designed to generate a signal at a steady voltage. The objective of the transmission is to vibrate molecules along the complete length of the cable at an identical frequency.

You can think of this as being like sending water through a pipeline. You want the water pressure at the end of the pipe to be relatively the same as water pressure at the beginning of the pipe.

Of course, molecules vary depending on the type of network media that are in use on the network. For example, as illustrated in Table 3.1 page 87, thick coaxial cable can carry the network signal five times the distance of twisted pair (you'll learn more about specific network media later in this chapter). This means that the signal begins to drop off after 100 meters if twisted pair network medium is used, which is called attenuation (Figure 3.4).

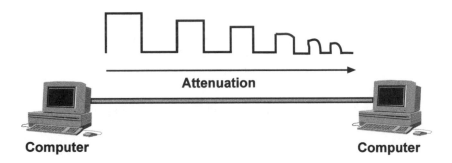

Figure 3.4
Attenuation occurs when the signal doesn't have the strength to reach the end of the network.

Attenuation isn't acceptable since packets become unable to reach the end of the network. Engineers solve this problem by either changing the network media or by using a device called a repeater, which retransmits the signal (see "Repeaters" on page 100).

Tech Talk
Attenuation: the weakening of the network signal over a network media.

Twisted Pair

If you look closely at a telephone wire, you'll notice that there are many fine strains of copper twisted together within a plastic sleeve of insulation. This is called a twisted pair wire.

The twists do more than provide strength to the strains. They also reduce the chance of picking up stray signals called crosstalk. Likewise, the insulation is used to isolate the strains from the environment (i.e., floors and walls along the path of wires).

Tech Talk
Crosstalk: interference from a signal generated by an adjacent cable.

There are two types of twisted pair wires. These are unshielded (UTP) and shielded (STP) (Figure 3.5). A shield is a foil or wire mesh sleeve that is sandwiched between the copper strains and the plastic sleeve that absorbs any stray signal from entering the cable.

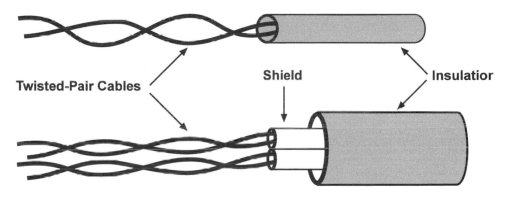

Figure 3.5
There are two kinds of twisted pair wires: shielded and unshielded.

Both wires are similar except the shielded twisted pair is thick and less flexible than unshielded twisted pair, and that makes shielded twisted pair more difficult to install. In addition, shielded twisted pair requires a grounding connector.

These issues translate into a higher cost to install a shielded twisted pair than an unshielded twisted pair. However, shielded twisted pair offers greater transmission security and reduces the likelihood a stray signal will interfere with transmission.

Unshielded twisted pair wires are classified by a category that certifies the maximum amount of bits that can be transmitted per second across the wire. These classifications are listed in Table 3.2. Notice that a faster rater of speed is achieved by using a higher category number because there is less resistance to the signal by the cable due to the cable's size. The larger the cable size (i.e., higher category number), the less resistance.

Table 3.2 Classification of Unshielded Twisted Pair Wires

Category	Transmission Speed
3	10 MBPS
4	16 MBPS
5	100 MBPS

Coaxial Cable

If you look carefully at the cable wire that connects your TV to your cable or satellite system, you'll notice a single wire within a sleeve of insulation. This type of cable is called coaxial cable (Figure 3.6).

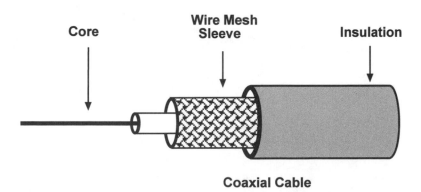

Core   **Wire Mesh Sleeve**   **Insulation**

Coaxial Cable

Figure 3.6
Coaxial cable has a solid copper core surrounded by insulation.

Coaxial cable, also known as coax, was the first type of cable used in networks. It consists of four types of material. These are a solid core of either a solid or twisted strands of copper, a layer of insulation, woven metal mesh, and an outside insulation layer.

The center core is used to transmit the signal. The metal mesh is used to ground the cable and protects the signal from interference caused by stray signals in the environment. The metal mesh attracts the interference and funnels it away from the center core.

Coaxial cables are used wherever there is heavy electrical interference and data needs to be transmitted over long distances. Table 3.3 contains a comparison of various network media, including coaxial cables.

There are two kinds of coaxial cable, which are categorized by the thickness of wire. These are called thick coaxial and thin coaxial. Thick coaxial cable has a higher transmission rate (i.e., bits per second) than thin coaxial cable. However, thick coaxial isn't flexible, making it difficult to install—and translating into a higher cost than thin coaxial cable.

Table 3.3 Characteristics of Network Media

Medium	Max Cable Length	Transmission Speed	Cost
UTP	328 ft	10–100 MBPS	Least
STP	328	16 50 MBPS	Moderate
Thinnet	607 ft	10 MBPS	Inexpensive
Thicknet	1,640 ft	10 MBPS	High
Fiber Optic	6,562 ft	100 MBPS–2 GBPS	Most Expensive

Fiber Optic Cable

No doubt you've read a lot about fiber optics in the press since major telecommunication companies like AT&T are replacing portions of their coaxial cable system with fiber optic cables. The reason for excitement about fiber optic technology is because it provides extremely fast data transmissions over long distances by using light waves.

Recall that in Chapter 2 we explored the electromagnetic spectrum, which categorized frequencies of waves. Each band of frequencies within the spectrum had unique characteristics. For example, our ears can detect a band within audio frequencies. Likewise, frequencies within the visible light band can be seen.

Fiber optic technology uses light waves to transmit a signal over a fiber optic cable. A fiber optic cable is a thin glass or clear plastic fiber within a sleeve that prevents the light signal from escaping and prevents stray light from interfering with the signal (Figure 3.7).

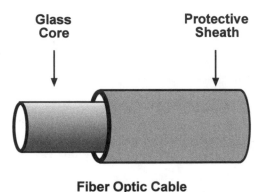

Fiber Optic Cable

Figure 3.7
Fiber optic cable has a thin tube of glass or plastic surrounded by insulation.

There are two kinds of fiber optic cable: single-mode and multi-mode. Single-mode fiber optic cable uses a single wave, and multi-mode mode uses multiple waves. This is similar to a single- and multi-lane highway.

Fiber optics is far superior to other media used in networks. However, fiber optic cables are expensive to install because of their delicate nature. The glass or plastic core and connectors must be perfectly clean. A spec of dust or residual from the material used to make the connection dramatically interferes with transmission. Any obstruction that prevents light from flowing freely retards the fiber optic signal.

As discussed in the first part of the chapter, data is encoded onto a wave by a transmitter and decoded from the wave by a receiver. Remember that light is also a wave of a specific frequency similar to a radio wave, except light waves have different characteristics. You can see light waves, but not radio waves. However, both waves can be modified slightly to represent data, as discussed in Chapters 1 and 2.

TRANSMITTING A SIGNAL OVER THE AIRWAVES....

Packets can be transmitted between computers without a hard-wired connection. Instead of using cables, packets can be transmitted over the airwaves in a wireless transmission. There are three kinds of wireless technologies used to send and receive data. These are infrared, radio, and microwave.

Wireless transmission intuitively seems to have the advantage over hard-wired networks because it eliminates the need to run cables throughout a building. While this is true, there are other considerations that currently limit the desirability of using wireless networks to satisfy general network requirements. These are cost, transmission speed, and transmission security.

Infrared Technology

Infrared is a band of frequencies within the electromagnetic spectrum that use a specific range of light waves to transmit a signal through the air. This is the same technology your TV remote uses to change channels. An infrared network requires line-of-sight connectivity between the transmitter and the receiver (Figure 3.8). Any object between them will break the connection.

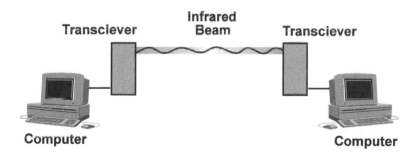

Figure 3.8
Infrared technology transmits information using an infrared wave, which is in the light portion of the electromagnetic spectrum.

Infrared is similar to light generated by a light bulb in that if you can see the light, then you can receive the signal. If something blocks your view of the light, then you cannot receive the signal. Likewise, another light shining in the same area can interfere with viewing the light. The same is true with infrared in that other infrared waves are generated naturally and by other devices, which can interfere with the infrared signal.

There are two types of infrared networks. These are point-to-point and broadcast networks. A point-to-point infrared network carefully focuses the infrared beam to a particular receiver. This is like shining a flashlight into a long tube. Only the person at the end of the tube or within that vicinity can see the light.

A broadcast infrared network does not focus the beam but instead allows it to disperse in various directions. This enables the signal to be transmitted to multiple computers, but requires those computers to be within the vicinity of the infrared transmitter, which is closer than in a point-to-point infrared network.

Radio Technology

Probably the most common kind of wireless network in use employs radio technology to transmit packets encoded onto radio waves. A radio wave is a band of frequencies within the electromagnetic spectrum that can travel in 360 degrees over the air and through many physical obstructions.

While radio wireless networks seem to overcome limitations posed by infrared technology, they have drawbacks. Most radio frequencies are controlled by the U.S. Federal Communications Commission and require an FCC license before a wireless radio network can be established. Radio wireless is also vulnerable to eavesdropping and interference from stray signals.

There are three types of wireless radio networks (Figure 3.9). These are low-power single-frequency, high-power single-frequency, and spread-spectrum. Low- and high-power single-frequency networks are similar except for the range the signal can travel.

Low-power single-frequency covers an area of 30 meters, which is about the area of a small building. This is the least expensive wireless radio network. In contrast, a high-power single-frequency wireless radio network can cover a metropolitan area.

Security is a concern when using low- or high-power single-frequency technology because the signal can be received by anyone who has a device tuned to the radio frequency. Of course, packets can be encrypted to hinder the information from being reassembled by the cyber snoop.

A spread-spectrum wireless radio network is an alternative to the single-frequency networks. It uses multiple frequencies to transmit the signal using one of two methods. These are direct-sequence modulation and frequency hopping. This makes it difficult for someone to electronically eavesdrop on the transmission.

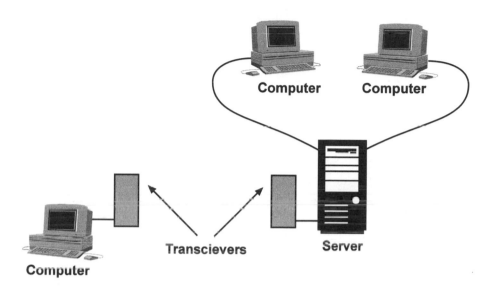

Figure 3.9
Wireless radio networks transmit information using radio waves.

Tech Talk

Direct-sequence modulation: a process in which bits of a packet are sent over multiple frequencies at the same time. The receiver reassembles the packet.
Frequency hopping: a process of sending a packet over a rotating set of frequencies.

Let's say there are 10 members of a track team. Each member is simultaneously running in his or her own lane on the track. In computer terms, each track team member is a bit, collectively the team is a packet, and the lanes are multiple transmission frequencies.

If you want to see all the members of the track team, you need to look at all of the lanes at the same time. This is similar to how you want to receive the packet using direct-sequence modulation (DSM) because each bit of the packet is transmitted on its own frequency. Therefore, if you want to see all the bits that comprise the packet, you must receive the frequencies used to transmit each packet. Frequency hopping is like having each member of a track team run behind each other in the same lane, then having the coach signal to change to a specific lane in the middle of the run.

Both the transmitter and the receiver know which frequency is used to transmit the signal based on a set of rules established before the transmission occurs. A timing interval is used to determine when to change to another frequency. Packets are then re-assembled in the order in which they arrive.

Microwave Technology

The term "microwave" is probably familiar to you since you probably use microwaves for cooking and maybe to receive direct television broadcasts. Microwave is a band of frequencies within the electromagnetic spectrum that travels in one direction.

There are two kinds of microwave networks. These are terrestrial and satellite (Figure 3.10). Terrestrial networks use microwaves to transmit signals across a terrain, such as between two buildings in an office complex. The signal can be received as long as there is an unobstructed view between the transmitter and the receiver. Since there are natural and man-made obstacles on earth, terrestrial networks must be designed carefully to avoid obstacles. Satellite networks also use microwaves for transmission, however, it is less likely the transmission will be obstructed in space than on the Earth.

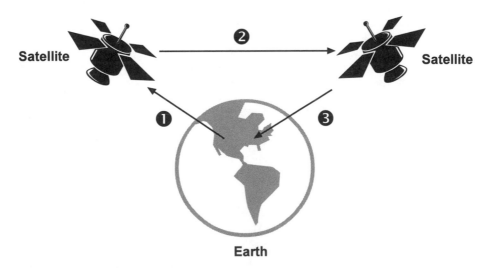

Figure 3.10
Data is sent from and Earth station, to a satellite (❶), then to another satellite (❷), and back to an Earth station (❸).

Satellite networks use microwaves to send and receive packets between a satellite ground station and a satellite. The same technology is used between satellites to relay packets around the world.

Although satellite transmissions can travel great distances relatively quickly, the speed may not be suitable for real-time communication.

Tech Talk

Real-time communication: the type of communication we experience during a telephone call, when someone speaks then waits for the other person to respond.

The transmission speed is slightly slower than terrestrial communication and this delay causes an unnatural pause in the communication. You probably notice this delay in a live international television broadcast in which a news anchor questions a field reporter who is located on the other side of the globe.

AFTER THE CABLE ....

Cables converge to form a highway of a computer network across which packets of information travel to their destination. A computer network is similar to a system of highways in that there are many on and off ramps that lead to other roadways, which are called network segments (Figure 3.11). Segments are connected using an assortment of connectivity devices.

Connectivity devices are electronic versions of information handling processes that we're familiar with. Let's follow a letter sent through the U.S. Postal Service to illustrate these processes.

A letter that you drop in the mailbox is picked up and carried to your local post office, where it is determined if the letter is addressed to someone in your town or outside of your town. This is similar to sending a packet to someone on your segment of the network or to someone on another segment. In this example, your local post office is a connectivity device that links your town to the rest of the postal system.

A letter destined for outside your town is transported with other similarly addressed letters to a regional postal center. There, letters are sorted by zip code into two general categories: post offices within the region and other regions. The regional postal center, too, is a connectivity device in the postal system.

Letters are then passed along to the appropriate local post offices or regional centers, where they are again sorted until their reach the cubby in the postal carrier's shelf for the destination address.

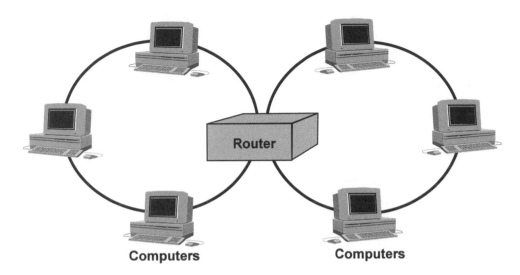

Figure 3.11
A network segment is a standalone network that is connected to a larger network.

There are seven types of connectivity devices that are used to route and control the flow of packets across a network. These are a repeater, a hub, a switch, a bridge, a router, a brouter, and a gateway.

Repeaters

Attenuation is a critical factor in the transmission of signals over a network (see "Transmitting a Signal Over a Cable" on page 89). The energy that sets electrons into a wave motion dissipates according to the length of the cable. Therefore, new energy must be applied to the signal to carry it over longer distances.

A repeater (Figure 3.12) is a connectivity device that links two lengths of cable. When a signal is received, circuitry in the repeater gives a boost of power to the signal so it can complete its journey. There are two ways in which a repeater strengthens a signal. These are amplification and regeneration. Regeneration of the signal produces a clearer signal than is achievable through an amplifier because a new, identical signal is generated rather than amplifying the incoming, existing signal.

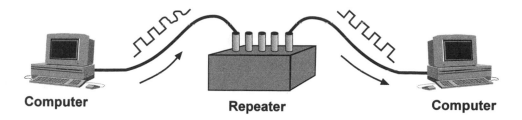

Figure 3.12
A repeater adds new power to a signal to overcome attenuation.

Tech Talk
Noise: the term used to describe interference in a transmission.

A repeater used in a baseband network amplifies the signal similarly to how the amplifier circuits in a stereo amplify sound. The circuitry doesn't "touch" the signal except to give it increased energy.

A repeater used in a broadband network regenerates the signal; the repeater receives the signal as a network device would receive it. However, instead of processing the packet, the repeater retransmits it in a manner similar to the way in which the originator device transmitted the packet originally.

Repeaters work at the physical layer of the OSI Model and can link various kinds of network media (i.e., coaxial, twisted pair). However, repeaters do not translate signals between various network architectures, which you'll be learning about later in this book.

Hub and Switches

A hub (Figure 3.13) is a device that connects nodes to a segment of a network. Node is a term used to describe any device (i.e., computers, servers) that is connected to a network. In the postal system example used earlier in this section, the post office is a hub that connects all of the homes and businesses in the town and concentrates postal communication in one location. It is because of this feature that hubs are also called concentrators.

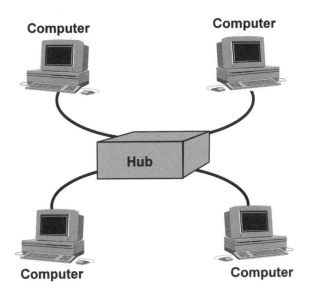

Figure 3.13
A hub concentrates connections from network devices to a central point in
the network.

Tech Talk

**A concentrator: a device that concentrates network traffic in a central
location, then sends packets to all nodes on the network. The network
card on each network device determines if the packet is addressed to
its device.**

A cable leading from each node is plugged into a port in the hub. Hubs typically
have 8 or 16 ports, but can be linked with cables to expand the network to include additional nodes. This is called chaining hubs, much like railroad cars are coupled together to form a train.

Packets travel around the network inside the hub before embarking to each node.
Hubs are used in the Star network design, which is discussed in the next chapter, and
work at the physical layer of the OSI Model.

Three types of hubs are used in a network: passive, active, and intelligent. A
passive hub is the elementary hub and provides basic connectivity among nodes. Simply, it joins ends of cables together to form a network.

An active hub is similar to a passive hub in that it connects nodes. However, an active hub also fulfills the role of a multiport repeater by regenerating the signal before sending it to the destination node.

As with the other types of hub, an intelligent hub joins cables together and also acts a switch to reduce network traffic.

Tech Talk

Multiport repeater: a device that receives signals from any one of multiple nodes on the network, then relays the signal to all nodes.

Hubs connect cables from nodes and redistribute incoming signals to all nodes. While hubs serve as a mechanism for distributing packets over the network, they also send packets to all nodes rather than the destination node. This increases traffic flow over the network needlessly.

A network switch, also known as a switching hub, reads the destination address of each packet and retransmits the packet only to the destination node. Other nodes are unaware of the transmission, which streamlines the flow of information over the network.

A switch reads only the physical address of the network device and knows which port on the switch is connected to that device. Switches work at the physical and data link layers of the OSI Model.

Bridge

A bridge (Figure 3.14) is a device that connects two or more network segments. It acts like a bridge that provides a pathway between two towns over a river and is part of the roadway system of both towns.

Imagine two network segments comprised of nodes connected to a hub. A node is any device connected to the network and a hub is a central point in the network where nodes are connected. A bridge is connected to both hubs. The bridge is a device on both network segments. That is, the bridge has a physical address on both segments and receives packets sent across both segments.

The bridge reads the physical address of a packet to determine if it is addressed to a node on the network segment. If so, then the bridge discards the packet. However, if the address is on another segment, then the bridge sends the packet to another segment where it is delivered to the destination address.

A table of physical addresses is maintained within a bridge, which is used to direct the packet to the appropriate segment. However, a network broadcast is transmitted if the physical address isn't contained in the table. This can cause a broadcast storm.

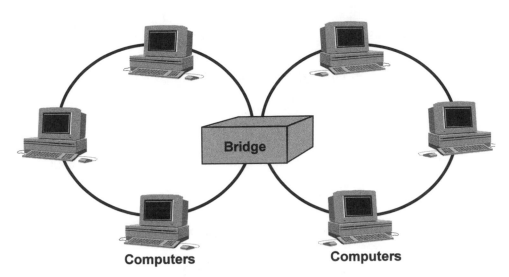

Figure 3.14
A bridge joins together segments of a large network.

Some bridges have the intelligence to detect when a broadcast packet reaches its destination, at which time the address table is automatically updated This tends to reduce the need for future broadcasts and dampens the likelihood of a broadcast storm.

Networks that use a non-routable protocol use a bridge to join network segments. However, networks that use a routable protocol use a router (discussed later in this chapter) instead of a bridge.

> ### Tech Talk
> **Network broadcast: the transmission of a packet to all nodes on every segment of a network.**
> **Broadcast storm: a degradation in network performance caused by the transmission of many packets to all nodes on every segment of the network.**

Bridges work at the data link layer of the OSI Model and must be used on like networks to join networks of the same architecture. That is, bridges are not designed to translate between an Ethernet network and a network running Novell NetWare. (We'll cover network architecture in the next chapter.) Instead, bridges are designed to divide a large network into segments.

While a bridge reduces traffic on a large network, there is a drawback. There is a small delay in transmissions because a bridge must read each packet to determine the destination address. This delay might go unnoticed on a network with relatively low traffic, but could bottleneck busy networks.

Routers and Brouters

Routers (Figure 3.15) work like bridges and are used to divide a large network into segments with the router connecting segments. Routers also have addresses on each segment and redirect a packet to other segments based on the network address. However, routers do not broadcast packets and therefore cannot cause a broadcast storm. A broadcast storm caused by a using a bridge makes unnecessary traffic on the network. A router does not broadcast packets, but instead knows valid addresses through the use of a router table.

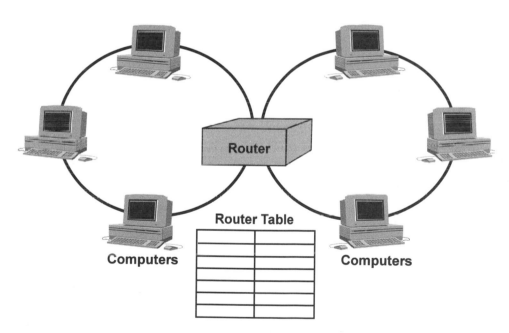

Figure 3.15
A router contains a table used to redirect packets to other network segments.

Routers work at the network layer of the OSI Model. They use the logical network address rather than the physical network address to route packets to their destination located outside the segment of the node that originated the packet.

Routers are also able to connect different network architectures. So networks that are dissimilar can communicate with each other by using a router. However, these networks must employ routable protocols or a bridge or a brouter must be used.

Tech Talk
Routable protocol: a set of network architecture rules that enable packets to retransmit across network segments by a router.

A router can be a self-contained device or a computer that contains multiple network cards and runs router software. This is unlike hubs, switches, repeaters (all discussed later in this book), and bridges that are stand-alone devices.

Nodes on network segments are identified by their address in a routing table. A routing table contains the addresses of nodes and the paths that can be used to reach the node. This may sound confusing at first, but the concept is similar to routing airplanes.

Let's say that you want to travel from New York to San Francisco. The fastest route is direct. However, you could take a plane to Chicago, then to San Francisco. Another route might be from New York to Atlanta to Los Angles, then to San Francisco. These alternatives appear to be more time-consuming than going direct, but under certain circumstances, such as San Francisco being fogged in for three hours, alternate routes might make sense.

The same is true with a large network comprised of many segments, which are also called subnets. Segments are interconnected. Assume there are three segments. We'll call them A, B, and C.

Segment A is connected directly to segment B by a router. Likewise, another router is used to connect segment A to segment C. Still another router is used to connect segment B to segment C. This leaves alternative routes for a packet sent by a node on segment A to travel to segment C. If one route is closed due to technical difficulties, then an alternative route is tried.

A packet can have many hops between the node that sends it and the destination node. The purpose of a router table is to retransmit the packet along the path with the fewest hops. In our example, the direct link between segment A and segment C is the best route. This consists of one hop. However, if this route is closed, then the next best route is to send the packet from segment A to segment B, then to have segment B send the packet to segment C. This increases the number of hops to two.

Imagine the number of hops that can exist on a very large network. When the shortest path is closed, a delay is experienced while a series of routers uses various alternative paths to transport the packet over the network.

Tech Talk

A hop: the transmission of a packet to a router or final destination.

Each router on the network has the same routing table, which must be maintained by a network administrator. Someone must determine the routes and enter them into the table. There are two kinds of routers: a static router, which uses fixed routing tables, and a dynamic router, which automatically updates other router tables when a change in made to one of the tables. Dynamic routers are ideal for larger networks that use multiple routers because the network administrator needs to maintain only one routing table.

Routers communicate with each other using one of two common routing protocols. These are the Router Information Protocol (RIP) and the Open Shortest Path First protocol (OSPF). The major difference between RIP and OSPF is that RIP routers send their entire routing table to all the routers to keep each table updated. OSPF sends only the changes to the routing table, which reduces network traffic.

A brouter is a device that can operate like a bridge or a router depending on the protocol the network architecture uses. Brouters join together, unlike network architectures, and therefore must be able to handle both routable and non-routable protocols.

A packet transmitted by a network that uses a routable protocol causes the brouter to act as a router and read the logical address to forward the packet. The physical address is used for non-routable protocols as a bridge forwards a packet. Brouters work at both the network and data link layers of the OSI Model.

Let's say that your network uses a routable protocol. Therefore, you can use a router to link segments of the network. However, a bridge needs to be used if the network does not use a routable protocol. Likewise, a brouter is used if some network segments use a routable protocol and others do not, because a brouter can act like a router or a bridge.

Gateways

A gateway (Figure 3.16) is a device that translates network signals, usually between unlike networks, such as between a PC network and a mainframe network, or between a mainframe network and a UNIX network. A gateway is typically not a stand-alone device but software running on a computer connected to both networks.

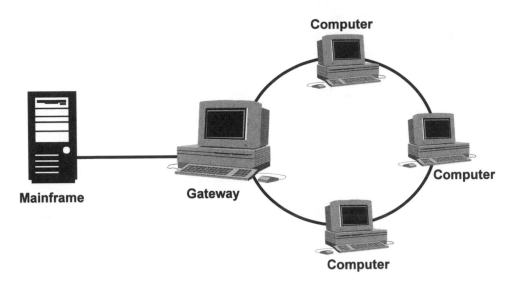

Figure 3.16
A gateway joins together segments of a large network.

For example, a PC on a network segment can be used as a gateway between the PC network and the mainframe. Packets destined for the mainframe are sent to the PC, which retransmits them to the mainframe. Replays from the mainframe are sent to the PC, which sends it along the PC network. Gateways are used frequently to translate e-mails between unlike networks.

SUMMARY ....

A network card connects a network device, such as your PC, to the network media, which in many networks is a cable. When the network card receives information, firmware on the card sends an interrupt over a designated interrupt line to tell the CPU to stop what it is doing and process the incoming packet.

Incoming packets are stored in memory on the network device that is shared with the network card or on the card itself, depending on the kind of network card used. Likewise, the network card might also have its own CPU that is used to process the packet without needing to use the network device's CPU.

Packets are transmitted to other network devices over a wire or a wireless path. A wired path is known as a cable that connects network devices. Network cables are like telephone cables, known as twisted pair, or like cable television cables, known as coaxial.

There are two kinds of twisted pair cables: shielded and unshielded. A shield is a mesh that surrounds the wires to absorb stray signals from entering the wire. Both kinds of twisted pair cables consist of strands of copper wire twisted to reduce the likelihood of a signal from another wire, called crosstalk, from reaching the cable.

There are also two kinds of coaxial cable: thick and thin. Thick coaxial cable is capable of transmitting a greater number of bits per second than thin coaxial cable, however, thick coaxial is more difficult and costly to install than thin coaxial.

Another kind of cable is fiber optic, which transports packets on light waves and is used in high-speed networks. Fiber optic cable can transmit in either single- or multi-signal mode.

Wireless networks use three kinds of technology to send and receive information among network devices. These are infrared, radio, and microwave technology. Infrared technology uses frequencies within the light band of the electromagnetic spectrum to transmit information in either one direction or broadcast 360 degrees. Any obstacle or stray infrared light can obstruct the signal.

Radio technology is similar to technology used to transmit radio broadcasts. The signal is sent either on a signal frequency or on switches between a set of frequencies, and has the same limitation as a radio broadcast.

Microwave technology uses frequencies within the microwave band of the electromagnetic spectrum to transmit a signal in a line-of-sight direction. That is, the transmitter and the receiver must be in a straight line without any obstacle in its way.

Each network device is called a node on the network and is connected to a hub. All packets are sent to the hub, where they are redistributed to all the nodes connected to the hub. However, a switcher can be used to send packets to only the destination node.

The type of network media used on a network determines how far a signal can travel over it. Each network media has a specified maximum distance, after which the signal will drop off and will not be received by a network card.

Using a repeater can extend a network's length. This device receives the signal, then gives it additional power to reach the end of the network.

Networks can be divided into smaller networks, called segments or subnets, to reduce the amount of traffic that flows over the larger network. Connecting a bridge, a router, or a brouter to the network creates segments.

A bridge receives packets, then retransmits them to other segments depending on the packet's physical destination address. If the address is unknown to the bridge, then the bridge sends the packet to all segments. This is called a broadcast and can lead to a broadcast storm, which slows network traffic.

A router also divides a large network into segments, but does not broadcast packets to all segments if the destination address is unknown. A router contains a table called a routing table, which lists the logical addresses of nodes and their corresponding segments. A routing table is created and maintained by the network administrator.

Routers can be used only on networks that use a routable protocol. Bridges can work with non-routable protocols. A brouter combines the capabilities of both a bridge and a router; it becomes a bridge if a non-routable protocol is detected and a router if a routable protocol is detected.

Bridges, routers, and brouters are used to connect segments of similar networks. They cannot be used to link segments of dissimilar networks, such as between a PC network and a UNIX network. A gateway is a device usually used to join dissimilar networks.

Summary Questions

1. What are the factors that must be configured in a network card?

2. Explain the various approaches used to increase the throughput of a network card.

3. What are the advantages and disadvantages of radio transmission?

4. What is the difference between a hub and a router?

5. How are interrupts used in network communication?

6. What are the advantages and disadvantages of wired and wireless networks?

7. What are the security concerns of each of the network technologies?

8. Explain the concept of attenuation and how to overcome it.

9. What are the advantages of using a switch over a hub?

10. Explain the advantages of using a router over a hub.

4 Networks: Linking Parts Together

In this chapter...

"A network is as strong as its weakest link."

Anonymous

Networks have a layout similar to a town in which streets are cables, and buildings are computers and other network devices. However, a layout of a town varies by town. Some have a center where all streets begin. Other towns have a single, long street. Most towns have a mixture of layouts.

Networks, too, have various layouts, called topologies, each having its advantages and disadvantages. In this chapter you'll explore network topologies and learn about:

- an electronic highway

- network topologies

- bus topology

- star topology

- ring topology

- mesh topology

- hybrid topology

- network architecture

- network protocols

REALITY CHECK..

Aerial photos of a major highway interchange show a jumble that looks like spaghetti splattered on the floor. Follow one roadway up and over another, then beneath still another strand a mile or so away. It's a maze without any dead ends, and it's amazing how engineers devise a structure that funnels thousands of vehicles through relatively the same space at the same time without delays or collisions.

After a few years, the once smooth-flowing interchange takes on the appearance of a parking lot, with an increased number of vehicles inching along, cutting each other off, some colliding.

Sitting in traffic, I begin to question the engineers' wisdom and ability to forecast the increased traffic that seems so obvious to us self-proclaimed highway engineers. I always hope that the chief highway designer is in the car behind me. After spending hundreds of millions of dollars and taking longer than it took to build the Empire State Building, highway designers still can't get it right.

To be fair, moving traffic along a highway involves science, design, and a "crystal ball" that accurately projects traffic flow for the foreseeable life of the highway. Unfortunately, engineers have not yet developed an infallible crystal ball, and this is at the crux of perpetual traffic jams.

Designing a computer network is fraught with many of the same challenges that face highway engineers. Instead of roadways of concrete, cables and airwaves are used. Instead of vehicles powered by fuel, electronic envelopes, called packets, travel the network powered by electricity. To prevent traffic jams on the network, engineers must use their crystal ball to estimate the amount of traffic expected to flow over it.

While building materials are different between a highway and a computer network, each roadway has the same objective: to move traffic efficiently between multiple origination and destination points .

A computer network involves scientific principles, which you explored in Chapters 1 and 2; components, which were explored in Chapter 3; and a plan to assemble those components into a working network. In this chapter, you'll learn the basis used to develop a network plan.

AN ELECTRONIC HIGHWAY ....

I like to use the highway metaphor when explaining how computer networks are built because the similarities are parallel. There are two major design considerations for every highway. The first is the layout of the highway, such as where to lay the concrete and construction overpasses. The other is the set of rules that vehicles must follow when using the highway. These are speed limits and other rules of the road.

Computer networks also have these design considerations, although engineers use technical jargon to describe them, and sometimes these terms are incorrectly used interchangeably by professionals.

Engineers call these topologies and architectures. Simply said, network topology is the layout of the highway, and the architecture is the set of "rules of the road."

For example, the topology of a network lets technicians know the type of wiring to use to build the network and what other network devices (i.e., hubs) are necessary to successfully transmit a signal from one node to another on the network.

In contrast, the architecture of a network tells technicians how packets of data are to be transported throughout the topology, such as how to avoid packets colliding with each other.

Tech Talk

Network topology: the system that defines the network media (i.e., wiring) and how the network media are configured.
Network architecture: the system that defines the standards used to communicate over the network.

Design specifications for a network topology and architecture are fairly standardized in the industry, which makes it relatively easy for network engineers to plan a network. However, implementing those plans is another story. Practical considerations usually stand in the way of installing a network quickly.

Let's say that you want to become the hero of your company by spearheading the effort to upgrade its computer network. You think you can probably have this baby up and running, purring like a kitten over a weekend.

If life could only be that simple. The reality is that you can talk-the-talk with the technology staff because conceptually you know the considerations that are involved in designing a computer network. And you might be able to apply topology and architecture rules to devise a preliminary design. However, as my plumber keeps reminding me, if it was that easy then the professionals would have been out of business years ago.

The devil in any technical project is in the details—those little things that cannot be remedied intuitively. I learned this the hard way when I tried fixing my car. I tried to avoid the pitfalls experienced by most shade-tree mechanics and signed up for an adult education auto repair class at a local technical school.

The first lesson was changing spark plugs. The instructor rolled the engine attached to an engine stand in front of the class and proceeded to show us how to unscrew, then screw in spark plugs. A simple task. That was until I tried doing this on my own car—in the street under the shade of a tree.

The spark plugs were buried some place among wires and other components in a position I could touch and unscrew. That is except for one spark plug. I could touch it alright, but hours after trying to get a wrench on it—not to mention scraped knuckles —I had no idea how anyone could remove this spark plug. This was nothing like the nice, clean, and fully exposed engine shown in class.

Ah, the tricks of the trade. A mechanic at the dealership knew exactly my experience. After chuckling a few minutes, he let me in on the secret. Cars are designed for the assembly line, not for the repair shop. Then he pulled out a special tool built especially to remove that problematic spark plug.

Computer networks are also fraught with pitfalls that professionals know how to handle, so don't be afraid to step up to the challenge of taking the lead on upgrading a network. However, avoid overstating your position until you confer with network engineers.

For example, many communities have laws that require a special coating be placed on wires that are installed between floors. Most office buildings are designed with a space between the ceiling and the flooring above. The special coating retards any fire that might be generated by the cables.

Likewise, there might be restrictions on the installation of network wires. Contractors need to be contacted, bids received, a contract awarded, parts ordered, and a schedule devised.

Then there are those physical restrictions in the building similar to the elusive spark plug in my car. Anyone who has ever tried to run wire in a house knows you need a clean passage so the wire can be snaked through the walls and across ceilings. The same kind of passage is also necessary to run network cables—and those passages may not exist because the architect never anticipated a need to run network cables.

NETWORK TOPOLOGIES.....................................

A topology of a network defines how nodes are linked to each other using wire or wireless connections. As mentioned in Chapter 3, a node is any device, such as a computer, a server, or a printer, attached to the network.

There are four common network topologies (see Table 4.1). These are the bus, ring, star, and mesh. Each describes the actual network wiring and the path the data follows over the network. These concepts were confusing the first time I heard them. Intuitively, I assumed the data path and the network wiring were one and the same. They are not.

The network wiring is called the physical topology and the data path is called the logical topology. Let's jump ahead a little and briefly explore two topologies (discussed in detail later in this chapter) that will illustrate the difference between physical and logical topologies.

We'll use the star (see Figure 4.4 on page 120) and ring topologies (see Figure 4.6 on page 122) for this example. Imagine a cable leading from each node and ending in a central location called a hub (see Chapter 3). This is a star topology because the wires form a star. Now imagine all nodes are connected to each other to form a ring. This is a ring topology.

The token ring architecture (see "Network Architecture" on page 126) uses the star topology as the physical topology and distributes data (i.e., data path) within the ring located inside the hub.

Table 4.1   Advantages and Disadvantages of Network Topologies

Topology	Advantages	Disadvantages
Bus Topology	The cable and hardware used are inexpensive. Simple to understand. Can be easily extended.	Difficult to troubleshoot. Every connection may have to be checked to find the problem. Increased network traffic decreases network performance. Physical length of the network is limited.
Star Topology	Failure of a computer will not stop the network. Troubleshooting is easy. Easy to add computers to the network.	Cabling can be expensive because a separate cable is needed for each computer. Failure of the hub stops the network.
Ring Topology	Provides equal opportunities for all computers to transmit data. Simple installation. Signals do not degrade as much as other topologies.	Failure of any node stops the network. The network must be stopped while the new connection is added. Distance is limited.
Mesh Topology	Uses the advantages of other topologies.	Difficult to troubleshoot. Difficult to maintain.

Bus Topology

The simplest way to connect nodes to form a network is to use one cable and connect each node to the cable, which causes all network traffic flows across a single cable. This is called the bus topology (Figure 4.1).

There are two methods used to connect a node to the cable. These are using a special connector or using a drop cable. The T-connector (Figure 4.2(a)) is the special connector used to join a network card to a bus network.

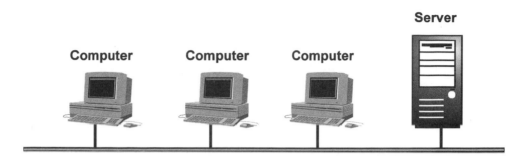

Figure 4.1
A bus topology links all network devices to the same cable.

Tech Talk

The T-connector: a device that looks like the letter "T." The top of the T is inserted into the cable much like a plumber taps into a pipe. The vertical bar of the letter screws onto the network card.
Drop-cable: the cable that extends from a node to the bus cable.

Many networks that are designed around a bus topology also use coaxial cable as the network media. Coaxial cable can carry a signal up to 500 meters, depending on whether thin or thick coaxial cable is used (see Chapter 3). The quality of the signal begins to drop off beyond that distance. A drop-cable or a T-connector is used to join a node to a thin coaxial bus, and a vampire clamp (Figure 4.2(b)) is used to do the same if the bus is a thick coaxial cable.

A vampire clamp has metal teeth that extend from the core of the drop cable and bite through the insulation of the thick coaxial cable making connection to the core of that cable.

Coaxial cable is available in various lengths. Using a barrel connector can extend these lengths. The barrel connector resembles a barrel (Figure 4.3) with each end screwed into the ends of each cable.

When you send an e-mail over a bus network, it is divided into pieces called packets (see Chapter 3) and sent over the network cable. Each computer looks at the destination address of each packet to determine if the packet is addressed to that computer. If it is, then the computer processes the packet, otherwise the packet is ignored.

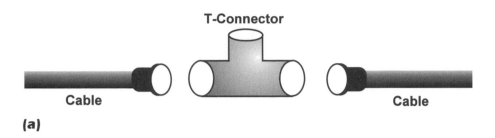

(a)

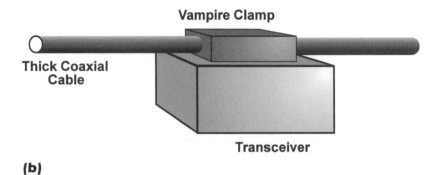

(b)

Figure 4.2
(a) A T-connector joins thin coaxial bus, and **(b)** a vampire clamp connects thick coaxial cables to backbone networks.

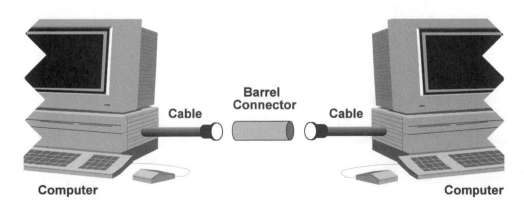

Figure 4.3
A barrel connector joins together two coaxial cables.

When you envision the bus topology, you may assume that the ends of the cable are connected to each other. This seems to be a natural assumption to make, but surprisingly a bus is a single wire that looks like a straight line rather than a circle.

A phenomenon of bus topology is bounce-back, so named because the signal transmitted over the cable returns when it reaches the end of the cable. This tends to unnecessarily increase traffic over the network because the signal has traveled to each node on the network by the time the signal reaches the ends of the cable. A device called a terminator is installed at the ends of the cable to prevent a signal from reflecting back on the cable. This means that once the e-mail reaches the end of the cable, the signal containing the e-mail is removed from the cable by the terminator.

Tech Talk

Bounce-back: a phenomenon that occurs when a signal reaches the end of a cable, reverses direction, and continues along the cable. A terminator at each end of the cable is used to prevent this.
Terminator: a device connected to the end of a bus to absorb the signal and prevent bounce back.

A bus topology is ideal for small networks because it provides an inexpensive way to connect nodes, since additional network components, such as a hub, are not required. However, a bus topology isn't without some disadvantages, the most critical of which is the repercussions of a break in the cable.

For example, in a bus topology network, you wouldn't be able to send an e-mail if there was a break in the cable because the path between your computer and the other computers on the network is broken.

Star Topology

If you imagine an octopus with a square body and tentacles reaching in all directions, you've just pictured a star topology (Figure 4.4). The body of a star network is a hub (see Chapter 3), which is a connection box for all cables in the network.

A hub is similar to the electrical panel in the basement of your house. Wires from each outlet converge in that location and enter the electrical panel through a port, which is associated with one of several circuit breakers in the panel. A hub also has a port for each node on the network.

The electrical panel receives electricity from one port (via the power company) and distributes power to all of the other ports. The hub does the same except the signal can be received from any port. However, a switching hub can be used, which redirects packets to only the port that contains the destination node.

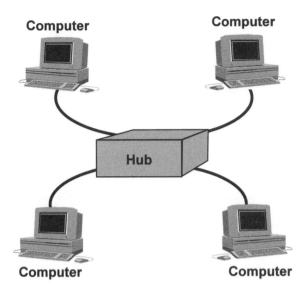

Figure 4.4
A star topology connects all devices to a central hub.

Let's say you send an e-mail again. However, this time it is sent over a network that uses the star topology. The e-mail travels from your computer to a central location called a hub. Since all computers that are connected to the network are also connected to the hub, it is easy for the hub to redirect the e-mail to the destination computer.

The cable leading from a network device to a hub is called a drop cable, which in a star topology is typically a twisted pair cable. This makes star networks less expensive and easier to wire than a bus topology that uses coaxial cable.

The star topology has a number of other advantages over bus topology. For example, the network continues to operate even if a problem arises from a drop cable. That is, a drop cable can be removed from the network without disrupting network operations.

You can add more network devices to a network that uses a star topology by connecting the device to an open port in the hub without having to disrupt other devices on the network. If a port isn't available, then another hub can be connected to the network. A port on each hub is connected to extend the number of ports available on the network (Figure 4.5).

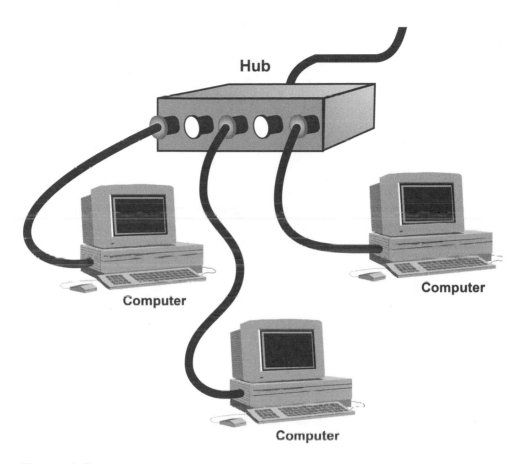

Figure 4.5
Hubs are connected together to extend the length of a network.

The hub gives an advantage to the star topology over the bus topology, but the hub is also a drawback. The cabling is the primary expense in a bus topology since network devices connect directly to the network cable. However, the star topology requires buying cables and a hub, making the hub an additional expense over the bus topology.

So is a bus topology cheaper than a star topology? Call in the accountants if you ever need to answer this question because you must consider factors other than cabling and network devices.

Ring Topology

Each node on the ring topology is an integral part of the network, just as if it was a piece of network cable. Here's how it works. A packet sent from the originating node is passed to the node's downstream neighbor, who examines the packet's destination address, and if it is not its address, passes the packet to its downstream neighbor (Figure 4.6).

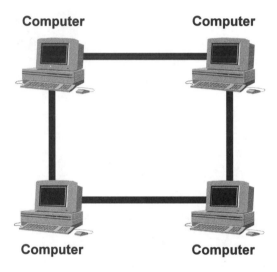

Figure 4.6
Each network device is an active part of the ring in a ring topology.

This electronic game of hot potato continues until either the packet reaches its destination or it is returned to the node that originated the transmission. This ensures that each node on the network receives all packets. However, as you might surmise, this benefit opens the network to certain risks.

Let's say that one of the nodes is offline or disabled for some reason. Network traffic comes to a halt because the network path is broken. To further complicate matters, technicians could find it difficult to locate the network device that is causing the problem because each node must be examined individually to verify that it is operational.

Mesh Topology

A mesh topology provides fault-tolerant security using redundant links. That's a mouthful of technological jargon. As with all the networking concepts you've learned so far in this book, there is a meaning that makes it a little easier to understand.

Fault tolerant describes something all of us wish for in any device. That is, the device never breaks down. Nothing works forever, but engineers are able to design a device so that it keeps going when a failure occurs. You can say that the device tolerates faults in the system.

Tech Talk

Fault tolerant: a feature that ensures that a network continues to operate in the face of a network component failure.

For most of us, a problem with our computer isn't a major disaster (although it might seem so at that time). We first try a lesson from the Bill Gates repair school—reboot your computer—which many times does the trick. (I wish he had invented the automobile. Wouldn't it be nice if whenever your car acted up all you'd need to do is turn it off and restart it?)

Wall Street firms, hospitals, and other organizations whose livelihood depends on fast access to information cannot afford to have their network stop operating for any amount of time. This is why engineers created the mesh topology that has built-in redundancy; if a part of the network fails, another part takes over. Redundancy is designed into a mesh network by using multiple links to nodes.

Let's say that your business requires constant e-mail service even if a server or a cable becomes disabled. You'll require a mesh topology similar to Figure 4.7. In a standard topology there would be a single server, a hub, and one set of cables to service the four computers in this example.

However, redundancy is necessary if you need to always be available if any of the four computers wants to send e-mail. Notice in Figure 4.7 that we have doubled the number of servers, routers, and cables that are found in a standard network topology.

If a cable, a server, or a router fails for any reason, there is a backup in place and operational. That is, e-mails and other information sent to the primary server are also sent to the backup server, enabling the backup server to immediately take over for the primary server without requiring technicians to do anything.

Many mesh networks use a router (see Chapter 3) to direct traffic along the best path to the designation address. A router can detect an outage along the network and then locate an alternate route for the packet. The quick change in direction might cause a fraction of a second delay in arrival time, but this is tolerable when compared to the alternative of a complete network failure.

The mesh topology is able to react to a network problem immediately without the need for manual intervention by a technician. However, this comes at a high price. The expense of cabling is enormous when compared to other topologies because of the added cable redundancy. There is also the difficulty of expanding the network because multiple cable links are required to add one node to the network.

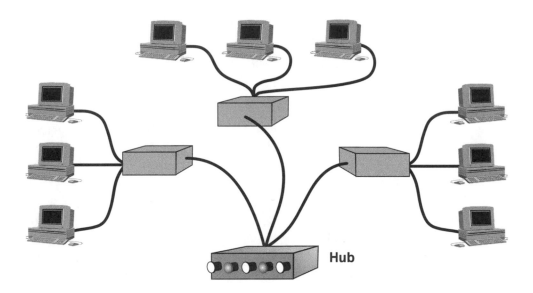

Figure 4.7
Star ring network.

Let's say we wanted to expand the four-node network to 10 nodes. Four nodes require eight cables and 10 nodes require 45 cables. Thirty seven new cables must be installed to increase the network by six nodes. You can begin to see how cost will become a significant factor before long.

Hybrid Topology

Just when you think you have a good understanding of network topology, engineers stir the pot with another topology called hybrid. To make matters more complex, this topology is a general term used to describe any combination of the other topologies.

Many networks use a hybrid topology so engineers can apply each topology to meet various situations throughout an organization, yet still be able to link all of them into one massive network.

The national highway system is a perfect analogy of a hybrid topology because various kinds of roadways join to enable you to get in your car and drive anywhere in the country. Your trip starts with the street outside of your house, which is likely to be a single-lane roadway permitting cars to travel in either direction on the street.

From there you travel on the main thoroughfare in your community. This roadway probably has two lanes and traffic control devices, such as a line dividing the street into two lanes and maybe a traffic light. Your trip continues to the local interstate where there are eight or more lanes marked by dashes and without any traffic lights along the complete stretch of highway.

A common hybrid topology is the star-ring topology. As the name implies, the star-ring topology is a combination of the star topology and the ring topology. If you could take an eye-in-the-sky view of the star-ring topology, you'd see only the star topology (Figure 4.8) because the ring is hidden inside the hub.

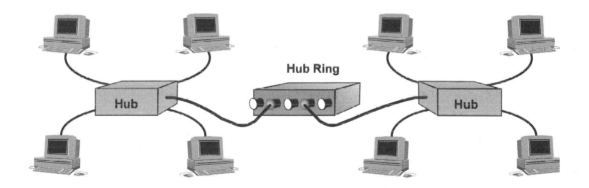

Figure 4.8
The star-ring hybrid topology has the characteristics of both the star topology and the ring topology.

A ring topology connects each node sequentially (see "Ring Topology" on page 122). A packet is transmitted to the next downstream node, which in turns passes the packet to its neighbor node.

A star topology connects each node using its own cable to the hub (see "Star Topology" on page 119). Packets sent by a node are retransmitted to all nodes by circuitry in the hub.

The star-ring topology uses individual cables to connect nodes to the hub. However, those cables are connected in a ring topology within the hub. This centralizes the ring to an accessible location while still maintaining the ease to connect nodes that the star topology offers. Of course, the network is still exposed to the same failure that exists with a ring topology.

A hybrid topology is used to tailor the right technology to the right situation and thereby balance the cost of technology with its benefits. For example, a large network might require only a segment of the network to be fault tolerant. Therefore, less expensive topologies can be used for other network segments.

NETWORK ARCHITECTURE ....

In the previous chapters, you learned how information, such as an e-mail, is sent from your computer by converting it into bits that are transmitted over a network. The network consists of computers and other network devices that are connected with a cable in an arrangement called a topology.

Network engineers needed to come up with a way to efficiently transmit information over a topology, and in doing so derived another level of complexity called network architecture. The best way to understand the concept of network architecture is to imagine the layout of a town.

All streets in this imaginary town begin at the center of town. This is similar in design to the star topology. However, this layout can become confusing to motorists, especially if all streets allow traffic to flow in both directions and the streets are only wide enough for one car to pass at a time.

A more efficient approach to using this layout (topology) is to designate each street as a one-way road and have some lead toward the center of town and others lead away. This is the general concept behind network architecture.

For example, suppose there are four nodes on the network: three computers and a server. Each is connected to the hub using a network card. One would expect that the next step is for a node to transmit a packet over the network, which is a likely scenario. However, what would happen if two nodes transmitted at the same time? Boom! A collision would occur.

As you might expect, this problem is addressed by the network operating system. Various components of the network operating system ensure that network traffic does not become a bumper car derby by enforcing rules determined by the network architecture.

There are five sets of rules, each known as a network architecture, used to ensure that packets flow freely over a network. These are Ethernet, Token Ring, ARCnet, FDDI, and Localtalk.

Ethernet

Ethernet is the daddy of network architecture, with roots going back to the late 1960s, when Xerox, Intel, and DEC got together to develop a way to transmit computer information over a cable. Their efforts were fine-tuned in 1982 to form the modern-day Ethernet. Ethernet standards describe how to provide traffic flow over a network and how to lay out a network to ensure that there is sufficient energy to send packets to every segment and node (see Table 4.2).

Table 4.2 Details of the Ethernet Specifications

	10BaseT	10base2	10Base5
Maximum number of hubs and repeaters on the network	4	4	4
Maximum segments on the network	1024	5	5
Maximum length of each segment	328 feet (100 meters)	607 feet (185 meters)	1,640 feet (500 meters)
Maximum number of segments that contain nodes on the network	1024	3	3
Maximum number of nodes on each segment	1	30	100
Maximum number of nodes on each network	1024	90	300
Minimum distance between nodes	Less than 1.6 feet (0.5 meters)	1.6 feet (0.5 meters)	8.2 feet (2.5 meters)

The initial problem solved with the Ethernet standard was how to prevent pack-ets transmitted by two nodes from colliding. The Ethernet solution was a reactive, rather than proactive, approach. The assumption was made that packets will be trans-mitted simultaneously and will collide. So engineers devised rules that define the ac-tion to be taken after the collision. This rule is called the Carrier Sense Multiple Access with Collision Detection Media Access Method, simply known as CSMA/CD (Figure 4.9).

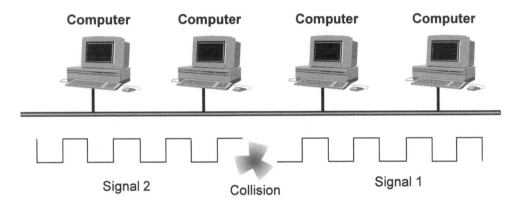

Figure 4.9
CSMA/CD requires transmitting devices to listen for a collision after sending a packet.

Tech Talk

CSMAC/CD: a method that requires software on network cards to listen to the network after transmitting a packet to hear if there is a collision. If so, then they must retransmit the packet after waiting a random time interval.

At first, this method seems fraught with problems. Waiting a second or two be-fore sending the packet again will delay the response time to such a degree that every-one on the network will complain. Besides, nothing prevents the packets from colliding the next time it is retransmitted.

These are good observations, but not in tune with the network speed. A second is too long between the transmission and retransmission. However, network cards re-transmit in a fraction of a second, so even if another collision happens it will not likely impact the response time. If it does, then engineers expand the network by opening new segments, thus reducing the amount of transmissions over a particular segment.

The other problem solved with the Ethernet standard was how to ensure successful transmission over various kinds of network media (i.e., cables). The solution was to devise three standards, each describing the number of segments, nodes, hubs, repeaters, and the length of cables on the network. These standards are 10BaseT, 10Base2, and 10Base5 (see Table 4.2 on page 127).

. . . .

DECODING THE SECRET BEHIND THE ETHERNET STANDARD

Who in the world came up with the 10BaseT and the other Ethernet standards? It seems engineers like to make up terms that require an engineering degree to understand. Why couldn't they use English words or at least label them standard A, standard B, and standard C?

The reason is that the name of an Ethernet standard contains its definition—as long as you know how to decode the definition. In contrast, the labels A, B, and C are meaningless unless you already know their definitions. The 10 implies the network can transmit packets at 10 megabits per second (MBPS). Base implies the network uses baseband technology for the transmission (see Chapter 2). The T implies that twisted pair cable is used for the network. The 2 implies thin coaxial cable is used and the 5 implies thick coaxial cable is used for the network.

10BaseT

The 10BaseT specification requires the network to use a hybrid topology that is a combination of star and bus topologies. Cables are arranged in a star topology leading from each node to a hub.

This is referred to as a physical star topology because the hub cables are connected inside to form a bus topology, which is know as a logical bus topology. Both active and intelligent hubs can be used in a 10BaseT network. The network must use category 3 or category 5 unshielded twisted pair cabling (see Chapter 3).

10BaseT networks are popular because they are inexpensive, easy to install, and the use of active or intelligent hubs makes it straightforward to locate trouble spots along the network. However, the network is limited to 1,024 segments, each of no more than 328 feet. Other rules are described in Table 4.2 on page page 127.

10Base2

10Base2, also known as Thin Ethernet, requires a thin coaxial cable be used in a bus topology. A continuous cable stretches the complete length of the network and BNC T connectors are used to link nodes to the bus. The cable must be RG-58 A/U or the military equivalent called RG58 C/U. Both categories use a stranded core. However, the military requires their cables to be shielded from stray signals. Another category called RG-58 /U is also acceptable to the 10Base2 standard, but is considered less reliable than the RG58 A/U and RG58 C/U because a solid core rather than a stranded core is used. A solid core provides a continuous body of copper rather than strands of copper, each having its own small core.

Engineers devised a special rule to ensure a smooth transmission of packets across a network. This is called the 5-4-3 rule, which states that the network is limited to five segments, four repeaters, and three of those segments can contain nodes (Figure 4.10). Therefore a maximum of 30 nodes can be connected to a segment and the entire network is limited to 90 nodes.

You don't need to be an engineer to realize the limitations of a 10Base2 network. This is why this standard isn't found in large networks and instead is used for smaller networks, such as in training rooms.

10Base 5

10Base 5, also known as Thick Ethernet, requires RG-8 thick coaxial cable. This, like the 10Base2 standard, uses a bus topology and follows the 5-4-3 rule. Nodes are connected to the cable by a tap, such as a vampire connection (see Figure 4.2(b) on page page 118), which is a device that pierces the cable to make the connection. One hundred nodes can connect to each segment, which results in a maximum of 300 nodes on the network.

The expense of thick coaxial cable makes a 10Base5 an expensive solution to a networking problem. However, 10Base5 networks are sometimes used to join 10Base2 networks to form a backbone network.

Tech Talk

Backbone: a central network path that interconnects other networks, much like the human backbone houses the central nervous system, which links nerve branches.

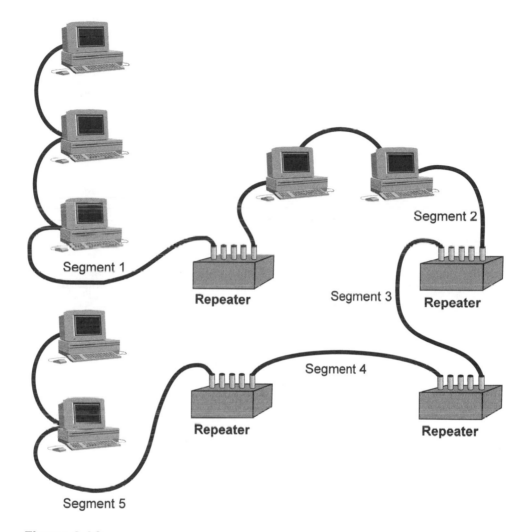

Figure 4.10
The 5-4-3 rule specifies the number of devices that can be connected to a
network segment.

Fast Ethernet

Fast Ethernet is an enhancement to the 10BaseT standard. Fast Ethernet increases the
speed of the network from 10 MBPS to 100 MBPS by requiring the use of two pairs of
category 5 twisted pair cables or four pairs of category 3 twisted pair cables. Another

requirement is that all devices on the network be configured to handle 100 MBPS. Devices that cannot keep up with this speed simply cannot be used on the network.

A variation of the Fast Ethernet standard is called 100Vg-AnyLAN, which is designated a voice grade (Vg) network because it can transmit voice communications at an acceptable rate, as well as data communication. AnyLAN implies that a bus or ring topology can be used for the network.

100Vg-AnyLAN doesn't use CSMA/CD to control access to the network. Instead it uses the Demand Priority Access method, in which packets are prioritized to gain access to the network.

Token Ring

I like to think of Token Ring as the hot potato of the network architecture. A node must receive the hot potato before it can transmit a packet over the network. The hot potato is called a token.

Tech Talk
Token: an empty packet that is passed to each node on the network.

The first node that logs onto the network creates the token and passes it to the next node. This pattern continues until the last node logs off the network. A node that receives the token examines it to determine if it contains information. If it doesn't, then the node has a choice to fill the token with information—which is to send as a packet—or to hand the empty token to the next node in the ring (Figure 4.11). Only one token is transmitted on the network at any time, which prevents packets from colliding as they make their way around the network.

Token Ring uses a hybrid topology, which is a combination of the star and ring topologies. The star topology is used to connect nodes to a hub within which a ring topology is used to complete the path to each node. A hub used in the Token Ring architecture is called a Multi-station Access Unit (MAU).

A Token Ring network can move information at either 4 MBPS or 16 MBPS, depending on the configuration of network devices. There are three types of cables used in a Token Ring. These are shielded twisted pair (STP), unshielded twisted pair (UTP), and fiber optics. The selection of cable determines the maximum distances of the network. UTP can reach 45 meters, while fiber optic cable extends the network to more than a kilometer.

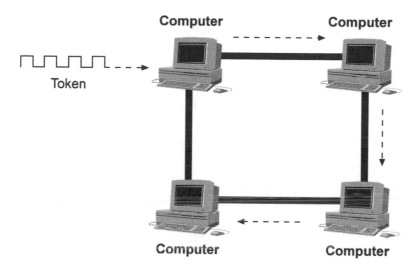

Figure 4.11
Each device on a Token Ring network needs to receive a thoken before the device can transmit a packet over the network.

Each node on a Token Ring has the responsibility to keep information flowing by passing the token around the network, which helps to handle heavy network traffic much better than Ethernet. Nodes also have another responsibility: to monitor the reliability of other nodes on the network. I call this the buddy system.

Each node monitors its nearest upstream neighbor on the network to ensure that the neighbor is alive and well. If the neighbor is unable to keep up with other nodes on the network, its downstream neighbor transmits a special packet called a beacon to all nodes, notifying all of them that an error has occurred.

Each node responds the same way when they get the beacon. Immediately, nodes including the node that transmitted the beacon run a self-test and remove themselves from the network if there is a problem. Nodes also examine the token to see if the node that caused the error sent the token. If so, then the token is removed and a new token is created.

ARCnet

I mentioned that Ethernet was the daddy of networks. Well, ARCnet is the granddaddy in the network family and first made its appearance in 1977. There are still a few ARCnets in operation, although Ethernet has replaced most of them.

ARCnet can be set up with star, bus, or hybrid topology using unshielded twisted pair, coaxial cable, or fiber optic cables to connect a maximum of 255 nodes. Both active and passive hubs are used, although at least one active hub must be on the network.

Data is transmitted across the network and each computer reads and processes data addressed to it and ignores other data. A token is passed around the network. Only a computer with the token can transmit data.

There are 255 addresses available on the network identified by numbers 1 through 255. Addresses are manually set using dip switches on the network card in each computer. Tokens are passed around the network based on the network address.

For example, computer 1 sends the token to computer 2. Computer 2 sends the token to computer 3, and so forth. A limitation of the ARCnet is that the next computer might be the farthest away from the computer sending the token. This could mean longer transmission delays because of the distance the token must travel.

Here's what happens when the network is started. The computer with the lowest address, called the station identifier, sends a query over the network asking if another computer has a higher address. If there is no response, then the computer increments the address and repeats the query until it receives a response.

Once a response is received, the computer sends the responding computer the token. The computer that receives the token repeats the same process. Once all the computers respond, the ARCnet is considered configured and is ready for operation.

FDDI

A newer member of the network clan is the Fiber Distributed Data Interface, known by its acronym: FDDI. This is a fast, long-distance highway that supports up to 100 MBPS with up to 62 miles (100 kilometers) between nodes. FDDI networks are commonly used as the backbone that links several smaller networks.

Engineers designed FDDI networks to be fault tolerant. Fiber optic cables are used to form two ring topologies. The first ring, called the primary ring, handles network traffic. The second, called the secondary ring, takes over if the primary ring fails. Network traffic is sent in the opposite direction to compensate for the error (Figure 4.12).

The FDDI network uses an enhanced version of the Token Ring architecture. Although each node can transmit only if it receives the token, FDDI networks accept multiple packets to be transmitted at the same time. In addition, a priority system is used that allows some nodes to be given higher priority over others. For example, a server might take precedence over a computer because it is responding to a previously transmitted request.

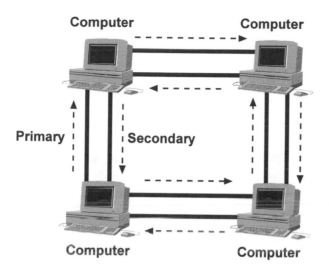

Figure 4.12
FDDI is used to transmit data over fiber optic cables.

When a lot of data needs to be transmitted across a long distance quickly, then the FDDI is the network to do the job since it transmits information at the speed of light. However, don't rush out and demand to have an FDDI installed in your office. You'll be in for a surprise once you get the bill. FDDI networks are expensive and difficult to install and maintain.

LocalTalk

LocalTalk is the network architecture developed by Apple Computer for the Macintosh computer, and it supports both Ethernet and Token Ring architectures, called EtherTalk and TokenTalk, respectively.

Originally, LocalTalk used shielded twist pair cables in a star or hybrid topology. However, firms other than Apple Computer modified the network to accept unshielded twisted pair cables. Up to 32 nodes can be linked to a LocalTalk network.

LocalTalk uses a variation on the Carrier Sense Multiple Access with Collision Detection Media Access Method (CSMA/CD) (see "Ethernet" on page 127). The LocalTalk method is called Carrier Sense Multiple Access with Collision Avoidance Media Access Method (CSMA/CA).

You'll recall that in CSMA/CD a node listened for a collision after transmitting a packet. If a collision is detected, it waited a random time period before retransmitting the packet. In CSMA/CA, a node is required to listen for traffic on the network before transmitting the packet, which dramatically reduces the likelihood of a collision occurring on the network.

Most Popular

Table 4.3 contains a summary of the advantages and disadvantages of each architecture. The most popular architecture is Ethernet using 10Base2, 10Base5, 10BaseT, or 10BaseF. 10Base2 and 10Base5 use coaxial cable in a bus topology. 10BaseT uses unshielded twisted pair in a star topology. 10BaseF is the primary selection for a backbone network that uses fiber optics to connect other networks.

Table 4.3   Advantages and Disadvantages of Network Architectures

Architecture	Advantages	Disadvantages
Ethernet 10Base2	Simple to install Inexpensive	Difficult to troubleshoot
Ethernet 10Base5	Long distances	Expensive Difficult to install Difficult to troubleshoot
Ethernet 10BaseT	Inexpensive Simple to install Easy to troubleshoot	Limited distance
Ethernet 10BaseF	Long distances	Expensive Difficult to install
Ethernet 100BaseT	Fast Simple to connect Easy to troubleshoot	Limited distance Expensive
Ethernet 100VG-AnyLAN	Fast Simple to connect Easy to troubleshoot Used with Ethernet or Token Ring	Limited distance Expensive hardware

Table 4.3 *Advantages and Disadvantages of Network Architectures (Continued)*

Architecture	Advantages	Disadvantages
Token Ring	Fast Reliable	Expensive Difficult to troubleshoot
ARCnet	Inexpensive Easy to install Reliable	Slow Poor interconnection with other systems
LocalTalk	Simple Easy to install	Slow Limited size
FDDI	Very fast Long distances Secured Resistant to EMI	Expensive Difficult to install

NETWORK PROTOCOLS...

Just when you think you've learned all the rules of networking, you're hit with another set called network protocols.

Network topology defines how the "highway" is laid out. Network architecture sets the rules of the road, such as how traffic gets on and off the highway. Network protocols define the expected behavior of drivers while using the highway.

Technically, network protocols are standards for data communications, which are supported by a network architecture. In fact, a number of network architectures support more than one network protocol and can handle multiple protocols being used at the same time.

In Chapter 2 you learned about the OSI Model that defines the process for communicating over a network. The process is divided into seven subprocesses, called layers. Each layer is defined by a set of rules called protocols that specify how data is handled at that level. Manufacturers of network software and hardware incorporate those protocols into their products to ensure that their products will be compatible with the existing network.

Network protocols are grouped into sets of compatible protocols known as protocol suites, but commonly referred to as a protocol stack, much like the layers of the

OSI model. Network technicians select the network protocol stack to use on the network when they connect your computer to a network.

Tech Talk
Protocol suite: a set of compatible protocols used to communicate over a network.

This sounds a bit confusing, so let's clarify the situation with an example. The OSI Model defines how one layer communicates with another. That is, the different layers need only to standardize the format of data they send to and receive from other layers. Once the layer receives the information, it can process it any way it wants as long as the output of the process is in the format the next layer requires.

This is like you sending a letter. You give it to the U.S. Postal Service in a particular format (i.e., the destination address and your address on the outside of the envelope and the letter inside the envelope). You expect the letter to be delivered to the destination intact. You don't care how it gets there as long as it gets there in one piece.

The U.S. Postal Service acts similarly to a network protocol that follows the OSI Model. However, there are other ways you can send letters. You can use other protocols, such as Federal Express, United Parcel Service, and an assortment of other such services.

Each of these services expects to receive the letter in the same format as you prepared it for the U.S. Postal Service, and you expect the letter to be received intact. Each service uses its own method to get the letter to the destination. Some services are better than others and you can choose which to use just like the network technician can choose which network protocol to use.

There are a number of distinctions between network protocols. These include reliability and the way in which a connection is established with the destination node. For example, a protocol might increase throughput of the network by not acknowledging packets when they are received. This reduces the amount of network traffic significantly since one—not two—transmissions are required for each packet sent over the network.

Another distinction is the way that a communications protocol connects the sending and receiving nodes. There are two common methods. These are using a connection-oriented protocol or a connectionless protocol.

Let's say you send an e-mail on a network that uses a connection-oriented protocol. The e-mail isn't transmitted until the destination computer is ready to receive it. In contrast, on a network that uses a connectionless protocol, the e-mail is transmitted without first contacting the destination computer.

**A connection-oriented protocol: a rule that creates a virtual circuit connection with the destination node before a packet is transmitted.
A virtual circuit: a connect that exists only for the duration of a transmission.
A connectionless protocol: transmits packets without first making a connection with the destination node. That is, packets are sent regardless of whether the destination node is ready to receive them.**

There are five commonly used network protocol stacks. These are TCP/IP, NetBEUI, IPX/SPX, AppleTalk, and DLC. Table 4.4 lists their uses.

Table 4.4 Common Network Protocols

Protocol	Typical Use	Routable Protocol (see Chapter 3)
TCP/IP	Large networks such as the Internet, intranets, and extranets	Yes
NetBEUI	Small Windows networks	No
IPX/SPX	NetWare networks	Yes
AppleTalk	Apple Macintosh networks	Yes
DLC	IBM mainframe networks	No

TCP/IP Suite

One of the most popular protocol stacks is the Transmission Control Protocol/Internet Protocol (TCP/IP) protocol suite. You no doubt have heard this term bantered around by the office network guru since it is the protocol suite used for the Internet.

Many large corporations adopt the TCP/IP protocol suite for use internally in their Intranets, which is a private internet within a corporation. This is because the TCP/IP protocol suite provides a broad range of protocols that offer a useful set of features. These include TCP and User Datagram Protocol (UDP), Network File System (NFS), Serial Line Internet Protocol (SLIP), and Point-to-Point Protocol (PPP). The downside of using the TCP/IP protocol suite is the need to hire a specialist to administer the network, which isn't as necessary with the other protocol suites.

TCP is a connection-oriented protocol and UDP is a connectionless protocol. Both are used to transport packets over the network. NFS is the network file system protocol that enables nodes on the network to share files.

Tech Talk

NFS: the network file system that works on the application layer and makes files on a remote computer appear as a subdirectory on a local computer.

SLIP is the Serial Line Internet Protocol, which was the first protocol used to access the Internet using a dial-up access. SLIP works on the physical layer of the OSI Model, but does not provide security.

PPP is the Point-to-Point Protocol, which is an improved version of SLIP. PPP offers security, data compression, and error control. In addition, PPP dynamically assigns network addresses to nodes as they log on the network. This means when you log on the Internet using PPP, your computer is assigned a temporary address on the Internet. This address becomes available to another computer once you disconnect from the Internet.

IPX and SPX

Novell NetWare was one of the first networks used in corporations primarily as a way to share files among computers. IPX, known as Internetwork Pack Exchange, and SPX, Sequenced Packet Exchange, are the protocol stacks used on NetWare networks. IPX is the connectionless protocol and SPX is the connection-oriented protocol.

NetWare networks are able to connect to Windows NT by using NWLink, which is Microsoft's implementation of these Novell NetWare protocols. IPX and SPX are suitable for small networks, not larger networks, which use TCP/IP.

Tech Talk

Internetworking: a method that divides the data link layer into the Logical Link Control (LLC), which manages flow control and error corrections between network devices, and the Media Access Control (MAC), which controls how the network card accesses the network.

NetBEUI

IBM and Microsoft got together and developed NetBEUI as the protocol for the Windows file sharing and communication standards for workstations, which is known as the Network Basic Input/Output System (NetBIOS).

NetBEUI is ideal for small networks because it is an efficient protocol. However, NetBEUI is not widely supported outside the Windows community. Another drawback is that NetBEUI cannot be used with routers, therefore a bridge must be used to connect segments of the network (see Chapter 3).

AppleTalk

Apple Computer developed a suite of protocols called AppleTalk so Macintosh computers can share files and printers. AppleTalk is flexible; it can be used with Ethernet, Token Ring, or Localtalk network architectures.

Although AppleTalk is built for Macintosh computers, Microsoft created a link to Windows NT called the Microsoft Services for Macintosh (SFM). SFM enables Macintosh computers to access Windows NT services.

DLC

IBM developed a transport protocol called the Data Link Control (DLC) for use with IBM's mainframe Systems Network Architecture (SNA). This is the protocol used for networks to communicate with mainframes. DLC is also used to communicate with certain kinds of network printers, such as the Hewlett Packard JetDirect. However, TCP/IP is becoming preferable to DLC.

. . . .

IEEE STANDARDS

You may be asking yourself who makes up these rules used to communicate over a network. One of the major rule-making organizations is the Institute of Electrical and Electronic Engineers (IEEE).

Imagine how difficult it would be if network hardware and software manufacturers developed their own standards. None of their products would work with each other. The industry foresees such problems and turns to the IEEE to develop rules, known as standards.

The IEEE launches a project and assembles leaders from the industry to create standards. Projects are given a number and standards are identified by a value following a decimal point. For example, the IEEE launched Project 802 in 1980 to develop standards for networking, which are contained in Table 4.5.

Table 4.5   IEEE Networking Standards

Standard	Description
802.1	Internetworking and the OSI model
802.2	Logical Link control (LLC)
802.3	CSMA/CD Ethernet media access method
802.4	Token bus media access method
802.5	Token ring media access method
802.6	Metropolitan area networks
802.7	Broadband technologies
802.8	Fiber optic technologies
802.9	Hybrid voice and data networking
802.10	Network security
802.11	Wireless networking
802.12	High speed LANS

SUMMARY ....

A computer network is similar to a highway; they both have a layout, rules of the road, and standards by which every driver is expected to meet. In network terms, these are network topology, network architecture, and network protocols.

Network topology is how cables and network devices merge together to form the electronic highway. There are five types of network topologies: bus, star, ring, mesh, and hybrid.

A bus topology consists of a single cable, much like a strand of spaghetti, in which the ends are not connected. Attached to the cable are nodes, which are network devices, such as a computer. Packets that travel the length of the cable must be trapped by devices called terminators to prevent them from traveling back over the network.

A star topology resembles a spider—each node is connected to a hub. The hub receives a packet from a node, then distributes the packet to the other nodes. The ring topology consists of a single cable similar to a bus except the ends of the cable are connected to each other. Each node intersects the cable and thus becomes part of the network path and is required to receive, then pass along every packet.

A mesh topology uses redundant connections to each node to provide a fault tolerant network. That is, backup connections are already in place and automatically become activated if a connection to a node has an error.

A hybrid topology is a combination of two or more topologies, such as the star and ring topologies in which nodes are connected to a hub using a star topology, but inside the hub nodes are connected using a ring topology.

There are five kinds of network architectures. These are Ethernet, Token Ring, ARCnet, FDDI, and Localtalk. Ethernet uses Carrier Sense Multiple Access with Collision Detection Media Access Method to control access to the network. The CSMA/CD method requires each node that transmits a packet to listen for a collision with another packet. If a collision is heard, the packet must be retransmitted.

Ethernet also has rules that describe the number of devices and segments that can be used in a network. This is called the 5-4-3 rule. There are several Ethernet standards, each defining the speed at which data can be transmitted using a particular transmission type and using a specific kind of cable. The standards are described in the name. For example, 10BaseT is interpreted as 10 MBPS speed using baseband transmission technology over twisted pair cable.

Token Ring requires a node to obtain a special packet called a token before the node can transmit information over a network. The token is created by the first node to log on the network and is passed to its neighboring node, which in turn continues to pass the token around.

ARCnet is the granddaddy in the network family and first made its appearance in 1977. There are still a few ARCnets in operation although Ethernet has replaced most of them.

FDDI is a network architecture designed for fiber optic transmission and can transmit data at 100 MBPS for up to 62 miles.

LocalTalk was developed by Apple Computer and is used to network Macintosh computers. LocalTalk uses Carrier Sense Multiple Access with Collision Avoidance Media Access Method. CSMA/CA requires a node to listen for network traffic before transmitting a packet.

Network protocols are rules that define how the various steps in the transmission process are handled. Network protocols are grouped to form a protocol suite or stack in which each protocol in the stack is compatible with the others.

Two of the more popular network protocol stacks are TCP/IP and IPX/SPX. TCP/IP is the network stack used to communicate over the Internet and intranet. IPX/SPX is used for the same purpose but with Novell NetWare networks.

Many network devices, such as a computer running Windows, can use a number of network protocol stacks simultaneously.

Questions

1. What are the advantages and disadvantages of a mesh topology?

2. What is the difference between network topology and network architecture?

3. Create a network layout diagram for 10Base2 architecture.

4. How does a star-ring topology work?

5. Why would a hybrid topology be used for a network?

6. What kind of network would use a TCP/IP Suite?

7. What technology is used to connect a Macintosh to a Windows NT network?

8. Why are different protocol stacks available for network communication?

9. Describe the technology used to create a backbone.

10. Why is there a need to specify a maximum length for a network?

5 Networks: Connecting over a Wide Area

In this chapter...

They Said It...

*"No distance is too far to prevent you from
keeping in touch with a friend."*

Anonymous

A crucial benefit of a network is the ability to share information with network de-vices located around the world. This is possible through the creation of a wide area network that enables local area networks to exchange data over long distances.

Wide area networks use a variety of technologies, including cabling and wire-less, to transfer data. In this chapter you'll explore wide area networks and see how they work. You'll learn about:

- the telephone system

- switched and dedicated services

- the layout of private lines

- signaling and store and forward switching

- private branch exchange (PBX)

- wide area networks

- types of lines and services

- ISDN

- DS1

- T1, T2, T3, and T4 lines

- virtual private networks

- frame relay network access method

- ATM network access service

- fiber optic network

- wireless networks

REALITY CHECK...

We had completed a new international system for a major Wall Street firm when word got out that they were looking for someone to introduce the system to the firm's Pacific Rim offices. In technical terms this is called a free two-week tour of Hong Kong and Tokyo, with enough frequent-flyer miles to cover the cost of a summer vacation!

However, to my surprise, the demo of the system would be shown from our offices in New York at 2 P.M.—Hong Kong time! That meant 3 A.M. New York time.

What happened next still excites me. I was able to take over a computer in Hong Kong from my desk in New York. Everything I saw on my screen was also seen on the Hong Kong computer. Every time I clicked the mouse or pressed a letter on the keyboard in New York, the computer in Hong Kong responded the same way nearly instantaneously.

Just think: My keystrokes left my keyboard and traveled without interruption to Hong Kong in a fraction of a second, and the image on their screen made the return trip in the same length of time. Let's not overlook the fact that I was holding a telephone conversation with them throughout the demo.

Instantaneous communication over vast distances appears miraculous to most of us. However, after reading the first few chapters of this book, you realize there must be a scientific explanation for this miracle—and there is. In this chapter, you'll explore the technology used to connect computers between office buildings located anywhere from across the parking lot to around the world.

THE TELEPHONE SYSTEM.....................................

Alexander Bell probably never fully appreciated his contribution to society. Can you imagine life today without the telephone? Bell and his long line of fellow inventors, scientists, and engineers have enabled us to talk with someone around the world just as if the person was sitting in the same room with us.

Telephone technology is also the keystone that enables our computers to talk with one another regardless of where they are located in the world—as long as the computer is connected to the telephone system. My systems demonstration in Hong Kong couldn't have taken place unless both our computers were linked to the public telephone system.

The first chapter of the book showed you the basic science of how this is done. The signal that leaves our telephone or modem enters a complex system, technically called the *public switch telephone network*. Think of it as the international super highway.

Tech Talk

Public switch telephone network: a network of cables and switches that route signals to any telephone on the network, based on the telephone number the caller dials.

We know the public switch telephone network simply as the telephone system that is at the end of the wire leading from our telephone. While this is true, the telephone system is actually a network of networks that are connected by a sophisticated set of switches, which is where the name *switch telephone network* is derived. A key feature of the telephone system is the capability to connect to various networks nearly instantaneously. This is called *real-time switching*.

Tech Talk

Real-time switching: the capability of the telephone network to connect to any point in the telephone system when someone makes a call.

Let's jump on a telephone call and follow it through the telephone system. Regardless of whether we are telephoning a friend or connecting to our Internet Service Provider (ISP), we are making a telephone call. The telephone system does not know if we are speaking, sending a fax, or sending a stream of computer data.

Our initial step is to dial a telephone number, which sounds like a series of strange tones played by the telephone. The sounds are called Dual Tone Multi-Frequency (DTMF). The telephone or modem generates two frequencies in the audio spectrum of the electromagnetic spectrum (see Chapter 1) for each number of the telephone number.

The tones are similar to those used by an electric keyboard, although I don't suggest trying to learn to "play" your telephone since this can become an expensive lesson. By dialing the telephone number, you are actually encoding the telephone number into DTMF, which is then sent to the central office of your local telephone company where it is decoded into an address signal of the telephone or modem that you are calling.

The central office is technically the other end of your telephone line. After the telephone number is deciphered, computers in the central office parse the telephone number. That is, the telephone number is broken down into components.

There can be three components. These are the area code, exchange, and the number that identifies the telephone within the exchange. The area code isn't required and calls without the area code are assumed to be located within the caller's area. The caller's area is shrinking in recent years because the telephone company is running out of telephone numbers within the older area codes. For example, at one time, a state might have had two area codes for the entire state. Today, one of those area codes covers perhaps only a few towns in that same state.

Here's one way to picture this relationship. My telephone is connected to a small network within the public telephone system. This is called an exchange, which is housed in the central office of my local telephone carrier. The first three digits that follow the area code identify the exchange.

When I call someone who is also attached to my exchange, my telephone call stays within the central office. You'll recognize this as a local telephone call, one that doesn't require an area code and normally is included in your monthly telephone charge.

The area code groups central offices within a metropolitan region of the country, although these regions are becoming smaller as the demand for telephone numbers increase. In general, we can say there are three networks. There is a network of telephones called the central office or exchange; the network of central offices called an area code; and a network of area codes.

The central office routes a call along the appropriate path on the network. If the first digit of the telephone number is 1, then computers in the central office assume that the next three digits comprise the area code and forward the call to the long-distance carrier (i.e., network of area codes) to process the call.

However, if the first digits represent a country code, then the central offices forward the call to the long-distance carrier, which in turn passes the call to telephone service in that country.

If the first digit is not a 1, then the computer in the central office assumes that the call is not a long-distance call and that it is destined for a telephone within the area code. However, a decision still must be made to determine if the telephone number is within the exchange or outside of it. The first three digits answer this question. If these digits represent the exchange of the central office, then the call is routed to the telephone that is assigned to the next four digits; otherwise the call is routed to the central office of the exchange.

Switched and Dedicated Services

Calls we dial ourselves use the switched service provided by the telephone company. The term *switched service* is the technical term used to describe something most of us do every day: make a telephone call.

The telephone company creates a temporary circuit between our telephone and the phone of the person we are calling. In the case of computers, our modem calls the remote computer's modem. The temporary circuit is called a *virtual circuit*. Intuitively, we have some notion of what the term *circuit* means and we usually conjure the image of a circuit board.

Tech Talk

Virtual circuit: a temporary connection between two points on the telephone network that disappears once a call is completed.

While the image is correct, we need to have a more formal definition to fully understand the concept of a virtual circuit. A circuit is a physical connection between at least two points, such as a string connected to two paper cups to form a crude telephone circuit. You can touch a physical circuit because, as with the paper cup telephone circuit, you can hold the complete circuit in your hands.

However, the term *virtual* changes this concept, because virtual implies that something appears real, but is a figment of our imagination. Anything virtual is not physical—you can't touch it.

Virtual and circuit used together to describe a circuit seems to be contradictory—a kind of paradox. Yet, virtual circuit actually describes the path of your telephone call. The telephone systems consist of a network of networks that are connected through a set of switches.

Each switch connects one network to another and several switches are used to connect the network in your telephone company's central office to a central office located on the other side of the country.

These connections create a temporary circuit between your telephone or computer and the one at the destination (Figure 5.1). The circuit exists for the duration of the telephone call. Once the call is completed, the circuit disappears. That is, the direct connection between your site and the destination no longer exists and must be recreated when you make another call to that remote location. This is a virtual circuit, which is the keystone of a switched service provided to you by your telephone company.

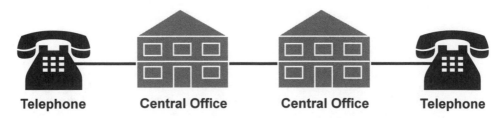

Telephone   **Central Office**   **Central Office**   **Telephone**

Figure 5.1

A temporary circuit exists for as long as the telephone call. (Redrawn with permission from Prentice Hall. Dodd, Annabel Z. The Essential Guide to Telecommunications. Upper Saddle River, NJ: Prentice Hall, 2000, p.125.)

Dedicated Service

The switch service is ideal for typical voice and remote computer access, such as when you and I connect to the Internet. We pay for the duration of the call, and the physical circuits and switches used to create our virtual circuit can be reused once our call is completed.

However, there are situations when dialing the telephone or modem becomes time consuming, especially when we are dialing the same telephone number frequently. I'm not talking about calling your friends. I am talking about a business calling another business, such as is the case with two Wall Street trading partners who pick up the telephone and the trading partner is already on the other end of the phone. No dialing is necessary

The telephone company makes a direct connection between both sites. This is called a *dedicated service*. The circuit isn't temporary and doesn't disappear when the receiver is placed back on to the telephone.

Tech Talk

Dedicated service: a permanent connection between two points on the telephone network. The connection remains intact after each call is completed.

Dedicated service is sometimes referred to as having a dedicated or private line between sites. The telephone company charges a flat monthly fee for this service, allowing an unlimited number of calls to be made between these sites. However, the dedicated line cannot be used to call anyone else since the dedicated service lacks the capability to receive, decode, and route telephone numbers to other locations. Companies frequently use the dedicated service to connect a computer to a remote site. This enables two locations to share information around the clock.

Although the advantage of using a dedicated line is obvious, especially for remote computer access, there are drawbacks. The company who rents the private line must manage dedicated lines. The telephone company manages switched service.

This may seem to be a trivial cost of doing business, but it isn't if a company has private lines connecting to multiple sites. A technical staff must be hired to track the inventory of lines and maintain and repair hardware needed to link to the dedicated service.

Dedicated lines are expensive, therefore they are typically used to handle communication that is critical to an organization's operation. And this critical traffic adds to the complexity of using a dedicated service because multiple lines are commonly use to link two sites. One line is used as the primary link and the other as backup in case the primary fails. Telephone companies have seized this complexity as an opportunity to offer expanded services, which includes the telephone company staff in place of a firm's technical staff managing their dedicated lines.

The Layout of Private Lines

In the previous chapter, you learned that the layout of a network is called the network's topology and since the telephone system is also a network, there is also a topology used to connect telephone cables. The topology of private (dedicated) lines plays an important role in the decision to use such lines to link to a remote computer because it affects costs and reliability of the connection.

There are four private line topologies that are offered by many telephone companies. These are *point-to-point*, *multipoint*, *star*, and *mesh*. A point-to-point topology is one in which both computers are connected using a single line, much like the way a string is used to connect the two paper cups in a primitive telephone. Of course, if something happens to the line, all communications between the two connections is lost and the connection cannot be re-established by redialing the remote computer's telephone number. This is because a dedicated service, rather than a switched service, is used.

The multipoint topology is designed to provide redundant connections between two sites. That is, more than one line is used to connect two locations. One line is designated as the primary line and the others are secondary or backup lines used in case the primary line fails.

The star topology (Figure 5.2) is used to connect multiple remote sites to one central location, called a *hub*. This is identical to the star topology described in the previous chapter except that the telephone company configures the private line network, which is used to connect to locations outside of a building. Organizations favor a star topology private network whenever there is a need to poll remote computers.

Tech Talk

Polling: the regular transfer of data between a series of computers located in remote locations. A central computer systematically calls (polls) each computer to initiate the exchange of data.

Let's say that you owned a chain of supermarkets. Prices for every product in the stores are entered into a central computer at the home office. Every evening when the stores close, the home office computer connects to each of the stores' computers and uploads the price list. This is referred to as *polling*, in which the home office computer "asks" the store's computer if it is ready to receive the updated prices.

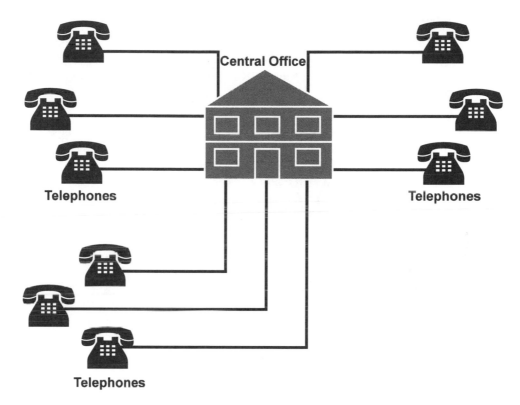

Figure 5.2
Multiple remote sites are connected to one central location, called a hub. (Redrawn with permission from Prentice Hall. Dodd, Annabel Z. The Essential Guide to Telecommunications. Upper Saddle River, NJ: Prentice Hall, 2000, p.150.)

The mesh topology is similar to the mesh topology used for local area networks, which was mentioned in the previous chapter. In a mesh topology, all nodes on the network are connected to each other to form a fault-tolerant network. If a private line becomes disabled, then one of the other lines in the mesh topology goes into action and keeps the lines of communication open to that node. A mesh topology ensures that the transmission will go through, but a high monthly cost is the price a company pays for such service. This is because there are a larger number of private lines used in a mesh topology than with other topologies.

Signaling and Store and Forward Switching

You probably have a good idea what is meant when I say that telephones provide two channels of communications. These two channels enable us to speak and to hear the person we call at the same time, similarly to the way we hold a conversation with someone in person.

This contrasts to the way a police officer in the field must pause after transmitting a call and wait for a response. Police radios use a single communications channel to send and receive a call.

However, there is more to the telephone system than meets the eye. The telephone system has a third communications channel that is used to manage a call, called Signaling System 7 (SS7). SS7 is like a stage mom who keeps a watchful eye over all her little children (telephone calls). SS7 is a signal that routes calls and provides a dial tone, a busy signal, Caller ID, and 800 and 900 number services. I mustn't leave out the most important information carried over this channel: tracking information used to calculate our telephone bill.

Tech Talk
Signal System 7: the third communications channel in the telephone network, used to manage telephone calls.

I think of the SS7 as the telephone network's own telephone network, since this is the way central office "talks" to your telephone and to other carriers. For example, once the central office decodes the first digit of the number you dial as a 1, an SS7 signal is transmitted to the long-distance carrier that you selected to say, "Hey! Wake up! This call is for you." The call is then turned over to the long-distance carrier for further processing.

SS7 is used by telephone companies to provide advanced services, such as voice mail, that do not require the sender and receiver to be available at the same time. This is known as *store switching,* which means information is collected from the sender and held until the receiver is online. Our normal telephone calls use forward switching, which sends our information to the receiver immediately.

Store switching offers a wide variety of ways to communicate over the telephone system. For example, one call can be automatically transmitted to many receivers and attempts to transmit can occur multiple times until the message is received. Likewise, information can be transmitted at off-peak times, which could reduce the cost of the call.

Private Branch Exchange (PBX)

Our telephones connect directly to the central office of the telephone company and for this privilege we usually pay a flat monthly charge plus another charge every time we make a phone call. Some calls are included in the monthly charge, while others, such as long distance calls, are charged based on the call. Cost of this service isn't too pricey unless we need to make and receive many calls simultaneously, such as in the case of a business.

Businesses are able to reduce the expense of telephone service by creating their own telephone network on their premises. This is called a *private branch exchange (PBX)*.

Tech Talk

Private branch exchange: a privately owned telephone system that performs the function of an exchange on the telephone network.

A PBX is similar to the central office of the telephone company in that all the telephones within the business converge into a central hub within the business. The central hub, which is a computer, routes telephone calls among telephones within the business and calls to a location outside of the PBX. That is, between the PBX and the telephone company.

The telephone company assigns the business a block of telephone numbers, such as 555-7000. The telephone company routes any telephone number between 7000 and 7999 for the 555 exchange to the business' PBX system (Figure 5.3). Computers in the PBX system decode the telephone number, then route the call to the proper telephone extension within the business.

PBX systems are economical because they reduce the need for telephone lines coming into the business. Let's say the business has 100 telephones. If you or I had 100 telephones, we'd require a telephone line for each one.

However, only a few telephones are used at the same time. This means that most of the 100 telephone lines sit idle, yet the company still pays the telephone company a monthly charge for those lines.

The PBX system interfaces with the telephone company through the use of special telephone lines, which are discussed later in this chapter. These telephone lines can handle many incoming and outgoing calls at the same time. The PBX computer assigns these lines to telephones within the PBX system when a caller needs them.

Based on experience, the business and the telephone company can estimate the number of telephone lines that are required. Typically, the number of telephone lines between the business and the telephone company are far fewer than telephones used in the business. In addition, the PBX system is used to route calls within the company without incurring charges from the telephone company.

Although a PBX system takes on the role of a telephone company's central office, there are differences that impede communications. For example, some PBX systems cannot be used with a modem to connect to a remote computer because the PBX system uses different technology than the telephone company uses when transmitting using a modem.

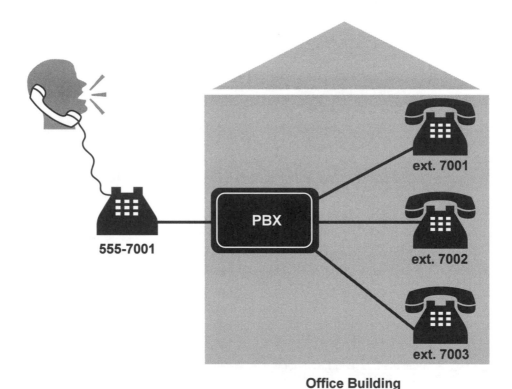

Office Building

Figure 5.3
A PBX saves organizations money by creating their own telephone exchange. (Redrawn with permission from Prentice Hall. Dodd, Annabel Z. The Essential Guide to Telecommunications. Upper Saddle River, NJ: Prentice Hall, 2000, p.49.)

WIDE AREA NETWORKS ....

In the previous chapter, you learned how information is transmitted over cables to computers within the same office. This is called a local area network (LAN). However, organizations are finding an increasing need to communicate with computers located at remote locations with the same speed and dependability that a LAN offers.

We've connected to a remote computer every time we dial up our ISP to surf the Internet. Our modem uses the telephone company's switched service to make the connection. However, large organizations use various services, including switched services provided by the telephone company and other firms, to create their own network, called a *wide area network (WAN)*. There isn't a computer in the world that cannot be connected to a remote computer with WAN technology, the foundation of which is the telephone system.

Tech Talk

Wide area network: a computer network that covers vast terrain, rather than being localized in one location, such as within an office building. Metropolitan area network: a computer network that covers a metropolitan region.

One of three switching methods is used to route data over a WAN. These are *circuit switching*, *message switching*, and *packet switching* (Figure 5.4). Circuit switching, as mentioned earlier in this chapter, is the method used to place our telephone call. Telephone switchers create and maintain a connection, called a virtual circuit, between our telephone and the remote telephone until we hang up the telephone. Circuit switching is referred to as a connection-oriented method because both the sender and receiver must be available at the time of the transmission.

Message switching is a connectionless method because no connection is made between the sender and receiver. Instead, messages are transmitted without knowing if the receiver is available. The telephone company stores messages and delivers them when the receiver is online.

Packet switching is also a connectionless switching method that divides messages into smaller units called packets, which was discussed in the previous chapter. This enables portions of the message (i.e., packets) to be sent to the destination using different routes rather than a virtual circuit. I like to think of this as a group of buddies going to a football game. They can squeeze into one van for the trip (circuit switching) or they can break up into three cars with each car taking a different road to the game (packet switching).

In the 1970s, large corporations used the X.25 protocol to connect to remote computers over the Public Data Network (PDN), which are circuits set up by carriers, such as Sprintnet and Tymnet. Devices called Data Terminal Equipment (DTE) are used to connect to X.25 PDN. Many of these devices had built-in support for X.25. Those that did not required a Packet Assembler/Dissembler (PAD) to convert from the DTE's protocol to the X.25 protocol, which is required to transmit over the PDN.

Although at the time the X.25 protocol was state-of-the-art, today it is looked upon as being too slow compared with other protocols and transmission methods discussed later in this chapter.

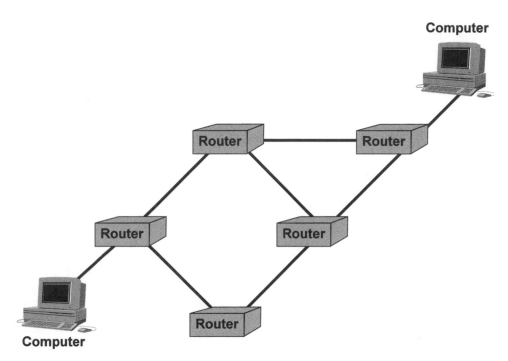

Figure 5.4
Packet switching is connectionless, dividing messages into packets.

Types of Lines and Services

Wide Area Networks connect to the public telephone system using various services and special lines that provide an efficient means of transmitting and receiving digital information over the telephone network.

Digital Data Service (DDS) was one of the first services telephone companies offered to carry digital information. DDS used a special device called a Channel Service Unit/Digital Service Unit (CSU/DSU) to connect remote computers using a dedicated line. The CSU/DSU is like a modem.

DDS ensured a higher transmission quality than those offered by the telephone company's dedicated analog line service and was able to transmit information at 56 KBPS. A limitation of the DDS is that a dedicated line is required, which prohibits connections to other remote sites.

MODEMS AND REMOTE COMPUTERS

A modem is your computer's telephone and translates information inside your computer into a signal that the public telephone network understands. This is called modulation and demodulation. Modulation is how a digital signal is converted to an audio signal. Demodulation is the reverse process.

The speed at which a modem can transmit information depends upon the common fastest speed of the modems involved in the transmission and the equipment used in the telephone company's central office.

The number of bits per second that the modem can transmit and receive is used to rate modems. Typically, these are 56 KBPS or 33.6 KBPS. For the longest time, I assumed that the modem with the highest rate guaranteed that my messages would travel at that rate—which is 56 KBPS.

Well, I was wrong because of two factors. First, the two modems involved in the transmission must agree on the rate. Older modems are not capable of communicating at 56 KBPS, so my 56 KBPS modem needs to slow down to a speed that an older modem can handle. This is like leading a family caravan of aunts and uncles on a weekend outing. You must travel at a speed they're comfortable with, otherwise you'll leave them in your dust and they'll get lost.

Another less-known fact about 56 KBPS modems is that you only get the benefit of that speed if the telephone company central office is using digital equipment. The same applies if your are using the modem to connect to your ISP.

This means that you can spend top dollar for a 56 KBPS modem and only be able to communicate on the Internet at a slower speed because your telephone company and your ISP may not be using digital equipment.

The telephone company overcame this limitation by offering Switched 56 service. Switched 56 is also a digital service; however, it uses circuit switching in place of the dedicated line. This enables a company to connect to one of many sites that also uses Switched 56 service by dialing a special telephone number. Switched 56 service has been replaced with the Integrated Services Digital Network (ISDN).

ISDN

ISDN is a term that you probably heard bantered around your company by the office gurus who think they're cool by having an ISDN line at home to link to the Internet. I'm not sure that they are so cool since an ISDN line is expensive and overkill for most of us. It's like having a souped-up sports car that can reach 100 MPH in 60 seconds, but is stuck behind a clunker in traffic.

In 1984, the telephone company introduced ISDN as an alternative to the analog telephone network, which is designed for voice communication rather than data transmissions. ISDN divides the communications line into channels, much like we have television channels. Each channel can handle a transmission at the same time.

There are two kinds of ISDN. These are called the *Basic Rate Interface (BRI)* and the *Primary Rate Interface (PRI)*. This is the standard consumer model.

BRI consists of three channels called B1, B2, and D. B1 and B2 are commonly called the B channels and each is used to transmit and receive either voice or data at 64 KBPS. The D channel is used to control the call. Think of the D channel as the telephone company's own private network to keep track of calls. Information is transmitted over the D channel at 16 KBPS. In some situations, the D channel can also be used to transmit data.

PRI contains 23 B channels and a D channel, which enables 23 phone calls to be made at the same time over the same line. Those calls can transmit voice or data. The D channel in PRI is also used to control the calls.

T1, T2, T3, and T4 Lines

The telephone company is able to offer various data transmission services and other wide area communication services because high-speed communications lines are used in place of the telephone cable that most of us have in our homes.

The high-speed lines are called *T carrier-lines*, of which there are four categories, T1 through T4. T1 and T3 lines are commonly found in data communications. Unlike our home telephone lines, T carrier-lines can be use to transmit on multiple communication channels. Each channel is capable of transmitting voice or data.

The category of a T carrier-line implies the number of channels that the line can transmit. T1 lines carry 24 channels, T2 lines 96 channels, T3 lines 672 channels, and T4 lines 4,032 channels. As you can imagine, the increase in the number of channels a T carrier-line carries is represented in the higher price a customer pays for the service.

Multiple channels offer customers a way to transmit and receive a lot of data within a short time period. For example, a T1 line can transmit 1.544 megabits per second (MBPS), the T2 line 6.312 MBPS, the T3 line 44.736 MBPS, and the T4 line 274.175 MBPS.

For most of us at home, using a T carrier to connect to a remote computer such as we do when using the Internet is more than we need. This is like buying a tractor-trailer to pick up our groceries at the supermarket. However, T carriers are a perfect way for businesses to economically transfer large amounts of information. This is similar to how a tractor-trailer is used by the supermarket to bring their shipment of groceries from the warehouse to the store.

T carrier-lines are slowly being retired as the cable of choice for data transfer and are being replaced with DS carrier-lines. A *DS carrier-line* uses fiber optic cables instead of the copper cables used in T carrier-lines. DS carrier-lines are categorized similarly to the categories used for T carriers. That Is, DS1, DS2, DS3, and DS4. These categories are equivalent to the number of channels and speed of their counter-part T carrier category.

DSL

You've probably heard of someone who set out to solve a problem and inadvertently made a great discovery. This happened at the 3M company when a research engineer who sought a new adhesive stumbled across one that didn't stick too well. Today we call it Post-it® Notes.

A similar situation occurred at Bellcore, one of the spinoffs of AT&T. In 1989, long before anyone dreamt of the e-economy, engineers were looking for a way to transmit video over the telephone network. Video contains a lot of information that must be transmitted quickly at 30 frames of video per second or continuity is lost be-tween frames.

Unfortunately, the telephone network is designed for voice transmissions and couldn't handle the demand of video. So, Bellcore engineers created the *Digital Subscriber Line (DSL)*. With the onset of cable television, however, the demand to pro-vide video over a telephone line diminished. But DSL is fast becoming the service of choice used to connect computers to the Internet.

Here's how DSL works (Figure 5.5). The telephone cable is similar to a highway in which lanes are like communication channels. Communication channels are defined by a frequency (see Chapters 1 and 2). Voice transmissions use frequencies below 4 Kilohertz (KHz) (4,000 cycles per second), although the telephone cable can handle a greater range of frequencies. It's these unused frequencies that engineers use to provide DSL service.

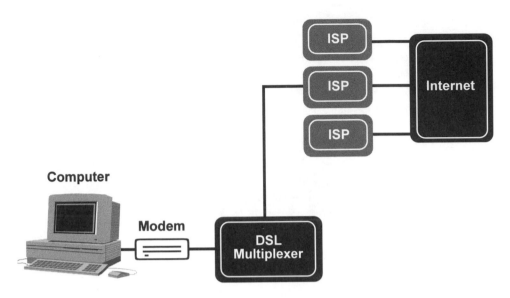

Figure 5.5
DSL uses multiple channels to transmit information quickly over a telephone network. (Redrawn with permission from Prentice Hall. Dodd, Annabel Z. The Essential Guide to Telecommunications. Upper Saddle River, NJ: Prentice Hall, 2000, p. 202.)

A DSL service uses a special DSL modem to transmit data using frequencies above 4 KHz. You could think of this as using the shoulder of the road to increase the number of vehicles that can travel over the highway at the same time.

Frequencies above 4 KHz are divided into 256 subchannels, each of which can transmit 32 Kilobits per second. Half the channels are used for transmission and the other half for receiving data. This technique is called *Discrete Multitone Modulation.*

Engineers use a compression algorithm to reduce the number of bits needed to transmit information, which increases the transmission throughput. Compression is the technique of representing a sequence of identical characters by fewer characters.

Let's say we needed to transmit 111110000000000 (remember data is represented as ones and zeros; see Chapter 2). We could rewrite this to say "5-1 10-0" using eight characters to represent 15 characters. This is an example of a compression algorithm, although a less sophisticated one than those used in data communication. When the transmission is received, software deciphers the compressed data into a full representation of the data.

DSL travels on the same telephone network as voice communication until the signal reaches the telephone company's central office, where the DSL signal is routed over the telephone company's data network. This relieves congestion caused by the convergence of voice and data that is transmitted by a standard modem. In contrast, data you send using a modem competes for the same frequencies as voice transmissions.

There are several versions of DSL (see Table 5.1). These are Asymmetric Digital Subscriber line, DSL Lite, High Bit-Rate Digital Subscriber Line, Very High Bit-Rate Digital Subscriber Line, Rate Adaptive Digital Subscriber Line, Symmetric Digital Subscriber Line, and Integrated Services Digital Subscriber Line.

Table 5.1 Types of DSL Services

Type of Service	Description
Asymmetric Digital Subscriber Line (ADSL)	This uses different transmission speeds to and from the customer. Typically, 8 Megabits are sent to the customer and information from the customer to the remote computer travels at 1 Megabit.
DSL Lite	This is the type of DSL service the IS guru has in his or her home. DSL Lite does not split the voice and data transmissions, therefore this is much slower than ADSL, yet still faster than using a traditional modem. DSL Lite is sometimes called Universal DSL.
High Bit-Rate Digital Subscriber Line (HDSL)	This is a premium service that is found more in businesses than with residential customers. Unlike ADSL, HDSL provides the same data transmission speed going to the customer that is sent from the customer.
Very High Bit-Rate Digital Subscriber Line (VDSL)	This provides a very fast communication. VDSL service uses a combination of copper cabling and fiber optic cables to provide a very high data-transfer rate.
Rate Adaptive Digital Subscriber Line (RADS)	This has the same features of ADSL, however adjustments are made in the signal speed to compensate for the various cabling that is used between the sender and the telephone company's central office.
Symmetric Digital Subscriber Line (SDSL) service	This has the advantages of HDSL, but with its own twist. SDSL uses the same transmission speeds to send and receive data, but the speeds are slower than those provided for in HDSL.
Integrated Services Digital Subscriber Line (ISDS)	This is similar to the ISDN service (see "ISDN" on page 160), however customers are charged a flat monthly fee, which is different than ISDN. In addition, ISDS does not transmit voice, which ISDN can do.

Virtual Private Networks

It wasn't too many years ago when telephone calls and the mail were the only means for businesses to interact with their business partners. An auto manufacturer, for example, mailed an order for parts to a vendor who then coordinated delivery using the telephone. Delay in communication and shipment was anticipated, so the manufacturer retained an inventory of parts on site.

Managers saw this system as inefficient and developed a just-in-time inventory procedure that required vendors to deliver parts to the plant a few days before the car was assembled. This eliminated inventory sitting around in either the vendor's warehouse or in the manufacturing plant.

However, just-in-time inventory placed a strain on the old way in which orders and deliveries were coordinated. The new system was too demanding for human intervention. Auto manufacturers turned to their computers to manage manufacturing, including ordering and tracking delivery of parts. This meant that automakers' computers needed to talk directly to the computers of part suppliers.

You can imagine how this volume of data transmission stretched the capabilities of existing data communications networks. The automotive industry turned to telecommunication carriers to help make their data communications operations work more efficiently. The solution was to create a *virtual private network (VAN)*.

A virtual private network, which is similar to the private telephone network that was discussed earlier in this chapter, uses a dedicated line to connect the manufacturer and the vendor. However, a goal for the virtual private network was to overcome the pitfalls found in a private network, which were network management and flexibility.

Tech Talk
Virtual private network: a private wide area network maintained by the telephone company that connects multiple business partners.

Private networks required the firm to hire a team of experts to control and maintain them. In addition, private networks are not flexible, especially when new sites must be incorporated into the network or when a growth in data traffic volume begins to clog it.

In contrast to a private network, a virtual private network uses the telephone company's management and facilities to create and maintain this wide area network. In the auto industry example, the auto manufacturer tells the telephone company the sites to connect and the telephone company makes it happen.

There are two kinds of communications networks used in large organizations. These are the PBX, used to route telephone calls, and a LAN, which is used to route data communication. However, there is a movement to converge these networks into a single communications network that can handle both voice and data communication.

Virtual Private Networks extend the reach of networks within the company to sites and computers that are located off premises by using a T1 line and a channel bank. A channel bank is a device that connects the company's network to the telephone company's central office and performs the task similar to a modem.

Frame Relay

You can think of a virtual private network as the highway that connects a site to a remote site, which is used to extend a local area network to a wider area. From reading this book, you realize that the "highway" is one piece of the data transportation puzzle. A method to ride on that highway is also required, which is called a network access method. Frame relay is such a method.

In the early 1990s, telephone company customers that owned private networks, that used a dedicated line to connect two sites, were offered the more efficient and less costly virtual private network. Frame relay made this possible because it defined a much faster way for routing messages over a wide area network than the X.25 protocol (see the discussion of X.25 on page 157).

Companies that use frame relay benefit from the reduced hardware requirements and multiple backup routes to the remote location, which are provided for by a virtual private network. They also benefit by the high-speed throughput of data over the virtual private network.

A virtual private network that uses frame relay requires that each node (see Chapter 4) be connected to the network using an access line and a Frame Relay Access Device (FRAD), which is similar to a model used to connect your computer to your Internet Service Provider.

A FRAD places information that is to be transmitted over the private network into an electronic envelope called a frame. A frame is similar in concept to a packet (discussed in Chapter 4). The frame has addressing information (bits that indicate where the information begins and ends), information for routing the frame to the destination, and information used by the telephone company for billing purposes.

Frame relay transmits information faster than its predecessor (the X.25 network access method). X.25 required error checking to be performed by each telephone company router that the message encountered during the transmission. Frame relay network access method performs less extensive error checking. Frame relay requires routers (see Chapter 3) at the receiving site to determine if an error has occurred in transmission.

The access line used in a frame relay network can be either a dial-up line or a dedicated line from each site to the telephone company's central office. Businesses that have an occasional need to use a frame relay network typically connect using a dial-up line while consistent network users find a dedicated line more economical.

Once transmission over a frame relay network is received, the FRAD retransmits the information over the organization's local area network, where the data is routed to the designated computer.

Frame relay networks are characterized by three criteria. These are the committed information rate (CIR), port, and the type of circuit. The committed information rate is the throughput rate that the telephone company promised. Transfer speeds range from 56 KBPS to 1.544 MBPS.

The entry point used to enter the frame relay network, which is called a port, affects throughput rates. A port can handle a maximum transmission speed. More than one access line can be connected to the same port and must share access to the port.

I like to think of a port as an entrance to a highway and access lines as lanes in the road leading to the highway entrance. I can speed through to the highway if I'm the only car on the access road. You can say that I'll be traveling at the highest port speed.

However, I'll need to slow down if someone is in the other lane and arrives at the entrance the same time I do. This means both of us will enter the highway at a speed slower then the highest port speed.

This changes drastically if the Presidential motorcade wants access to the same entrance at the same time I approach the highway. I'm stopped—although I think this unfair—and the motorcade is allowed to access the highway at the highest port speed. This is a way the government adjusts access to the highway.

The telephone company uses a similar method to ensure a guaranteed port speed by limiting the number of access lines connected to a port. Of course, the higher the committed throughput rate, the more a business can expect to pay for the service.

There are two kinds of circuits available for use in a frame relay network. These are a *permanent virtual circuit (PVC)* and a *switched virtual circuit (SVC)*.

Tech Talk

Permanent virtual circuit (PVC): a predefined, permanent virtual circuit that connects two sites for a fixed monthly fee.
Switched virtual circuit (SVC): a temporary virtual circuit that exists for the duration of the connection and for which a business is charged for the time of the connection.

We tend to think of data as being the only form of communication that is transmitted over a frame relay network, but voice can also be transmitted. Voice communication is different than data communication because we quickly detect any delay in transmission when we're speaking to someone on the phone.

Transmission delays are influenced by two factors, which are the size of the data that needs to be transmitted and the traffic on the network. A voice message contains much more information than the same message sent as data, such as in an e-mail. Therefore, a special voice compression technique must be used to temporarily shrink the size of the voice message for transmission. The message is restored to its full size once the message is received. This is similar to data compression techniques discussed in Chapter 4.

The frame relay network can distinguish a voice message from a data message and gives voice messages priority over data messages whenever both are in contention for the network. This enables the telephone conversation to flow smoothly without pauses.

ATM

Let me begin by saying that this has nothing to do with the Automated Teller Machines (ATMs). The first time I heard ATM used by some guys in IS, I assumed the company was going to install another ATM machine in the lobby. Wrong! Instead, the company was installing a wide area network that uses *asynchronous transfer mode (ATM)* to access the network.

ATM is a new and improved way to transmit information over long distances. I use the term "information" because ATM technology is designed to carry voice and data as well as video and multimedia, all at speeds up to 2.5 gigabits per second.

The popularity of ATM, also known as ATM network access service, is because ATM frees businesses from using separate switching networks for each type of information the firm needs to transfer. Instead of having one network for voice, another for data, and a third for video (i.e., video conferencing), an organization can consolidate by using one ATM network.

The key to ATM technology is its capability to provide a different quality of service over the same network. This is known as *QoS*. For example, voice and video communications require a different service quality than data communications because we expect an instant response during a phone conversation or when we watch a movie, yet we'll accept a slight delay when data is transmitted.

ATM is able to offer fast transmission rates and variation in service quality because of the way it works (Figure 5.6). Voice, data, video, and multimedia information is divided into smaller units similar to the packets used on a Local Area Network (see Chapter 4). However, packets in an ATM network are called *cells*.

Each cell holds 53 bytes, but only 48 of those contain the information that is being transmitted. The other five bytes, called a *header*, contain information that is necessary to control the transmission, such as routing information, error checking data, and the priority of the cell. The fixed size of the cell enables routers to automatically know when the cell ends. If the cell were a various length, each router on the network would need to read each byte looking for the byte that signals the end of the cell. The time looking for the end of the cell is saved when a fixed cell is used.

You might think that 53 bytes is skimping a little. More bytes in the cell would obviously reduce the number of transmissions. But there is logic behind the design.

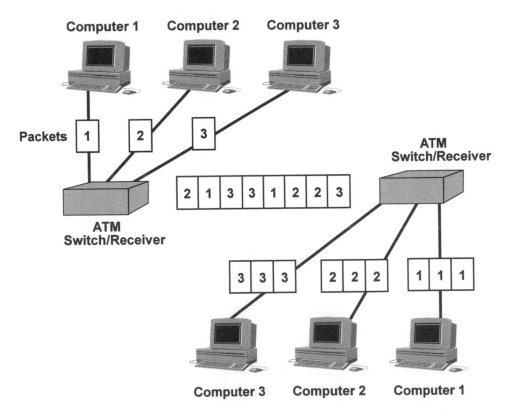

Figure 5.6
ATM transfers data quickly over long distances because data is broken into tiny packets.

A smaller cell actually increases the throughput of the network. You'll recall from the previous chapter that the destination node examines the information to determine if a transmission error has occurred. If so, then a request is made to retransmit the information. So if the cell contained 100 bytes of data, all 100 bytes must be sent again. However, less transmission time is required when a small cell is used. Instead of 100 bytes, the ATM network needs to transmit 48 bytes of actual information in a cell containing 53 bytes.

ATM is a connection-oriented network in which the network determines if the destination address is online and if so, it creates a virtual circuit between the sender and receiver. Each cell is then transmitted over the same path to the destination node. The ATM equipment is housed in the telephone company's central office and is connected to the business using a dedicated T carrier or a fiber optic equivalent.

Fiber Optic Network

Fiber optic networks will bring a convergence of interactive computer software and video will open new ways for us to learn and be entertained similar to the way television revolutionized the radio news and entertainment.

A key difference between voice/data and video/multimedia is the quantity of information that must be transferred over a short time span.

A frame of video, for example, is represented by many more bytes than is used to display a Web page. While we expect a Web page to be stationary, except perhaps for a small animated ad, we require video to be fully animated at a rate of 30 frames per second. You can think of this as displaying 30 Web pages on the screen every second.

Your computer has the horsepower to present video on your monitor's screen. However, the telephone system is just getting the engines to transport video and multimedia at the rate that will let you view and transmit video and other formats that require a lot of information to be sent in a second.

The new horsepower is coming from fiber optic technology and the fiber optic network called the Synchronous Optical Network (SONET). SONET is a mouthful, but the concept is easier to understand.

Information is encoded into light waves that are transmitted through a tiny thin tube of glass or plastic (see Chapter 4). This means information is traveling faster than a speeding bullet (which travel slightly faster than the speed of sound) and without the help of Superman. Information transmitted using fiber optics travels at the speed of light.

Here's how I describe the difference between the speed of sound and the speed of light to my students, without confusing the issue with math. All of us at one time have witnessed a lighting strike. What occurred first, the flash of light or the loud blast? The flash of light! The lighting strike causes both the flash and blast to occur at the same time. However, light waves travel faster than sound, giving you the appearance that the blast occurs a second or so after the flash.

SONET uses that difference to speed more bytes over the network than can be transmitted over copper cables. In addition, SONET can transmit many signals from various sources on the same cable at the same time. This is referred to as *multiplexing*. You can think of this as a highway intersection in which there are many on-ramps leading from different roadways.

Those on-ramps can be from existing network connections, such as ATM, Internet, and T-carriers. This is made possible by the layering design of SONET. There are four functional operations in SONET, which are called *layers* (Figure 5.7).

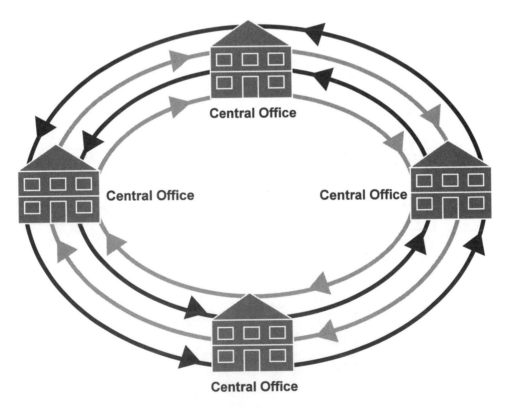

Figure 5.7
SONET transmits data at the speed of light over long distances, using fiber optic technology. (Redrawn with permission from Prentice Hall. Dodd, Annabel Z. The Essential Guide to Telecommunications. Upper Saddle River, NJ: Prentice Hall, 2000, p.218.)

The first layer is called the photonic layer. This is where electronic signals are converted to optical signals and optical signals to electronic signals with a device called a multiplexer. This is similar to the modem in your computer.

The second layer is called the selection layer and is responsible for monitoring the optical signal along the network. The third layer is called the line layer, which is like traffic control at the entrance to the highway. Its job is to combine signals from various users into a uniform format. In technical terms, this is called synchronizing and multiplexing multiple streams into one stream. The fourth layer is called the path layer, which assembles and disassembles information into frames similar to packets used in a LAN.

SONET uses a bidirectional ring topology. The primary ring is used to transmit traffic and the second ring, called the protect ring, is used as a backup in case the primary ring becomes disabled. Telephone companies offer various levels of service over SONET (see Table 5.2).

Table 5.2 Levels of SONET Services

Levels of Service	Throughput Speed
OC-1	52 MBPS
OC-3	155 MBPS
OC-12	622 MBPS
OC-48	2488 MBPS
OC-192	994 = 53 MBPS

Wireless Networks

Who could imagine even a few years ago that Star Trek technology would become reality in our lifetime? I remember Captain Kirk flipping open a handheld communicator ordering Spock to beam him aboard the Enterprise. Traveling on a light beam is still scientific fantasy, but the communicator exists today in the form of a palm computer and cellular telephones that double as a mobile link to the Internet. Advancements in wireless technology have made all this possible.

I tend to take it for granted that technology has become commonplace in everyday life. For example, once someone at a radio station in Missouri interviewed me by telephone. A listener called in from his car and asked me a question. I had to stop for a moment. I was in my attic in New Jersey on the phone with a radio station halfway across the country answering a question from someone driving in Kansas.

Today we're starting to see a blur between cellular telephones and handheld computers. You can buy a cellular telephone that connects you to the Internet to receive stock quotes, e-mail, and browse your favorite Web site, and there's probably a palm computer that can be used as a cellular telephone.

Engineers call these devices "smart" devices because they truly are intelligent mobile communicators rather than a cellular phone or handheld computer. The Internet is the driving force for the rapid development of smart devices because it offers the rich content people on the move demand.

The cellular network is the backbone of wireless connectivity to the Internet. Smart devices are able to receive information from the Internet by using Wireless Application Protocol (WAP). WAP defines how information is to be transferred between the digital cellular network and the Internet. Other software on the smart device is used to modify the layout of Web pages to fit on the smart device's small screens. For example, graphic images too large to fit on the screen are not displayed.

BLUETOOTH TECHNOLOGY—THE WIRELESS NETWORK

Bluetooth technology uses low-power radio transmission to connect network devices without cables, and can maintain the network connection even if the network device, such as a computer, is on the move.

Wireless networks have been around for years in the form of infrared light transmissions, which required a clear line-of-sight between the infrared transmitter and the network device. However, offices typically have obstructions, such as walls, that inhibit widespread use of infrared wireless networks.

Bluetooth technology overcomes the line-of-sight limitation by using radio waves instead of light waves to transmit network information. Radio waves travel in all directions from the transmitter and can penetrate obstructions such as walls.

The key to Bluetooth technology is the low power used to broadcast the signal, allowable because the broadcast is limited to within approximately 400 feet, which is expected to be extended to nearly 4,000 feet radius. The current radius is perfect for a wireless network in an office.

Radio transmissions are vulnerable to interference and security breaches. Interference occurs from transmissions broadcast on frequencies close to the frequency Bluetooth technology uses . Security breaches are possible because any receiver tuned to the Bluetooth technology frequency can receive the signal.

Bluetooth technology overcomes both problems. Short data packets are used to maximize throughput and dramatically reduce the effects of interference. Packets that experience transmission errors are retransmitted, however, the short size of the packet becomes advantageous because it shortens retransmission time. Bluetooth technology transmits at 1 megabits per second.

Security is provided by using frequency hopping at 1600 hops per second. This practically eliminates the chance that the signal will be intercepted. Bluetooth technology also uses two additional security measures. Data is encrypted before being broadcast. Even if the signal is intercepted, the receiver still requires the key to decipher the data. Furthermore, Bluetooth technology employs an authorization scheme that permits only authorized devices to access network data.

Some see Bluetooth technology as a great value to business travelers who currently need to carry an assortment of cables and connection devices to have their PCs link to networks outside their offices. The PC will have a Bluetooth technology transceiver that can communicate with networks in other offices and hotel rooms.

Signals broadcast using Bluetooth technology can simultaneously carry both data and voice and redefine mobile computers, mobile phones, and similar devices. For example, a cellular phone using Bluetooth technology can easily become a mobile computer both inside and outside of the office.

Pick up a copy of <u>Bluetooth Revealed</u>, by Brent Miller, for an in-depth look at Bluetooth technology.

Cellular Networks

If you've seen the ads that try to talk you into signing up for a cellular telephone, you probably realize that there are two types of cellular networks. These is an analog cellular network and a digital cellular network. An analog cellular network uses analog technology (see Chapter 2) to use variations in the signal to encode information. In a digital cellular network, digital technology is used to encode information as one of two values : a zero or a one (see Chapter 2).

The analog cellular network dates back to the 1970s, when AT&T expanded its offerings to include mobile telephone service. It wasn't until mid-1995 when IBM developed the technology needed to digitize information over the cellular network.

IBM's objective was to overcome the shortcomings of analog cellular transmissions when data instead of voice is transmitted.

Cellular networks are composed of transmitting and receiving towers strategically positioned around the country to link mobile telephones (Figure 5.8). These are called base stations, each of which has a defined coverage area called a cell and links the cellular network to the telephone network. As long as you turn on the telephone, cell phones communicate continuously with base stations as the cell phone moves through the network. When you place a call with your cell phone, the phone broadcasts a signal that is received by the base station nearest your location.

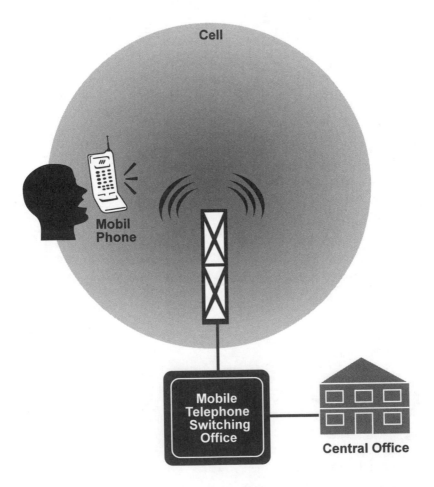

Figure 5.8
Cellular networks link mobile communication devices to telphone-based networks. (Redrawn with permission from Prentice Hall. Dodd, Annabel Z. *The Essential Guide to Telecommunications*. Upper Saddle River, NJ: Prentice Hall, 2000, p. 319.)

Your signal strength decreases as you move farther away from the base station. Before your signal reaches the outer limits of the base station, the cellular network transfers it to a base station closer to your new location. This is called a handoff, and it causes the connection to be dropped for a fraction of a second before the next base station picks up the signal.

We rarely notice the handoff during the telephone call, but this split-second gap is noticeable when data instead of voice is transmitted and is sufficient to cause errors in transmissions. The lack of capability to handle errors is a drawback to using the analog cellular network for sending data to a remote computer.

Data transmission errors occur regardless of whether the network is wired or wireless. However, data network protocols are designed to trap and correct errors and analog cellular network protocols are not designed for error control.

The problem stems from the fact that analog cellular networks transmit one long burst of information whereas data communication networks break up the information into small pieces called packets, frames, or cells.

To compound the problem, an analog cellular network can either transmit or receive data, but it can't do both at the same time. This is called half-duplex. Duplex transmission is used by the wired-based telephone, which enables us to send and receive simultaneously. That is, analog cellular networks work similarly to how walkie-talkies work. Only one person can talk at a time.

Let's say that you are sending a large message over an analog cellular network and an error occurs in the transmission because your call was handed off to another base station. Let's also assume that the remote computer is smart enough to detect the error, similar to how a destination computer on a LAN recognizes that an error has occurred.

The remote computer is unable to notify your mobile computer about the error because it cannot transmit the error message at the same time that your mobile computer is transmitting data.

IBM realized the power of the cellular network to free data communications from wired networks, so its engineers developed the Cellular Digital Packet Data (CDPD) protocol, commonly known as IP wireless.

Here's how CDPD works. Each mobile computing device is assigned an IP address, much like an IP address is assigned to computers on a TCP/IP network (see Chapter 4). A fixed IP address is important in reducing errors that occur when a call is handed off to another base station.

Your cellular telephone is assigned to a port in the cellular network. A port is an entry point into the network's base station and is identified by a unique port number. The port is reassigned every time your call is handed off to another base station.

Sometimes there are problems with the handoff and the cellular network is unable to re-establish the connection. For example, you are beyond the range of the first base station that has your original port assignment and the new port has not been assigned in the next base station.

A fixed IP address resolves this dilemma because your call is identified by your unique IP address, which cannot be lost by a handoff. If you are out of range of the first base station, the connection can always be reestablished by using your IP address.

A special modem called a CDPD modem is used to transmit small bursts of encrypted data over the existing analog cellular network. A burst frees the communication channel to transmission error messages by the receiver.

Cellular networks promise to free computers from being tied down to wires. However, new technology is required to fulfill those promises because cellular network transmission is slow compared with speeds required for data communications.

Analog transmissions have a throughput of 9,600 bits per second and CDPD improves throughput to 14,400 bits per second. These speeds are sufficient for remote entry of delivery information, inquiring about an order status, or providing remote access to e-mail. However, they are not sufficient for full access to the Internet.

Inside Digital Wireless Services

Cellular networks provide the topology for data communications of the network. This is similar to how cables are connected together for a LAN. Digital wireless services use the IP wireless protocol to transmit data over the cellular network just as the TCP/IP protocol is used to transmit data over a LAN.

The FCC reserved a set of frequencies within the radio frequencies of the electromagnetic spectrum for cellular communications. You can think of this as a fixed number of lanes on a highway.

Engineers developed multiplexing techniques that enabled each frequency to carry more than one call at a time. This is possible because each call is divided into packets that contain control information. Control information includes the receiver's IP address, much like every car on the highway has a driver who knows the address of his or her destination.

There are three techniques used to multiplex transmission on a digital cellular network. These are Code Division Multiple Access (CDMA), Time Division Multiple Access (TDMA), and a third generation wireless standard called 3G.

CDMA uses a spread-spectrum approach to transmission, in which the data is transmitted over more than one frequency. This increases the throughput of data over the network. CDMA also utilizes the soft handoff method when transferring a call to another base station. During the handoff, transmission from the mobile phone is held up until the connection is made with the next base station. The mobile phone temporarily stores the data in on-board memory as a way to keep transmission from the computer flowing into the transmitter.

WIRELESS APPLICATION PROTOCOL (WAP)

The Internet is going to have its cable clipped by WAP, the wireless application protocol. WAP sets the rules for wireless communication with the Internet by using mobile devices, such as cellular telephones. Application developers used WAP to create microbrowsers, e-mail applications, mobile handset messaging, and telefaxing, among other types of software.

WAP was created in 1997 by the WAP Forum, founded by Ericsson, Nokia, Motorola, and Unwired Planet. Over one hundred companies, including software developers and telecommunication carriers, have since joined the Forum.

WAP focuses on two areas: an application language used to create WAP enabled applications and transmission protocols used to communicate with the Internet.

The Wireless Markup Language (WML) is used to create WAP applications. WML is a subset of Extensible Markup Language (XML), which is used to develop Web applications. XML uses tags to describe how a browser is to handle text within a Web page (see Chapter 6). WML specifies the types of tags an application programmer is to use to enable the Web page to work with WAP devices.

Transmission protocols represent layers of the OSI Model (see Chapter 2) and consist of the application layer, session layer, transaction layer, and transport layer. WAP also specifies a security protocol. WAP protocol functions similarly to the transport protocol specified in the OSI Model. However, the WAP protocol addresses the special requirements to exchange information using WAP devices.

WAP applications provide easy and secure access to banking, messaging, and entertainment available over the Internet by using mobile devices. Furthermore, proprietary information that is normally found on an intranet, such as data contained in corporate databases, can also be accessed using a WAP device and a WAP application.

You'll find more information about WAP in <u>WAP Essentials</u> by Jouko Vierumaki.

In contrast, TDMA divides each frequency into time slots. Every call is assigned a time slot, much like the way computers share a network printer. Each waits its turn to use the frequency. 3G multiplexing techniques are still in development and use both CDMA (called CDMA 3G) and TDMA (called TDMA 3G) to increase throughput to 56 KBS and beyond.

Mobile Radio Networks

A forerunner of the cellular networks is the private radio network. Private radio networks are used by organizations such as government agencies, trucking companies, and service companies to communicate with employees in the field. You may call these networks by their informal but more descriptive name: two-way radios.

The FCC set aside a range of frequencies for use by private radio networks. All transmissions on these frequencies are isolated from the cellular and standard telephone networks, so there is no way for an employee in the field to use the private radio network to make a telephone call.

Early private radio networks transmitted only analog information, but this soon expanded to digital communication as the need for paging and messaging services materialized. Today, many delivery services, such as Federal Express, use a private radio network to provide wireless package tracking. You've no doubt seen a driver scan package information into a mobile computer device, which is then transmitted over the private radio network to the company's computer.

Although an organization can buy a private radio network, many find leasing time on another company's private radio network more economical. Telephone companies provide such a service called Specialized Mobile Radio (SMR) network services.

Satellite Networks

Probably the most revolutionary wireless technology is satellite networks. Just the sound of the name conjures images of Captain Kirk and the Enterprise and begins to take the fiction out of science fiction.

We've heard about satellites being sent into space and of millions of dollars spent to send work crews up there to perform electronic maintenance, yet most people know little about how satellites are used in communication.

Most satellites are repeaters that receive microwave signals from Earth and then rebroadcast the signal to another satellite or to a receiver on Earth. Repeaters are used in computer networks, too, as discussed in Chapters 3 and 4.

Although a satellite costs about $15 million to launch, this is far less expensive than placing a series of repeaters, called relay stations, around the world. A satellite has a wide, unobstructed view of Earth, which enables it to retransmit the signal to a large area regardless of the terrain.

The first generation of satellites was used for military purposes and was stationed in an orbit that rotated at the same speed as the Earth's rotation. This is called geosynchronous and stationed the satellite at a fixed location 22,300 miles above the Earth's surface.

It wasn't until satellites were used for commercial purposes that a characteristic of a geosynchronous satellite became a problem. The problem was a delay in communication. The time it took for a signal to be transmitted to the satellite and received by the Earth station was too long for both commercial data and voice communication. Customers expected instantaneous transmission to which they were accustomed with wired communication.

The solution was to shorten the distance between the satellite and Earth from between 435 to 1,500 miles. This is called a Low Earth Orbiting Satellite (LEOS). Two other problems arose. First, LEOS covered a smaller area of Earth, which meant more satellites were required to give the same coverage area as geosynchronous satellites cover.

The other problem is LEOS' location. A change in the distance above the Earth also changed the speed at which LEOS orbits it. They are no longer in geosynchronous orbit. This means they travel faster than the rotation of the earth, which means ground stations have to locate a LEOS before beginning communication.

Another type of satellite is called the Middle Earth Orbit (MEO), which orbits between 6,000 to 13,000 miles above the planet. Geosynchronous satellites, LEOS, and MEO all have something in common. Their life expectancy is between 7 and 15 years, because of the wear on solar cells that power the satellites and because of the outdated technology used in the satellites.

Pick up a copy of *Fundamentals of Wireless Communications* by Andy Dornan for more information about wireless communication.

SUMMARY ....

Data can be shared among computers located within the office by using a local area network (LAN). Likewise, data can be shared with computers outside the office by using a wide area network (WAN). At the center of WAN is the telephone system.

The telephone system provides the network cabling, routers, and other devices necessary to transmit data to practically any point in the world that is covered by the telephone network. WAN uses one of two ways to link to the telephone network. These are by switched or dedicated service.

A switched service creates a virtual circuit to the remote computer and keeps the circuit alive until transmission is completed, much like the technology used to complete a telephone call. A dedicated service creates a fixed circuit to the remote computer, which is available 24 hours, seven days a week. A dedicated service is also known as a private line.

There are four private line topologies that are offered by many telephone companies. These are point-to-point, multipoint, star, and mesh. Point-to-point topology connects two computers to the same circuit. The other topologies enable multiple computers to connect to the circuit and provide various recovery options if a transmission line fails.

Businesses and large organizations are able to save costs by owning their own telephone exchange, which is called a private branch exchange (PBX). A PBX is a telephone network within an organization that connects all of the business' telephones and communication devices and becomes a private offshoot of the telephone company's network. Outside calls to the business are sent by the telephone company to the business' PBX, which distributes the call to the appropriate telephone within the business.

Telephone companies offer various wide area network services. These include Digital Data Service (DDS), Integrated Services Digital Network (ISDN), and Digital Subscriber Line (DSL).

DDS was one of the first services telephone companies offered to carry digital information. It was replaced by ISDN, which divides the communications line into channels, much like we have television channels. Each channel can handle a transmission at the same time. DSL is quickly replacing ISDN as the service used to connect to the Internet because unused frequencies are used to transmit data.

Telephone companies also offer a virtual private network, which enables businesses to create an exclusive wide area network. A virtual private network is created and maintained by the telephone company.

Wide area network services are provided over high-speed lines called T carrier-lines, which are commonly known as T1, T2, T3, and T4 lines, or their equivalent fiber optic line. Special wide area network protocols are used to specify how data travels over a wide area network. These protocols include X.25, Frame Relay, and asynchronous transfer mode (ATM).

X.25 protocol was the first used in a wide area network and required routers along the network to check for transmission errors. Frame Relay improved upon X.25 by requiring the destination computer to check for errors, not all the routers used in the transmission. This dramatically increases the throughput of data. ATM improved upon Frame Relay by dividing data into small pieces called cells that can be quickly transmitted to the destination using various paths. ATM also uses QoS technology to provide different quality of service over the same network. For example, voice communication would have a higher priority than data transmission because voice communication requires a real-time response without any pause in transmission.

Synchronous Optical Network (SONET) is becoming the standard for wide area networks because it uses fiber optic technology to transmit data faster than copper cables.

Wide area networks can use cellular, radio, and satellite technology to distribute data over vast areas. Cellular networks use the cell phones and intelligent communicators to link to the telephone network. Cellular towers called base stations are strategically placed to transmit and receive calls. As the mobile device moves from one area to another, base stations handoff calls.

Private radio networks also provide a mobile data link between field personnel and the office. A private radio network is similar to the communication network used by police departments, in which communication channels are reserved for private transmissions.

Satellite technology is used to extend a wide area network to global locations. Data is sent using microwaves to an orbiting satellite, which retransmits data directly to an Earth station or to another satellite. Satellite technology provides an economical alternative to installing transmission relay stations throughout the world.

Summary Questions

1. **What is the difference between a LAN and a WAN?**

2. **What effect does the location of a satellite have on communication?**

3. **How is the cellular network used in a wireless WAN?**

4. **Why is ATM better technology than Frame Relay?**

5. **Why would a business use a virtual private network?**

6. **How does a PBX relate to the telephone system?**

7. **How does ISDN work?**

8. **What is the difference between stored and forward switching?**

9. What is the difference between switched service and dedicated service?

10. What are the different types of T carrier-lines and how do they differ from each other?

6 Networks: Internet, Intranets, and Extranets

In this chapter...

There's no doubt that the Internet is changing our lives. The Internet is likely to be the first place you go when you're planning a trip, trying to avoid crowds at the malls, or researching your child's homework.

Much is written about how we use the Internet to buy goods, find information, or make a claim in the cyber gold rush. However, what is the Internet—really—and how does it work? What is an Intranet or an Extranet? In this chapter, I'll take you behind the scenes of the Internet, Intranets, and Extranets and explore how these magic marvels work. You'll learn about:

- the Internet

- a bit of Internet history

- the Internet backroom

- the international flavor

- a walk behind the scenes

- surfing the Net

- the Internet connection

- Internet addresses

- Internet protocols

- Internet services

- the World Wide Web

- Internet security

- Internet privacy

- Intranets and Extranets

REALITY CHECK...

It wasn't too long ago that a former intern at Salomon Brothers, an international investment banking firm, told colleagues he was leaving the company to sell books on the Internet. Everyone laughed quietly and joked that he'd be back in a year.

Selling books on the Internet was an outlandish idea, especially when you consider leaving a promising position on Wall Street. A year passed and he never returned. However, his former colleagues did hear from him again when he became the "Man of the Year" for *Time* magazine. His name is Jeff Bezos. His company is Amazon.com.

The Internet is a wide area network that links computers, servers, and other networking devices. However, Bezos' imagination, and that of a long list of other visionaries, has transformed network hardware into a revolutionary concept that changes the way we conduct business.

Within a few years, Bezos has taken on the giants of the book publishing industry to become one of the major booksellers around the world. He is leading the gold rush in which practically anyone who has a good business idea can turn it into a viable business venture by going online.

INSIDE THE INTERNET ....

The Internet is a network of networks that is owned by no one and everyone. I agree this sounds more like legal mumbo jumbo, but this is a concise definition of the Internet. In previous chapters of this book you learned how cables, devices, and computers are linked to form a computer network called a local area network (LAN) (see Chapter 4).

A large LAN can be subdivided into smaller LANs called segments. In a sense, this is the same as the Internet except on a smaller scale. The Internet is a wide area network (see Chapter 5) of global proportions that is comprised of tens of thousands of segments.

Your company owns segments of your company's LAN. However, each segment on the Internet is independently owned by the organization that created the segment.

Let's say that the Internet is a co-op apartment building (Figure 6.1) in which apartments are network segments and the building itself is the Internet. Each resident owns his or her apartment, just like each organization owns its segment of the Internet.

Each apartment contains different items based on the apartment owner's wants. Some apartments may have a piano, others a monster TV, still others a professional kitchen. The organization that runs the co-op building does not tell each apartment owner what they can or cannot have in their apartment.

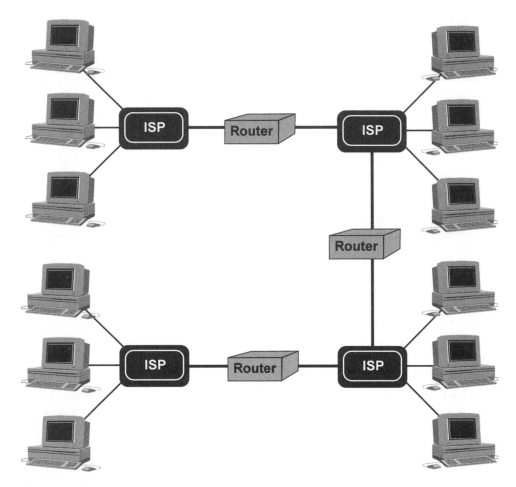

Figure 6.1
The Internet is a network of networks. (Redrawn with permission from Prentice Hall. Comer, Douglas E. The Internet Book. Englewood Cliffs, NJ: Prentice Hall, 1997, p. 110.)

The Internet works the same way, in that some segments will store games, others music, and still others e-commerce businesses The organization that oversees the Internet has no authority to control the material stored on any segment of it.

Visitors to the co-op apartment can wander the common hallways and knock on doors of any apartment. The apartment owner opens the door, then decides whether or not to allow the visitor into the apartment.

In Internet terms, you and I can log on the Internet and use the vast array of network cables to knock on the doors of Web sites. The owner of each Web site determines if we are allowed in to visit. The Internet cables, which are basically the telephone network, are like the hallways in a co-op apartment building, and the Web sites are located on segments of the Internet.

Once inside an apartment, the apartment owner grants us permission to freely roam the apartment or restricts us to certain rooms or activities, such as watching the monster TV, but not allowing us to change the channel. This is similar to restrictions found on some Web sites, where the Web site owner controls which Web pages you can access.

The co-op building is managed by a consortium of apartment owners whose job it is to establish rules for using the common areas of the building. For example, visitors must enter the co-op building using designated entrances. They must use the elevator to reach the desired floor. They must use the apartment number to identify the apartment they want to visit, and they must knock on the door of the apartment and wait to be invited into the apartment.

You probably surmise that the Internet also has rules developed by a consortium of segment owners. These rules are called *protocols* and they define the standards that must be followed for interacting with segments of the Internet.

For example, the entranceway to the Internet is through a portal usually supplied by an Internet Service Provider (ISP), which is discussed later in this chapter. After logging on the Internet, we use a Web site address to locate a segment of the Internet and we use our browser to knock on the door of the site.

The Web site follows Internet protocols and displays a page called a *home page*, which greets us similarly to how the apartment owner greets us at the door. Likewise, through our browser we follow certain protocols to interact with the Web site just as we follow certain mannerisms when interacting with apartment owner.

So the original statement that the Internet is a network of networks that is owned by no one and everyone is true. No one person owns the co-op apartment building, yet each apartment owner owns the co-op apartment building.

Tech Talk

Home page: the first Web page that is displayed when you visit a Web site.

A Bit of History

For once, the federal government has done one thing correctly by giving birth to the Internet. The U.S. Department of Defense launched a project in 1969 to electronically connect government scientists at universities throughout the United States so they could easily, quickly, and securely share information.

This project, the Internet, made its way into the world in a "delivery room" tucked away in a corner of the University of California, Los Angeles. The delivery room was really a computer room and the Internet was known as ARPANET. (Who but the government would give their new offspring a name like ARPANET?) ARPANET is the acronym for Advanced Research Projects Agency Network.

An objective of ARPANET was to keep lines of communications flowing in the event of a nuclear attack. Today, this may seem less of an issue than in the days of the Cold War, when the U.S. Department of Defense thought such an attack was probable.

Engineers used technology developed in 1962 by the Rand Corporation, one of the pioneers in the computer industry, to ensure that data could be transmitted over the network even if a portion of the network became disabled. The technology is called *packet switching* (see Chapter 5).

Tech Talk
Packet switching: the technique of dividing information into small pieces and placing each piece into an electronic envelope called a packet, which is transmitted over a network.

Information that was transmitted over the ARPANET was stored in packets, which also contained the destination address, the sender's address, and error checking information. A packet was sent to the destination computer by traveling along one of multiple paths. If a path (transmission line) became inoperable, then a device called a switch, first created by the Bolt Beranek and Newman (BBN) company, rerouted the packet along a different path.

The dangers imposed by the Cold War dissipated by 1984 and so did ARPANET. However, with approximately 500 universities actively using ARPANET, it didn't make sense to disband it. Instead, ARPANET was renamed the Internet and three years later turned over to the National Science Foundation to administer.

Faculty, students, and computer hobbyists who managed to get onto the Internet soon found its services very useful. You're probably familiar with the Internet e-mail service; other Internet services, such as newsgroups, Telnet, and FTP might be unfamiliar.

Tech Talk
Internet services: various methods that are available to exchange information over the Internet, such as e-mail, Telnet, FTP, and newsgroups.

A *newsgroup*, sometimes called a bulletin board, is a place on the Internet where someone can post a notice, a question, or an answer to a posted question. Let's say a student is tackling a technology problem and needs help. She can post the problem on a newsgroup and wait for another Internet user to post a solution. Newsgroups cover a variety of topics and still exist today, although commercial Web sites are taking over the role by offering interactive chat rooms.

As discussed later in this chapter, Telnet and FTP let you connect to a remote computer linked to the Internet. The Telnet service enables you to log on the remote computer and interact with it as if it was on your desk. The FTP service enables you to transfer files between your computer and the remote computer much like how you copy a file from a floppy disk to a hard disk. Both Telnet and FTP are also available today on the Internet.

Interacting with the Internet in its early days required good technical skills, since you had to log on the remote computer and locate the file that contained the desired information using commands. There was no one greeting you at the door with a home page.

The first major improvement to the Internet came in 1989 when the World Wide Web was created. The World Wide Web is a way information is organized on the Internet (see "The World Wide Web" on page 207).

The Internet and the early World Wide Web were text-based and lacked the graphical elements that Web pages have today. Anyone who wanted to surf the Internet in those days had to use special programs that required them to learn commands to interact with those programs. Commands were typed into the computer, primitive by today's standards in which we point and click our way through the Internet.

This system changed in 1993 when engineers that the University of Illinois developed Mosaic, the world's first browser for the World Wide Web. Internet users were no longer required to learn strange-sounding commands to find information on the Internet. Instead, they could point and click, then see information in a mixture of text and graphics.

The Internet Backroom

Every organization has a "backroom" where the powerbrokers make decisions about how the organization will run. The co-op apartment building has the co-op board, composed of apartment owners who establish and enforce rules for operating the apartment building. The Internet, too, has a group that creates rules for it. Actually, there are several groups, each of which oversees an aspect of Internet operations.

In 1992, a nonprofit group called the Internet Society (ISOC) formed to develop policies to "govern" the Internet. (Govern is probably too strong a word to use to describe the ISOC's purpose.) The ISOC formally adopts standards recommended by leaders of a particular aspect of the Internet. Once adopted, hardware manufacturers and software developers are responsible for making sure their products adhere to the standards. However, there is no Internet police force to catch violators. Instead, the desire to have their products work seamlessly with the Internet is the only motivation necessary to enforce the standards.

Internet Corporation for Assigned Names and Numbers (ICANN) handles policies that affect Internet addresses. ICANN is the successor of the Internet Assigned Numbers Authority (IANA), which was the original government agency selected to manage Internet addressing standards.

ICANN is a private international organization. This is the group that created .com, .net, .org, and other top-level domain names, which are discussed later in this chapter. The Internet Network Information Center (InterNIC) is the service run by Network Solutions, Inc. to register Internet names and addresses.

In addition to managing Internet addresses, there are two other aspects of the Internet operation that needed to be organized. These are hardware and software used to keep network traffic flowing, and the way information is accessed over the World Wide Web.

Traffic standards, as I like to call them, are created by the Internet Engineering Task Force. The IETF is a branch of the Internet Society and the Internet Operator's Providers Services (IOPS.ORG). The IETF focuses on standardizing the TCP/IP protocol, which is discussed later in this chapter. IOPS.ORG is a consortium of telecommunications carriers, such as AT&T, GTE, and MCI WorldCom, that set hardware standards to ensure that data is routed efficiently over the Internet.

Tech Talk
TCP/IP: protocols used to transmit data over the Internet.

The World Wide Web Consortium (W3C) sets standards for how information is shared on the World Wide Web by using a browser to link Web pages. The three leading members of the 150-member W3C are The MIT Laboratory for Computer Science, the French-based National Institute for Research in Computer Science and Automation, and Kieo University in Japan.

The International Flavor

The Internet evolved from a computer network financed by the U.S. Department of Defense and has grown to encompass areas around the world that are serviced by a telephone network. This includes North and South America, Europe, Asia, Australia, and some African countries.

Compatibility among national telephone networks is the key to giving the Internet worldwide reach. The Post, Telegraph, and Telephone (PPT) agency within each country manages telephone networks in many European countries. For example, this enables the German telephone network to communicate seamlessly with the Italian telephone network.

On a more international scale, the International Telecommunications Union (ITU) is an organization of national telephone companies that adopt telecommunication standards which, if adhered to, ensure continuity among telephone networks around the world.

However, a dilemma arose when the ITU adopted the X.25 network protocol (see Chapter 5). The X.25 protocol is an older transmission protocol used for computer networks and is incompatible with TCP/IP, which is the protocol used to transmit data over the Internet.

By the mid-1990s, a group of universities and research labs formed a cooperative and created EBONE, which is the European Internet Backbone. Members of the cooperative pay a fee that goes toward leasing dedicated lines between the EBONE and the U.S. Internet.

EBONE is divided into three layers called levels (Figure 6.2). Each country is connected to the top level of EBONE. You can think of this as a network of countries. Each country has its own Internet network that connects regions within the country. Think of this as a network of regions inside a country. The lowest level of EBONE exists within each region and is used to link local Internet sites to the regional Internet. Regional Internet networks consist of a network of Internet sites.

A Walk Behind the Scenes

Let's take a behind-the-scenes look at what happens when you the surf the Net. Your trip begins when your computer dials your ISP using a dial-up program. The dial-up program handles communication between your computer and the ISP's computer.

An ISP is an organization that sells connections to the Internet at a reasonable price. Anyone can become an ISP if they are willing to invest in hardware and communications lines. The objective of an ISP is to lease a dedicated T carrier-line from the telephone company for a monthly fee, then sell a portion of that time to people like you and me for a smaller monthly fee.

Before you made your first call with your computer, you needed to do a little "under the hood" tinkering to get the dial-up program working properly. This tinkering made sure your computer and the ISP's computer used the same communications protocol (see Chapter 4).

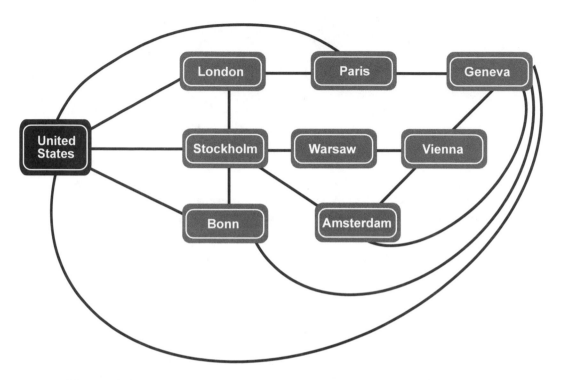

Figure 6.2
EBONE is the European Internet backbone that links regional networks in
several countries to the Internet backbone. (Redrawn with permission from
Prentice Hall. Comer, Douglas E. The Internet Book. Englewood Cliffs, NJ:
Prentice Hall, 1997, p. 77.)

Tech Talk

**Internet service provider (ISP): an organization that provides
inexpensive access to the Internet backbone.**

Once the dial-up software is configured (the technical term for tinkering under
the hood), a click on the dial-up icon begins your trip. Your modem dials the ISP's
telephone number, then waits for the ISP's computer to answer the call. Your ISP has
rooms of modems that connect the telephone company's central office to its local area
network using T carrier-line (Figure 6.3) (see also Chapter 5).

Your modem and the ISP's go through a handshaking procedure during which
they say "hello" to each other and agree to the transmission speed. After these formal-
ities, the ISP's computer requests your ID and password before giving you access to
the ISP's local area network.

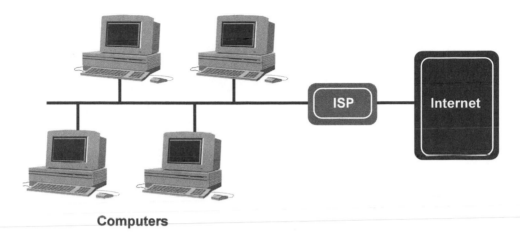

Computers

Figure 6.3
An Internet service provider links computers to the Internet backbone. (Redrawn with permission from Prentice Hall. Dodd, Annabel Z. The Essential Guide to Telecommunications. Upper Saddle River, NJ: Prentice Hall, 2000, p. 308.)

You can enter your ID and password into the dial-up software either when you set up the software or every time you connect to the ISP. The ID and the password are assigned to you when you sign up with the ISP.

The ISP's computer receives your ID and password, then compares them to data stored in its computer. If the data don't match, the ISP's computer transmits an error message to your computer prompting you to re-enter the information. Otherwise, the ISP's computer sends a message indicating that you have successfully connected to their network.

The ISP also assigns your computer a temporary Internet address called an IP address, which is discussed in detail later in this chapter. The IP address is similar to having your own "www...com" except your address is a number that is reassigned when you disconnect from the ISP.

Tech Talk
IP address: Internet protocol address, which is the unique address assigned to every network device.

The connection to the ISP is similar to being connected to your company's local area network. That is, the line of communication to the network is open and you need to run software on your computer that utilizes services on the LAN. After the connection is made, we click the browser icon and the ISP is transformed into our Internet portal.

Tech Talk
Portal: the place where you enter the Internet.

SURFING THE NET...

You can surf the Internet by entering the name of the Web site you want to visit into the browser, then pressing the Enter key or clicking highlighted text or a graph on the current Web page. In either case, the browser transmits the Web site name to the ISP's computer.

What you think of as a Web site's address is really just an alias because the IP address is the true address. For example, *www.amazon.com* is an alias for a specific IP address. We can remember the alias easier than trying to remember an IP address. (See the "Internet Address" section later in this chapter.)

The alias and the IP address are stored online in an Internet directory (Figure 6.4), which is used to compare the alias a user enters into a browser with the IP address.

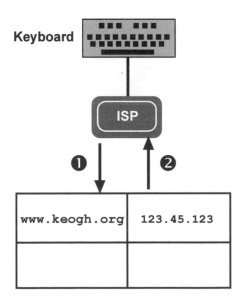

Figure 6.4
A name of an Internet site is translated into a unique Internet address before connecting to the site.

The Internet directory is a database stored at various central computers on the Internet and maintained by the Internet Network Information Center (see "The Internet Backroom" on page 189).

The ISP sends a request for the location to one of the databases and within a fraction of a second the Internet address is returned to the ISP. The ISP sends a message to the Internet address asking for a particular file, which is typically *index.html* unless your browser specified a different file name.

The *index.html* is the name of the file that contains the first Web page of a Web site, which is called the Web site's home page. This is the first Web page you see when visiting a Web site. A Web page consists of text that appears in the browser and includes instructions, called source code, that tell your browser how to display the text.

These instructions are written in one or a combination of Internet languages that include HTML, XML, and Java. Some of these instructions tell the browser to display text in bold or to align it left, right, or center. Other instructions direct your browser to request and display other files that contain graphics, video, or sound, for example.

Tech Talk

Source code: the instructions that tell a browser how to display a Web page. You can see the source code by placing the cursor on the Web page, clicking the right mouse button, then selecting View Source from the pop-up menu.

Hypertext: text or a graphic that is associated with and linked to other text on a Web page or associated with another Web page.

You've probably noticed that some text is highlighted on a Web page. These are called hypertext links because the text references other information and by clicking the hypertext, the browser displays the referenced information. Hypertext can reference information contained in the same file, called a bookmark, or reference information stored in a different file, which may be a different Web page.

When you click hypertext, the browser looks at the name associated with the hypertext and determines if it is a bookmark or another Web page. It knows the difference by the way the Web programmer encodes the instruction.

If the name is a bookmark, then the browser locates the bookmark on the Web page and displays the corresponding text and graphics. Otherwise, the browser looks up the Internet address of the Web page name, contacts that Web site, and requests the file.

Sometimes hypertext links to a different Web site, in which case the browser requests the *index.html* file for that site. Other times hypertext links to a specific file at a

Web site. For example, I visited the CNN/*Sports Illustrated* Web site and found hypertext linked to baseball. Baseball is another page on the CNN/*SportsIllustrated* site.

As you've noticed, surfing the Internet is really requesting that a file contained on a remote computer be copied to your computer. Your browser then follows instructions in the file to properly display text and graphics.

JAVA™ PERKS UP A WEB PAGE

The office guru talks about Java™ in the coffee room at work—and her conversation has nothing to do with refreshments. Java is a programming language that consists of words that have special meaning to programmers and to your computer.

Programmers use programming languages to tell your computer how to do something, such as how to become a word processor. Java™ is one of many programming languages and is one that is used to give intelligence to Web pages.

For example, we've all seen scrolling text across a Web page. This is possible because a programmer writes a small Java™ program called an applet that instructs your computer about how to scroll text.

Engineers who created Java™ to work with a browser used a clever design to enable Java™ programs to run on any kind of computer, including PC, Mac, and UNIX computers. The design centers on using a Java™ engine.

Although the name conjures images of a device powering a rocket into space, the Java™ engine is much simpler to understand. It is a program designed for a particular computer. This means there is a Java™ engine for a PC and another for a Mac, and so on. The engine's job is to translate a Java™ program into instructions that a specific computer can understand.

Here's how it works. The programmer who created the Web page includes instructions written in the Java™ language as part of the page. Java™ instructions are clearly identified, so when the browser comes across them while reading HTML and XML instructions, it stops and runs the Java™ engine.

The Java™ engine picks up where the browser left off and translates the Java™ instruction embedded in the Web page and directs the computer to do something, such as scroll text at a particular location on the screen. Once the Java™ instructions are translated, the Java™ engine turns control back to the browser, which continues to read and follow the rest of the instructions on the Web page.

Java™ has an advantage over other programming languages because it is machine-independent. Programs written in other programming languages can run on specific computers, but not all computers.

For example, programs that run on a computer running Linux, an operating system used on many Internet servers, cannot run on a computer running Windows. Software manufacturers need to create a different version of their program for each type of computer. However, programs written in Java™ can run on any computer.

The Internet Connection

The Internet is seen as the modern day gold rush in which everyone is trying to stake their claim to a site that might be sitting over a vein that will make them millionaires over night. Today's prospectors are staking claims to Web sites, but not too many years ago those looking to profit from the Internet sought their wealth by becoming Internet Service Providers.

An ISP gambles that there will be more subscribers to its service than the maximum number of transmissions per month. An example will help to clarify the idea.

Let's say the telephone company charges an ISP $500 a month for a T carrier-line that can carry 24 transmissions at the same time. The ISP charges its subscribers $20 per month and tries to get as many subscribers as possible to sign up for the service. The gamble is that not more than 24 subscribers will connect to the Internet at the same time.

The ISP needs at least 25 paid subscribers a month to cover the cost of the T carrier-line and a higher number of subscribers is necessary to cover other expenses. The ISP has hardware, software, maintenance support, customer relations, and other expenses needed to keep subscribers happy. At some point, the ISP is betting that these expenses will be covered by monthly subscription fees and return a profit.

I like to think of an ISP as a health club. The health club purchases expensive training equipment, then lets us have unlimited use of it in return for a monthly fee. The health club owner is betting that more people will pay the fee and not use the equipment than those who will pay the fee and use the facility.

Communications carriers, such as the telephone company and cable TV companies, soon realized that they too could easily become an ISP and possibly offer faster transmission than that provided by traditional ISPs. For example, some telephone companies offer DLS service (see Chapter 5) and some cable TV companies offer special modems that connect your computer to their cable.

Another objective of an ISP is to keep transmissions over the T carrier-line to the Internet backbone at a minimum. This reduces the chance that additional T carrier-lines will be needed to accommodate subscribers.

Imagine an ISP as a local area network of subscribers that has one pathway to the Internet superhighway, which is a T carrier-line. Let's say that many subscribers to the ISP visit Amazon.com.

Each time a subscriber selects Amazon.com, the ISP goes to a remote computer and looks up Amazon.com's Internet address. This ties up a channel on the T-carrier line. However, the ISP can eliminate these trips if it copies the Internet telephone book to a server on the ISP's local area network. This way, the ISP uses its own copy of the Internet telephone book to find Amazon.com's Internet address without using a channel on the T carrier-line.

The reduced traffic from the ISP to the Internet backbone frees the T carrier-line for other Internet transmissions, which could reduce the number of T carrier-lines that need to be leased from the telephone company.

The Internet backbone is the interconnection of networks managed by network services providers called Tier 1 providers. These providers include AT&T, Sprint, MCI WorldCom, GTE Internetwork, and UUNET.

Tech Talk

Tier 1 provider: a telephone company that has a large network that connects IPSs and corporations directly to the Internet.

Tier 1 providers each have their own large networks, which connect to ISPs and corporations that want direct access to the Internet. The National Science Foundation created four central points where Tier 1 providers exchange data. I think of these like regional post offices where information is redirected to the destination network. These central points are called public peering centers, and instead of letters being exchanged, such as is done in a regional post office, public peering centers exchange data packets (see Chapter 5). Private Tier 1 providers run each of the four centers.

However, the rapid growth of Internet traffic has far exceeded the capability of public peering centers to keep up with demand. Tier 1 providers are overcoming this obstacle to growth by creating private peering centers that perform similar duties to those the public peering centers perform (Figure 6.5).

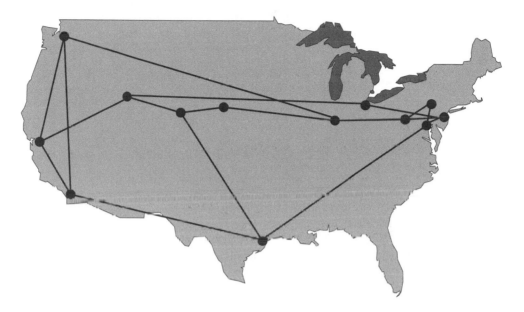

Figure 6.5
Tier 1 Internet providers connect together centers around the country to exchange information. (Redrawn with permission from Prentice Hall. Comer, Douglas E. The Internet Book. Englewood Cliffs, NJ: Prentice Hall, 1997, p. 69.)

Internet Addresses

Some business Internet addresses are worth millions of dollars, but most are like
mine, personal addresses that cost a few dollars a month to maintain rather than bringing in any revenue.

An Internet address is similar to a telephone number on the telephone network;
the address uniquely identifies a particular computer that is connected to the Internet.
The actual Internet address, also known as an IP address, looks something like this:
123.123.123.123.

This format of an IP address might appear strange to you especially if you are
familiar with entering the name that is associated with the IP address rather than the
address itself into your browser. For example, *www.keogh.org* is the Universal Resource Locator (URL) Internet name that is associated with my Web site. This is
called the *domain name*. Frankly, I don't know my IP address, which is not a problem
because my Internet Service Provider looks up the IP address whenever I connect to
my Web site by typing *www.keogh.org*.

A domain name implies the nature of the organization that owns a computer. You recognize this as .com, .org, .net, .gov, .edu, and .mil. These indicate a commercial business, a nonprofit organization, a network, an educational institution, a government organization, and a military organization, respectively. These are referred to as top-level domain names.

A word of caution: Don't assume the top-level domain name actually reflects the type of organization that owns the computer. Anyone can register a .com, .org, or .net IP address by filling out an online form and paying a registration fee. For example, an address that ends with .org can be used for a commercial venture.

The IP address consists of a setting of bits called *octets*, such as 111.222.333.444. A bit is a binary digit (see Chapter 2), although I like to consider a bit like a switch that can be turned on or off, with on representing a 1 and off representing a 0.

The IP address identifies more than a computer linked to the Internet. It also identifies the network that contains the computer. Earlier in this chapter, you learned that the Internet is a network of networks. The first two sets of numbers in the IP address are called the *subnet* and identify the network that contains the computer. The next two sets of numbers identify the computer.

Tech Talk
Subnet: the portion of an IP address that identifies a network.

This is similar to your telephone number, in which the area code identifies your metropolitan region, the next three digits represent your exchange, and the last four digits represent your telephone. An IP address is associated with one or more URLs. This is called mapping. For example, *www.instituteofe-commerce.com* and *www.keogh.org* are mapped to the same IP address.

The first set of characters entered before the Web site name (www) identify the Internet service that you request. You'll notice that if you type *www.keogh.org* in your browser, it automatically places "http" in front of the name, which identifies the Internet service you want to use to transfer files over the Internet.

Tech Talk
HTTP: HyperText Transfer Protocol, which is the Internet service used to transmit Web pages.

An Internet service has nothing to do with the type of Web site you can visit. Instead, it describes a feature of the Internet that you want to use, such as e-mail, FTP (to transfer files), and HTTP (to enter the World Wide Web).

You are probably familiar with e-mail and HTTP more than with FTP because most of us rarely transfer files directly on the Internet. We usually let the browser handle file transfer behind the scenes. We'll explore FTP in detail later in this chapter.

E-mail Address

The e-mail address is divided into two components that are separated by the @ sign. These are the name of the e-mail mailbox and the name of the computer that contains the mailbox. The name of the computer is called the domain name. The @ symbol was selected as the character to use for e-mail because it was unlikely that it would be used in a mailbox name or a domain name. In fact, @ cannot be used in a mailbox or a domain name.

The domain name is used by Internet devices, such as a router or a switch (see Chapter 4), to send mail to the proper computer, sometimes called the mail server (discussed in detail in Chapter 7). Once the mail arrives, the mail server uses the mailbox name to locate the proper mailbox on the server. If it is unable to find the mailbox, the e-mail is returned to the sender with a message stating that the mailbox is unknown. A mailbox is actually a directory on the mail server, similar to a folder on a computer's hard disk.

Internet Service Providers, especially those that host Web sites for other organizations, have a way to fool the system by assigning an IP address to a directory on their computer rather than to a computer.

Let's say that you want to have your own Web site and stake your claim to the billions of dollars that are expected to pour over the Internet. You can buy software that transforms your home computer to a Web server, then spend $500 a month plus an installation charge to connect your computer to the Internet backbone.

Or you can ask your Internet Service Provider to host your Web site for about $10 month plus setup charges. Don't expect to receive your own computer for that price. Instead, you'll receive a directory on the Internet Service Provider's computer.

You'll get to choose the name of your Web site, as long as it hasn't been reserved, and the Internet Service Provider will assign you an IP address that is associated with its computer. This IP address enables the Internet backbone routers and switches to find the computer on the Internet.

However, once a message arrives, the Internet Service Provider uses the IP address to locate your directory. This enables many of us to feed our dreams of making millions by owning a Web site, without spending thousands of dollars to set up a business.

The Internet is so hot that it is running out of IP addresses. There is a mathematical limit to the number of IP addresses that can be issued: 4,294,967,296. This is the number of bit combinations that can be represented by the bits used to store an IP address.

A similar situation is happening with telephone numbers. For example, each exchange (first three digits) can contain a maximum of 9,999 telephone numbers. And there can be a maximum of 999 exchanges for each area code, with a maximum of 999 area codes. My trusty calculator indicates that there can be 9,979,011,999 unique telephone numbers (9999*999*999).

Everyone overseeing the Internet realizes the seriousness of running out of IP addresses, and an effort has been launched to overcome this problem by creating a new version of the Internet Protocol.

Internet Protocols

The Internet is like a highway of interconnecting networks and computers, and as with every highway there are rules of the road. On the Internet, these rules are called Internet protocols, which were discussed briefly in Chapter 5.

Another way to look at this is to think of information flowing around the Internet as stuffed into electronic envelopes called packets (see Chapter 5). You can stick any kind of information in any format within an envelope, as long as the envelope is the standard size and is addressed properly.

Internet protocols are called Transmission Control Protocol (TCP) and Internet Protocol (IP), which are commonly referred to as TCP/IP. Together, they form an Internet protocol suite, which is discussed in Chapter 5.

IP is the protocol that specifies how to send and receive packets, called datagrams, over the Internet. Software manufacturers build software that follows these rules to ensure that information is transmitted properly.

Tech Talk

Datagram: a packet of information that is transmitted over the Internet.

Each datagram contains the IP address of the destination computer and the computer that sent the datagram. Routers and other Internet devices use the IP address to determine the most efficient path for reaching the destination address.

While the IP protocol handles addressing and constructing a datagram, the TCP protocol handles how to deal with transmission problems. A superhighway is connected by many interchanges of on and off ramps that join to approach roads. The Internet also has interchanges called routers and switches (see Chapter 4).

A bottleneck can easily occur when too many datagrams try to move through the same router at the same time. Software in a router does what most of us do when we become overwhelmed with information—ignores it. This is unacceptable for the Internet, so engineers developed the TCP protocol to manage the connection between two computers and redirect discarded datagrams to lesser-used routers.

Here's how TCP works (Figure 6.6). A timer begins when a datagram is sent. If all goes well and the datagram is received, the destination computer sends an acknowledgement, which turns off the timer. However, if the time expires before the acknowledgement is received, TCP sends another copy of the datagram since it is assumed a router discarded the original one.

TCP has the intelligence to adjust the time limit between transmission and acknowledgement based on conditions on the Internet. For example, more time is given to receive a response during peak traffic periods or when the destination is far from the sender.

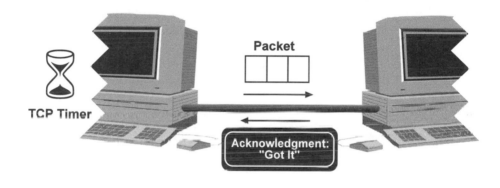

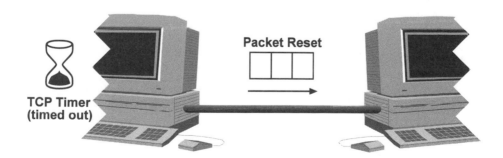

Figure 6.6
TCP starts a timer when a packet is sent. If time expires before an acknowledgment is received, TCP resends the packet.

INTERNET SERVICES ···

It is difficult to accept that there was a time when Amazon.com and Yahoo.com didn't exist. There wasn't any place on the World Wide Web to buy discounted merchandise. In fact, there was a time when there wasn't a World Wide Web, but instead a bare-bones Internet.

The Internet was designed to accommodate communication among researchers and scientists at universities and research institutions. The people who used it were happy with less fancy communications than we have become accustomed to on today's Internet. Any improvement over communicating by telephone, fax, or "snail" mail was seen as a triumph.

As mentioned earlier in this chapter, the Internet is a network of networks that consists of cables, routers, switches, and computers, along with software that obey Internet protocols to exchange information.

Engineers who helped build the Internet had to develop ways to package data transmissions that was efficient and easy to use. The packaging I'm referring to isn't data packets or datagrams, but Internet services.

I like to think of an Internet service as a consumer product much like services we use to transfer things from one place to another. I can transfer a few words that describe my new house by calling our friend. I can supply her with a play-by-play commentary on how I bought the house by transferring my thoughts in a letter and sending it by snail mail. If I really want to be eccentric, I can hire a moving company to tow the entire house to my friend's front door.

The Internet has services similar to the ones I just described except they are identified by formal names such as Telnet, e-mail, and FTP. Of course, I cannot overlook the World Wide Web.

Telnet

The Telnet service is similar to a telephone call; words we enter on our computer are sent directly to a remote computer. Like a telephone call, those words are not stored but, instead, displayed on the remote computer's screen.

In the early years of computers, before the Windows operating system or Macintosh computers hit the market, anyone who wanted to use a computer had to enter commands at an operating system prompt known as a command prompt. There weren't any fancy icons or lists of programs. Instead, everyone needed to learn commands that enabled him or her to control the computer.

For example, the command `dir` displayed the files and directories of the computer much like Windows Explorer does for a PC. You can still use commands if you display the MS-DOS Prompt window by clicking the Start button and then the Programs option in Windows.

The Telnet service enabled anyone who could connect to the Internet to take control of another computer that is also connected to it. Of course, the person who owned the remote computer had to grant access permission by issuing a login ID and password.

For example, I can access a computer at Columbia University, where I teach, by dialing my Internet Service Provider, then using telnet to dial the IP address of the computer at Columbia University. Once the computer "answers" the call, it sends my computer a log-in prompt, which are words that tell me to enter my ID and password. I enter this information on my computer, and it is transmitted to the Columbia University computer when I press the Enter key.

The Columbia University computer searches its password file to determine if my ID and password are valid. If they're not, a message is sent refusing me access to the computer. If the password and ID match, then an operating system prompt similar to the command prompt is sent to my computer. Then I can enter commands as if I was sitting in front of the Columbia University computer.

E-mail

Electronic mail, better known as e-mail, was born in 1972 when Ray Tomlinson, an engineer at Bolt Beranek and Newman Company (BBN) and one of the pioneers of the original Internet, needed a way to communicate with other engineers who were connected to the Internet. Tomlinson is the father of the @ sign in e-mail addresses.

E-mail enables you to use store-forward technology to electronically write your thoughts into a file and then copy the file to a remote computer, where another person can read it.

Tech Talk

Store-forward technology: a method of saving information to a file and then sending the file to a remote computer, where the file is stored until someone is available to read it.

What makes e-mail special is that the file can be addressed to a particular person at a particular computer connected to the Internet. This is possible because of the e-mail rules of the road called Simple Mail Transfer Protocols (SMTP), which are part of the TCP/IP protocol suite.

SMTP controls how e-mail is sent and received. However, SMTP is unable to handle attachments to e-mails. Engineers needed to develop a way to attach other files to an e-mail. This need gave birth to the Multipurpose Internet Mail Extension (MIME) standard, which specifies how attachments are to be associated with an e-mail.

Here's how MIME works. Keep in mind that an e-mail consists of a group of bits in which the first few bits identify the recipient and sender, followed by the e-mail message and bits that indicate the end of the e-mail.

Between the last bit of the e-mail message and the bit that identifies the end of the e-mail are bits that represent the attachment. The first few bits of the attachment identify the beginning of it and the type of file that is attached. The last bit of the attachment signifies the end of it.

Let's say that you attached a Microsoft Word file to an e-mail. The Word file is identified with the .doc file extension. This is the type of file. If you select a file with the .doc file extension, Windows assumes that Word is the program you need to read this file and starts Word automatically.

Archie, Gopher, and FTP

The original Internet was created for scientists and engineers who needed to exchange ideas through e-mail, and scientific works in the form of research papers and other documents. However, scientific works posed a new challenge. How would scientists and engineers know a scientific work existed? And how could they receive a copy of it?

Think about this a minute and you can appreciate the enormity of the problem. Let's say that I accumulated statistical data that described how to stop insects from eating apples. I wrote a formal scientific paper and placed it on my computer, then I told all my colleagues to go to the Internet and use Telnet to log on my computer and look at my paper.

This works well except for two limitations. My colleagues must read the paper online and cannot get their own copy. They cannot even print it because they are remotely connected to my computer, so any print commands they enter cause the document to print at my site, not theirs. The other limitation is that other scientists and engineers couldn't access the paper because they didn't know it existed unless the author told them. Many times the author was unable to spread the word about the paper and, therefore, the paper wasn't widely read.

You may be thinking, "Why don't they simply visit my Web page?". That's possible today, but until the early 1990s, Web pages didn't exist. However, there were three Internet services that were created to resolve these problems. These are Archie, Gopher, and the File Transfer Protocol (FTP).

The Archie and Gopher services were the forerunner of today's search engines. They enabled you to enter a keyword or phrase, and then Archie or Gopher searched the Internet for documents that matched the search criteria. The address of the remote computer that contained the document was returned as the results of the search.

The Archie Internet service was command driven, which meant anyone who used it needed to learn Archie commands to perform a search. The Gopher Internet service improved upon Archie by interacting with users through a menu instead of using commands.

Next, there needed to be a way to copy a document from a remote computer. Of course, e-mail could have been used for this purpose, but the scientist or engineer first needed to contact the author of the paper and ask that the document be sent as an attachment to the e-mail. This became cumbersome. The author didn't have time to respond to inquiries.

A better method was to use the FTP Internet service, which enabled the scientist or engineer to copy the file directly, without contacting anyone at the remote computer. The FTP Internet service required the person to connect to the remote computer and log in.

Obviously, the scientist or engineer didn't have an ID or password to gain access to the remote computer. However, owners of remote computers typically created a standard ID called "anonymous" and the password was the visitor's e-mail address. The password wasn't used to protect the site, but instead to record visitors. Everyone trusted other Internet users. Those were the days before computer viruses and cyber attacks.

After the scientist or engineer logged on the remote computer, he or she used FTP commands to locate the file that contained the document and to copy the file to his or her computer.

The World Wide Web

Surfing the Internet before the Web browser was created was a nightmare because you needed to learn a vocabulary of commands for every Internet service before you could become proficient using the Internet.

The main objective of the Internet is to foster an easy way for people to communicate, without requiring them to learn and use an archaic language. Tim Berners-Lee, a scientist at the European Laboratory for Particle Physics, agreed and took things into his own hands. He created a new service for the Internet called the World Wide Web (WWW).

The WWW specifies rules for finding and displaying information that is stored on a computer connected to the Internet, independent of a computer language and computer. These rules are called the HyperText Transfer Protocol (HTTP). You probably recognize HTTP as the first four characters displayed on the address bar of your browser. At the heart of HTTP is the HyperText Markup Language (HTML).

Tech Talk

HyperText Markup Language (HTML): a language that uses embedded tags to describe how a document is to be displayed in a browser and how it is to be linked to other documents.

Let's say you visit my Web site, *www.keogh.org*, by entering the address in your browser. The browser looks up the IP address associated with my site and requests the *index.html* file. This is usually the file that contains the Web site home page. The Internet Service Provider who hosts my Web site sends a copy of the *index.html* file to your computer, where your browser opens the file.

Your browser assumes that the *index.html* file is written in HTML, then reads each line of the *index.html* file looking for HTML tags (Figure 6.7) that tell the browser how I want the text to be displayed on your screen.

```
<HTML>
<HEAD>
<TITLE>Test Page</TITLE>
</HEAD>
<BODY bgColor=#ffffcc link="#3333ff" vlink="#3333ff" alink="#3333ff">
<P><IMG src="test.gif" ></P>
</BODY>
</HTML>
```

Figure 6.7
HTML uses tags to tell a browser how to display a Web page.

If I want the person viewing my Web site to see a mixture of pictures and text, I would use an HTML tag to tell the browser where to insert a specific graphic. This tag contains the name of the file and the name of the computer that contains the file, which the browser uses to request the picture file from that computer.

If you visit my Web site, you'll notice that I have links to many other sites. These are called *hyperlinks*, which are HTML tags that tell the browser the name of the file to request when someone clicks on the hyperlink. You recognize hyperlinks as colored text on the Web page or perhaps graphics that you can click on.

The hidden benefit of HTML is that any browser can read it on any computer. In contrast, a computer program can be run only on a specific computer platform. For example, WordPerfect is a word processing program that has versions for Windows and UNIX, which are different operating systems. You must have the proper version of WordPerfect for the operating system used on your computer. This is not the case with HTML documents since they can be viewed on any computer running a browser.

With the onset of electronic commerce and new technology, enhanced versions of HTML were developed. These include the Dynamic HyperText Markup Language (DHTML), Extensible Markup Language (XML), the Voice Extensible Markup Language (VXML), and SGML, which is the forerunner of XML.

DHTML is similar to HTML except the HTML code is generated by a program at the time a Web page is requested, rather than at the time the programmer creates it. For example, after you identify yourself by signing into a Web site, a program running on the site creates a personal greeting, which is displayed on the page. The Web pages that are not personalized are likely to be created once by a programmer and stored on the server waiting for your browser to ask for the page.

XML enables authors to create their own labels and fields, some of which have been standardized for electronic commerce. Let's say you have an e-commerce Web site that needs to exchange product information, such as prices, with other systems. You can create a product ID tag and a price tag that identifies information as the product identifier and the price of the product.

VXML enables you to interact with the World Wide Web using voice over the telephone. For example, you can ask for a weather report and receive a briefing over the telephone from a computer that is connected to the Web.

INTERNET SECURITY ....

The Internet is vulnerable to attack from people who seek to beat the system or cause cyber graffiti by leaving their name in a remote computer. There is an increased interest in protecting the Internet as more of our economy is conducted in cyber space.

There are many security issues involving the Internet because, as you've learned in this chapter, the Internet is comprised of many pieces, each of which must work together to provide successful transmission of information.

Let's identify points in a transmission where an attack can occur. The Internet is organized as a client/server network (see Chapter 7) in which at least one computer contains the information other computers want. The computer that contains the information is called a server and the computer requesting the information is called the client.

You and I are clients when we log on Amazon.com and browse its bookstore. Amazon.com uses a server to supply us with Web pages and eventually information that enables us to complete a transaction.

We begin our trip into cyber space by entering the name of the Web site that we want to visit, such as *www.amazon.com*. Our Internet Service Provider's computer looks up the actual IP address that is associated with *www.amazon.com*. Everyone assumes that the computer (a server) that contains the IP directory contains accurate information.

However, a cyber criminal could change the IP address associated with *www.amazon.com* in an IP directory. Keep in mind there are many copies of these "telephone books," so changing one may go undetected for some time.

A spoofing Web site operated by a cyber criminal can be substituted for the real IP address. Every request for your computer is passed to the spoofing site, which intercepts your request and forwards it to the real IP address. A sniffer program is used to search individual packets of data for confidential information, such as your credit card number. Next, *www.amazon.com* sends a response to your request to the spoofing Web site, which intercepts it before relaying it to your computer.

Tech Talk

Spoofing: occurs when an illegitimate Web site pretends to be a specific legitimate Web site.
Sniffer program: software that examines datagrams transmitted over the Internet for confidential information.

Information that is intercepted can be altered or left intact and used for illegal purposes without you or Amazon.com finding out until the cyber crime is detected. The most critical information in an e-commerce transaction is your credit card information. E-tailers, the name given to merchants on the Internet, protect credit card information by encrypting the data using a secured Web site. A cyber criminal still might intercept your credit card information, but the information is garbled and must be decoded with a special key.

Servers on the Internet are vulnerable to a frontal attack by cyber crooks trying to use various methods to gain access to IDs, passwords, and back doors that give them direct access to files located anywhere on the server.

Tech Talk

Back door: an entrance to a server that bypasses ID and password security measures.
War dialing: the technique in which a program dials sequential telephone numbers trying to detect those that are attached to modems.

For example, a cyber criminal might begin the attack by war dialing, in which programs are used to automatically dial thousands of telephone numbers trying to find those that are connected to modems. The idea is that where there is a modem, there must be a computer, which might contain interesting and confidential information.

Of course, the cyber criminal still needs an ID and a password to gain access to the server. Several techniques are used to overcome this obstacle. First, a password cracker can be used, which is software that tries to guess an ID and a password by attempting hundreds of combinations.

The good guys fight back by disconnecting the telephone call after three failed log-in attempts. Many times a call must be made to the administrator of the server to re-establish the ID. However, this too may not pose a problem because once the cyber criminal identifies the company that owns the server, he or she uses the social engineering tactic to gain access.

Social Engineering

Social engineering is used by smooth-talkers to make unsuspecting company employees give out IDs and passwords. For example, someone might call an employee and pretend to be a technician working with the IS department and ask the person to verify his or her ID and password. Of course, the "technician" gives the wrong ID and password, which the employee corrects, and the "technician" promises to correct the company's records.

Then there are those diehards who will dumpster-dive for the chance that someone tossed information about IDs and passwords in the trash.

Companies take a defensive position to fight off attacks by creating a *firewall* between their servers and the Internet. A firewall acts similarly to a brick and mortar firewall; the firewall separates two structures, which are spaced to ideally prevent dangerous people from attacking the main structure. In cyber space, the main structure is comprised of the servers within an organization.

Tech Talk
Firewall: a computer that filters every piece of information within the organization that is received from and sent to the Internet.

Some employees like to call a firewall "Big Brother" because it refuses employees access to specific Web sites that someone in the organization feels are not suited for viewing during business hours.

However, the primary purpose of a firewall is to trap Trojan horses, logic bombs, and malicious applets from gaining access to corporate servers. These are programs that can wreak havoc on a server.

Tech Talk

Trojan horse: a program that uses the same program name as a safe program, but contains instructions inside that could destroy files on the server.
Logic bomb: a program that is like a booby trap and sits quietly on the server until someone inadvertently triggers it. Once triggered, instructions in the logic bomb do a dirty deed on the server.
Malicious applet: a short program written in the Java programming language that is embedded into a Web page. The Web page seems like any Web page to you and me, but once it is opened, the Java applet can do all kinds of mischief, such as send erroneous e-mails or search for IDs and passwords stored on the computer.

One of the latest vulnerabilities of the Internet is denial of service, which causes such a traffic jam at a particular Web site that legitimate visitors are turned away. This has happened to Yahoo!, eBay, and other high profile Web sites.

The objective of cyber criminals who use this tactic is not to steal anything, but instead to deprive a company of business. Actually, denial of service is probably the least technical cyber crime and the most difficult one to prevent.

Here's how it works. Cyber criminals target both the IP address of the server and the IP addresses of routers and switches (see Chapter 4) that redirect packets to that IP address. Once these IP addresses are known, the criminal writes a program to send packets of data to those addresses. Although these IP addresses have the hardware and software that can handle high-peak traffic periods, there is a point when these IP addresses become overwhelmed and cannot process any more packets.

Cyber criminals know there is such a limit, but probably cannot measure it. So, they covertly distribute the packet-sending program to various Web servers and computers connected to the Web. Typically, they target computers at universities, which are less stringently controlled than those in corporations. Each program is timed to send a constant stream of packets to those IP addresses at precisely the same time and for the same duration, such as an hour. The congestion of packets at these addresses blocks legitimate packets from being processed, which can cause a slowdown of traffic on the Internet.

Internet Privacy

Privacy is a major concern of anyone who uses the Internet, especially when the media reports that information about us is collected covertly by some Web site operators. Many of us fail to realize that when we are connected to the Internet, another computer is connected to ours, theoretically making anything on our computer available to the remote computer.

You need to realize that when visiting a Web site, you are inviting the owner of the site to run software (i.e., the Web page) on your computer, yet you never know what that software is actually doing.

Some Web pages write small pieces of information to our hard disk called *cookies*. Cookies hold various kinds of information, such as the last time you visited the Web page or the credit card number you used to order merchandise from that Web site.

Many browsers warn you when a Web page is about to write a cookie to your hard disk and gives you the opportunity to reject the cookie. If you reject the cookie, the Web page might not be able to function properly. However, many Web surfers become annoyed by receiving constant cookie alerts and decide to turn off the alert feature on their browser. This leaves them totally vulnerable to cookies being written without their knowledge.

Cookies are not infallible because a cookie identifies the last person who used your computer to interact with the Web page. This can be misleading because the information may not pertain to the current visitor. I discovered this when I logged on Amazon.com and was greeted personally as Joanne, who is my daughter and the last person who ordered a book from that site.

Even if a Web page doesn't write cookies to your hard disk, it can still gather information about you without you knowing it by using hidden fields of information in the Web page.

Tech Talk
Field: a specific kind of information, such as a credit card number.

Let's say that you visited your favorite online merchant. As soon as you request its home page, the merchant knows which ISP you used and the city, state, and country of the ISP. Businesses and larger organizations, such as universities, are their own ISP, so just by visiting a Web site the owner of the site can identify the organization.

Every time you request a page from a Web site, your request and information about your Internet return address is recorded in a log file that can be analyzed by tracking software. This enables the Web site owner to know what pages you viewed, how long you viewed them, and the path used to move from page to page throughout the site.

For example, the home page is usually *index.html* and displays information that the Web site owner hopes draws you to other pages on the site. Tracking software reports to the owner which of those pages you visited and which you avoided.

You may say that this information isn't too important to you because your identity remains unknown to the Web site owner. This is correct until you supply information about your identity when you become a "member" of a Web site or when you buy something from that site.

Information that you provide is likely stored in a database along with information that tracks your visit to the Web site. Say that you become a member of a Web site that contains information about cars. As you surf through the site, you might spend a few minutes looking at a Lexus and another few minutes looking at a Mercedes Benz before leaving the site.

You don't give the visit a second thought; however, you've provided the Web site owner with information that can be sold to a third party. The owner knows your identity because you filled out an online membership form, which probably included your home address and your e-mail address. And you were probably asked to sign in to the site whenever you visit so you can take advantage of "special deals."

You might actually find good deals that aren't offered to nonmembers. However, by signing onto the Web site, its owner is able to relate you to a traffic pattern. The tracking software is likely to detect your interest in a Lexus and a Mercedes Benz because you spent more time looking at those Web pages than other pages.

When this information comes to the attention of the Web site owner, you can expect that your identity will be sold to merchants who are looking for customers seeking to buy a Lexus or a Mercedes Benz. Furthermore, your identity could be sold to merchants who sell other products to customers who own Lexus or Mercedes Benz cars.

There is a trend among online merchants to ask your permission to sell information about you to third parties. You might find such a request buried at the bottom of your membership form or online purchase request. Don't be surprised if the default setting gives permission to sell your information just in case you forget to make a selection. Some Web site owners are also enabling you to see and correct the *profile* that is built about you whenever you visit their Web sites.

Tech Talk

Profile: information stored by a Web site owner that describes products you purchase and Web pages you visit frequently. Profiles are used to display products and other information that might be of interest to you.

Corporations and other large organizations try to limit information inferred from a Web site log file by using a proxy server. A proxy server is a computer that is an intermediary between the Internet and servers within the organization. The identity of the server used to request a Web page is recorded in the Web site's log file. However, this information reflects the identity of the proxy server and not the actual server within the organization because the proxy server strips away the information of the actual server and replaces it with its own.

HONESTY MAY NOT BE THE BEST POLICY

Web site owners may not have all the relative information they think they have about visitors to their Web site. Clever Web surfers create virtual identities that conceal their true identity. For example, they create a ficticious name, then open a free e-mail account using that name. Instead of providing a Web site with their personal information, they provide a fake profile.

This enables the surfer to join free Web sites and participate in discussions without fearing that the site owner will learn any real information about them. This sounds dubious, but so are Web site owners who collect information about you and sell it to advertisers without your permission.

There's nothing illegal about creating a virtual identity as long as you don't attempt to defraud the Web site owner. For example, you must give legitimate information when making a purchase, but by then you should be comfortable dealing with that Web site.

INTRANETS AND EXTRANETS

Businesses are finding other uses for Internet technology besides communicating with anyone in the world. Two of those new uses are to use this technology to communicate within an organization and among business partners.

The term *Intranet* is used to describe Internet technology used on a local area network to provide e-mail, Web pages, and other communication methods to employees. Employees use the same browser used to access the Internet to access the company's Intranet. However, anyone who is not connected to the organization's local area network is unable to access the Intranet.

Intranets are used to distribute employee information, provide Web page-based forms that are completed online, and give authorized employees access to data stored in the organization's databases.

An Extranet (Figure 6.8) is frequently used to link business partners, such as suppliers, vendors, and trading partners, who conduct frequent business transactions with an organization. Let's say you provide office supplies to 100 businesses. Instead of the office staff quoting prices, checking availability, and tracking orders, every customer can do this by logging on your Extranet.

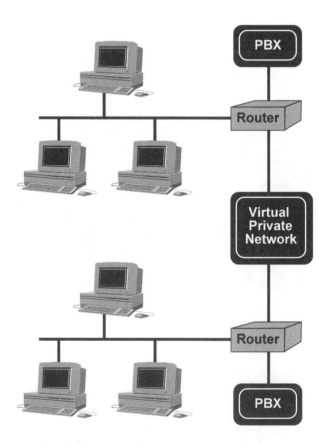

Figure 6.8
An Extranet connects business partners. (Redrawn with permission from Prentice Hall. Dodd, Annabel Z. The Essential Guide to Telecommunications. Upper Saddle River, NJ: Prentice Hall, 2000, p. 306.)

Typically, a customer uses the Internet address to visit your site, then uses an ID and a password to gain access to the Extranet Web pages. From that point, it is as if the customer is viewing a normal Web page.

An Extranet automates many of the normal business transactions that require human interaction but can easily be automated. Many inquiries require a sales assistant to look up the information in the company's computer system. The Extranet gives customers controlled access to that computer system.

Security is a critical concern to owners of Extranets since the owner is relying on the skills of the IS department to write a program that addresses all the facets dealing with a customer. The owner does not want incorrect information to be sent to the customer, nor does the owner want to frustrate the customer before he or she is able to talk to a person.

Extranets satisfy security concerns by using encryption, authorization, and integrity checks. Encryption mixes up data so it isn't easily read, as discussed previously in this chapter. Authorization requires the customer to use a unique ID and password to access the Extranet.

Integrity checks consist of logic written into a program to ensure that the interaction with the customer makes sense. For example, a small business that buys 10 reams of paper every month is unlikely to order 100 reams one month, so the Extranet ordering program would flag the order and bring it to the sales rep's attention.

SUMMARY ....

The Internet is a network of networks that links computers called servers that contain Web pages and computers called clients that request to see Web pages. The entrance point to the Internet is typically through an Internet Service Provider (ISP), which is an organization that sells access to the Internet for a small monthly charge.

An ISP leases one or more T carrier-lines from the telephone company, which enables the ISP to transmit and receive information on the Internet. Depending on the type of T carrier-line, the ISP will have a minimum of 24 communications channels over which data can be communicated 24 hours, 7 days a week.

Every telephone company has its own telecommunication network that links ISPs and organizations that directly link their servers to the Internet without going through an ISP. Telephone companies exchange Internet data at regional centers called peering centers. There are four public peering centers and many private peering centers operated by telecommunications carriers.

Every device on the Internet has a unique Internet address, which is a set of numbers. An Internet address, also known as an IP address, is often identified by a Web site name that is associated with the IP address, such as *www.keogh.org*.

You and I can visit a Web site by dialing our ISP, then using software called a browser to request and display Web pages. After entering the Web site name, the browser sends the request to the ISP, which searches the Internet telephone book to locate the IP address associated with the Web site name.

Once the IP address is found, the ISP contacts the Web site and requests a page. The first page that is requested is the site's home page, unless your request specifies another page. The Web page is sent to your ISP from the Web site and is passed to your computer, where the browser reads and displays the page.

A Web page is written using HTML or an enhanced version of that language called XML. Programmers who build the Web page insert HTML and XML tags into the page that tell the browser how to display the page.

In addition to tags that specify the text format, there are tags that tell the browser what graphics to display and how to link to other Web pages. These tags are called hyperlinks. A hyperlink is typically highlighted text or a graphic that, when clicked on, tells the browser to request either another block of text on that Web page or to display another Web page.

Information travels over the Internet in small electronic envelopes called datagrams. The TCP/IP protocol suite controls datagram traffic on the Internet. The Internet Protocol (IP) describes how datagrams are constructed and transmitted. The Transmission Control Protocol (TCP) is used to manage the transmission.

TCP, for example, requires a timer to be activated when a datagram is transmitted. If an acknowledgement has not been received when time has expired, then the datagram is resent because TCP assumes the first one was lost or discarded during transmission.

The Internet groups the different ways to transfer information over the Internet into Internet services. Four popular services are Telnet, e-mail, FTP, and HTTP (World Wide Web). The Telnet service enables a person to directly interact with a remote computer. The e-mail service enables people linked to the Internet to exchange electronic mail. The FTP service is used to copy files to and from a remote computer. HTTP is the service used to exchange Web pages.

Security and privacy concerns are a serious threat to the viability of the Internet as a tool for electronic commerce. Cyber crooks can use a variety of methods to gain access to a server or prevent legitimate visitors from accessing a server. Organizations whose servers are connected to the Internet use various techniques to thwart such attacks by password-protecting sites and using firewalls and proxy servers.

Anyone who visits a Web site must be on alert that the owner of the site might be creating a visitor's profile, which identifies you and your interests, and might sell your profile to a third party.

Internet technology is also used within an organization and its business partners by creating an Intranet and Externet. An Intranet is an organization's private Internet that enables employees to share information and access corporate data. An Extranet is also a private Internet, but it is used to link business partners, such as key vendors, and to track orders, sales, and other information typically exchanged by business partners.

Summary Questions

1. What are the differences between a Tier 1 provider and an Internet Service Provider?

2. What are the business objectives of an Internet Service Provider?

3. How are peering centers used on the Internet?

4. How do cyber criminals deny service to a Web site?

5. What are the privacy issues regarding visiting a Web site?

6. What security measures can a Web site owner take to thwart a cyber attack?

7. How does a browser work?

8. What are the components of an e-mail address?

9. What services are offered on the Internet?

10. Why are Extranets beneficial to businesses?

7 Networks: Client/Server Technology

"With all the money spent designing network servers, they still can't bring me a Coke."

Whenever you send e-mail, you are asking an e-mail server to do most of the work for you. This is because a client/server relationship exists between your computer and the e-mail server. Your computer is the client and asks the e-mail server to take and process your e-mail. All the processing is performed on the server, not on your computer.

E-mail is just one of many examples of a client/server model. In this chapter, you'll learn more about client/server technology and about:

- network operations
- network operations and clients
- network operations and servers
- print server
- fax server
- overcoming incompatible network operating systems
- the client/server model
- clients and requests
- servers and requests
- the client/server database

REALITY CHECK...

One afternoon, I tried to use a printer that had worked fine that morning, but that suddenly appeared to go to lunch and never come back. No matter what I did, nothing printed. So, I called the help desk. First, the technician asked if anyone else in my area had the same problem. I asked around and, sure enough, I wasn't the only one having problems printing at that printer. My response helped the technician identify that it wasn't my computer causing the problem.

The technician then asked if I was connected to WHMT3. WHMT3 was the network ID technicians assigned to the printer. It was clearly marked on the printer.

There was a brief pause in the conversation as I heard the tapping of keys in the background. Try it again, I was told. Sure enough the printer was humming again. The technician restarted the printer spooler, which is the program on the server that processes requests to print on printer WHMT3.

Our company, like most organizations, uses client/server technology to share printers among computers. Whenever anyone wants to print, the computer sends the document with instructions to a printer server, which is controlled by IS technicians.

NETWORK OPERATIONS ....

A network is similar to a computer. A computer is just a box of inanimate switches until the operating system, software such as Windows, is loaded. The operating system brings the computer to life. This is also true for a network. A network consists of cables, network cards, and other components that you learned about in previous chapters. It is the network operating system (NOS) that enables data to be transferred over these components.

Tech Talk

Network operating system: a set of programs that ensures reliable data transfer and handles a host of other functions that give a network administrator tools to manage the network.

A network operating system is similar to the operating system running on your computer. The network operating system manages the flow of data across the network and enables clients (like your computer) attached to the network to access network resources, such as files and printers, that are provided by network servers.

I like to think of a network operating system as a waiter who passes your lunch request to the chef, then returns with your order. In this scenario, you are the client and the chef is a network server.

There are two kinds of NOS: *Added-On Network Operating System* and *Inclusive Network Operating System*. The distinction between them is whether the NOS is included with client's operating system.

Tech Talk

Added-On Network Operating System: a network operating system that is added to a client's operating system.
Inclusive Network Operating System: a network operating system that is included in a client's operating system.

In the early days of computer networks, PCs used the Disk Operating System (DOS). Bill Gates and his pals, who developed DOS, never designed it to interact with a LAN because no one anticipated that computers would be linked. Therefore, DOS does not contain any network operating system software.

When LANs came into vogue, Microsoft created software called MS LAN Manager, which enabled PCs to connect to a LAN. MS LAN Manager is an example of an Added-On Network Operating System. Network software was built into newer operating systems, such as Windows NT, which is called an Inclusive Networking Operating System.

There are many clients (PCs) connected to a LAN, each capable of requesting access to one or more network servers simultaneously. The network operating system must be able to handle multiple requests. This is referred to as multitasking. Both the network operating system and the client's operating system must be a multitasking operating system. This means the operating system is able to handle incoming network traffic, such as e-mail, without disrupting the user's train of thought when writing a memo in a word processor.

Tech Talk
Multitasking: the operating system's capability to perform many tasks at the same time.

Here's how multitasking works. Within every computer there is a central processing unit (CPU), which is a chip that handles the processing of instructions and data inside the computer. Let's say that you run an application such as the word processor MS Word. Word is actually a program on your hard disk that contains many instructions, which the CPU processes sequentially. The CPU begins with the first instruction and continues working until the final instruction is executed.

While the CPU is happily following orders from Word, you could receive an e-mail from the network. The CPU is like you and me in that it can process only one instruction at a time, although some computers have more than one CPU or run an operating system that can logically spilt the CPU in half. In these situations, the computer can process instructions in parallel, which is called *parallel processing*.

Tech Talk
Parallel processing: a computer's capability to process two instructions simultaneously.

The operating system is able to detect when another task is more important to perform than the one currently being processed. When this occurs, the operating system interrupts the CPU and tells it to temporarily stop processing the current task and begin processing a new set of instructions.

This is what happens when you are writing a memo and you receive an e-mail. Instructions are processed so quickly (in microseconds) that you probably don't notice the word processor pause for a moment when the incoming e-mail is processed.

There are two ways in which a multitasking operating system manages multiple tasks. These are *preemptive multitasking* and *nonpreemptive multitasking*.

I like to think of the preemptive method like the way my boss asks me to do something. I really don't have a choice, so I stop what I'm doing and comply with her requests. The nonpreemptive multitasking is more like the way my kids respond to my requests. They might stop and do what I asked, but the probability of this occurring is slim.

> ### Tech Talk
> **Preemptive multitasking: the way the operating system controls when the CPU temporarily stops processing an application. The application cannot inhibit the decision.**
> **Nonpreemptive multitasking: the way the operating system requests an application to give up the CPU temporarily so another application can be processed. The application can ignore the request.**

Network Operations and Clients

The network operating system is divided into two parts: the *client* software and the *server* software. The client software is installed on every client's disk driver while the server software is installed only on a server. Collectively, the client software and the server software provide a secure way for clients to access resources on the server.

> ### Tech Talk
> **Client: a computer connected to the network that can request access to network services, such as a request to send a document to a network printer.**
> **Server: a computer connected to the network that provides network services, such as printing services, to network clients.**

The client software uses a network operating system program, called a redirector, to send a client's request for network resources to the network. The job of the redirector, also known as the requester or shell, is to monitor resource requests within a client's computer, then redirect requests for network services to the network. The server software receives and processes requests from the redirector.

Let's see how this works (Figure 7.1) by using the most commonly requested resource on a network, which is to access a file. You are familiar with how to open a word processing file stored on a hard disk. You select File|Open from the menu, then choose the disk drive and file. The same process is used whether the file is stored on your hard disk or on a network server.

The network computer used to store files is a *file server*. Think of a file server as a hard disk that everyone on the network can share. Anyone connected to the network that has permission to use the file server can save to and retrieve files from the file server's hard disk. This means you can save a spreadsheet to a file server and your friend can open the same file on her computer.

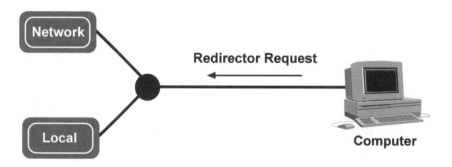

Figure 7.1
A redirector determines if a requested device is a local or network resource. If the request is for a network resource, the redirector passes the request to the network operating system.

Tech Talk

File server: a computer on the network that uses its hard disk to store files from network clients.
File manager: software used to copy, delete, and perform other organizational chores with files stored on your hard drive.

There is a good chance that you don't realize you are using a file server because network designers make the file server appear to be the same to you as your local hard drive. For example, you can use Windows Explorer to connect your computer to a network file server by assigning the file server to an unused drive designator. The term drive designator might sound strange, but you use it every time you access a file. You'll recognize the drive designator as the letter assigned to the disk drive, such as *A:* for a floppy drive and *C:* for a hard drive.

Technicians where I work assign *I:* for the network file server, which we commonly refer to as the *I:* drive. Any unassigned letter can be used for the drive designator for a file server.

Whenever I want to share a file with a fellow employee, I copy it from my *C:* drive to my *I:* drive without giving a second thought that I'm really requesting the use of a network resource—the file server.

The file server and the network are seamless on my computer. That is, I save and read files to and from the file server using the same techniques as saving and reading files to and from my hard disk or floppy disk.

Windows Explorer knows that *I:* isn't a drive on my computer, but a network resource. My request for the *I:* is then quietly passed along to the redirector, which "talks" to its friend the network operating system to complete the file transfer.

A similar process occurs when I print a document to a network printer. My computer's Print Manager associates a printer name with a network printer similarly to the way a local printer is identified. Of course, a technician creates this association by using the Add Printer Wizard on my computer. You, too, can use the Add Printer Wizard if you want to get down and dirty working with your computer.

Tech Talk
Local printer: a printer that is connected directly to a computer.

Before printing a document, I select the name of a printer using the Print Manager. The Print Manager displays the Print screen whenever I select File|Print from the menu. The name list box (Figure 7.2) lists the names of all the available printers, which includes the local printer and a variety of network printers. I wouldn't know which is local and which is network except the technician identified them for me when she gave me access to the printers.

Whenever I select a printer, the Print Manager knows if it is connected directly to my computer or if it is a network printer. The Print Manager sends all requests for the network printer to the redirector, which sends the document to the operating system for processing.

The network printer is connected to a print server, which receives documents from the request, then queues documents and sends them to the printer (see "Print Server" on page 232).

Network Operations and Servers

A network operating system consists of client software and server software, which in some cases, such as with Windows NT, reside both on clients and on servers. This might sound confusing, but let's say your are using Windows NT on your computer at work and it is connected to a LAN. Your computer has both the client and the server software on it.

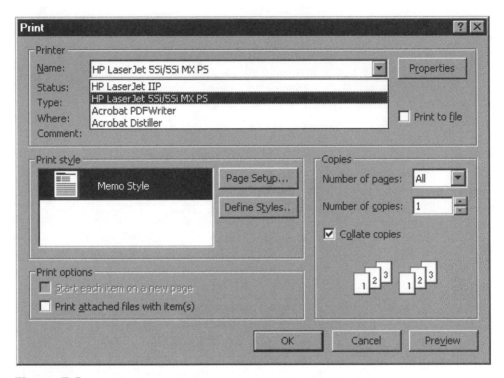

Figure 7.2
The network printer appears as a local printer on the client.

However, your computer is running only the client software. The server software remains unused and takes up space on your hard disk. Likewise, a network server also has both client and server software, but it runs only the server software.

Server software has three major roles on the network. First, it coordinates access to network resources by receiving requests from a client's redirector. Second, it provides the redirector with the requested resource, such as access to a network printer.

Server software also has the responsibility of limiting access to resources to only those clients who have the right to access it in a particular way. I like to call this the network cop.

For example, an application running on a client may ask the requestor to see a particular file located on a network file server. However, the server software will grant access to the server only if the client has permission to access it. A client needs access to the file server before it can read and write to the file.

The third job of server software is to administer the network. This includes a way to grant access to the network, based on rights granted to a user's unique network log-in ID. This happens when you log on the network.

Here's how the log-on process works. When you log on the network, the redirector on your computer displays a log-in screen that prompts you to enter your network ID and password. Network administrators, technicians who manage the network, assign each user a unique ID and password.

After you submit your log-in information, the redirector sends it to the primary network server for validation. The ID and password are compared with known users and if there is a match, the server makes network resources available to you.

Not everyone on the network can access all of its resources. The network administrator using network management software grants or removes specific privileges to access each resource, such as a printer or a file server. Network management software is also used to create and remove users from the network. Chapter 8 explores these security measures in detail.

It's a Setup

Although server software is supplied with many newer operating systems, it must still be installed on the server. The installation is an automatic process similar to the way you install software on your computer. You run Setup and the program handles the installation. However, there are times when some tweaking is required to get the server running efficiently.

You won't be required to install server software since installation is the technician's responsibility and is beyond the scope of this book. However, I'll give you a brief behind-the-scenes look at how this is done to give you insight into the job of a network technician.

Before the Setup program can flip all the right switches, it needs specific information supplied by the technician. The first piece of information is the name of the *network segment* where the server resides.

Tech Talk
Network segment: a local area network that is connected to a larger local area network.

Next, the technician supplies the Setup program with a name for the server. This is similar to the name of a Web site. Some technicians become creative when naming a server. Instead of using dreary monocles such as WHMT3, they'll call it Burt, Ernie, or Big Bird.

As discussed in Chapter 5, large computer networks are composed of smaller networks called segments (Figure 7.3). Each segment contains clients and one or more servers, and is identified by a specific name, called a workgroup name or a domain name.

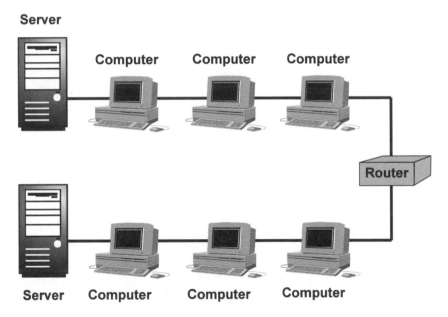

Figure 7.3
Each network segment contains clients and one or more server.

The redirector uses both the server name and the segment name to find the server on the network. I like to think of the server name as the name of a Web site that is translated into an IP address (see "Identifying the Server to the Network" on page 231).

Another question the installation program asks is if the server is the primary domain controller (PDC), the backup domain controller (BDC), or a stand-alone server. This sounds like more baffling technical jargon, but like any technical term, the concept of a domain controller is easy to comprehend.

By now you realize that there can be many servers connected to the network, each of which has a different role in network operations. For example, a server can be used to store applications, such as MS Word or MS Excel, that are shared among clients on the network. This is called an applications server. Another server can be used to store nonapplication files, such as spreadsheets and word processing documents. This server is called a file server. A common server on large networks is a print server, sometimes called a print spooler, which is used to temporarily store files until they are sent to the printer.

At least one server on a network segment is designated as the PDC, which is usually the first server installed on the network. The PDC server administrates the domain by enforcing network security, storing information about the domain and about network users. You can say the PDC server is the boss of bosses when it comes to the network domain.

Every boss needs a second-in-command to stand in when the boss isn't available, and that's the job of the backup domain controller. The BDC takes over network administration chores if the PDC becomes inactive.

A stand-alone server is a server that isn't designated as the PDC server, such as an application, file, or print server. Even the BDC can be a stand-alone server since most of its network duties are to sit and wait for the PDC server to become disabled.

Identifying the Server to the Network

A network server is like other clients on the network in that it, too, needs a network card before the server can connect to the network. The network card (see Chapter 4) is a circuit board that connects the server to the network cable. The server also needs to be told the protocol to use to communicate on the network (see Chapter 5) and an IP address (see Chapter 6).

Technicians configure the network card for a particular protocol suite. The most commonly used protocol is TCP/IP, although other protocols, as illustrated in Chapter 5, can be used in client/server technology.

The IP address is similar to a telephone number and uniquely identifies the server to the network operating system. The IP address consists of two parts. These are the network ID and the host ID. A host is a client. The network ID is used to identify all the hosts on the same network, and the host ID specifies a particular host. Each IP address must be a unique 32-bit value that consists of four sets of digits, each separated by a period, such as 145.133.6.132.

The portion of the IP address that identifies the network is called the subnet mask and is used to determine whether the target address is on the same network as the originator client or on a remote network. A typical subnet mask looks like 145.133.0.0, in which the first two sets of numbers specify the subnet and the second two sets are set to 0.

IP addresses are difficult to remember, so the network technician associates the server name with the IP address (see Chapter 6). On a Windows NT network, which is commonly used as the network operating system in businesses, the technician uses the Windows Internet Name Service (WINS) to create and store the server name. The server name associated with the IP address in a Windows NT network is called the NetBIOS name and the process of creating the name is called registering. WINS translates the NetBIOS name into the IP address whenever the name is used to request access to a network service.

Technicians also need to specify the router to use whenever an IP address cannot be found on the local network. The router is referred to as the default gateway for the server. Let's say a client sends a request to a print server expecting to print a document. However, the IP address isn't on the same network segment as the client. This means the IP address cannot be found. The network operating system makes an assumption that the IP address resides outside the network segment and therefore sends the document to the default gateway router, which tries to locate the IP address (see Chapter 5) on another network segment. A router is also assigned an IP address that is used to identify the router as the default gateway.

Print Server

I always complain whenever I leave my desk to pick up my documents at a printer located in a corner of the office. Compounding my frustration is when I wait 15 minutes for my one-page memo to print because someone who got in queue before me is printing a 100-page document.

My complaints fall on deaf ears because the printing gods in our company determined that remote printers are the most cost-efficient way to print. I can't fight city hall, although I could easily point out some employees are more equal than others and have a private printer attached to their computer.

Printing to a network printer is different than printing to a local printer because the network printer determines the order in which documents print. Here's a look at what occurs when you print to a network printer (Figure 7.4).

The print server temporarily stores the incoming documents in memory called a Simultaneous Peripheral Operation Online (SPOOL), also known as a spooler. Sometimes the print server is known as the print spooler.

There is a limited amount of memory available on the print server and during heavy demand, it runs out of memory. When this occurs, documents that can't fit on the spooler are temporarily stored on the print server's hard disk, which is typically large enough to handle most printing demands.

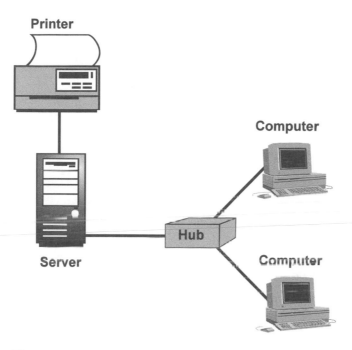

Figure 7.4
A network printer is shared among network clients.

The document that you print is called a print job and is logged in a queue in memory called a print queue. This is similar to a line at the grocery store—and sometimes there is a long line of documents waiting to print.

As a print job comes to the top of the print queue, the print server sends the document from the print spooler to the printer, then all the other jobs move up in the print queue. This makes room in the print spooler for a print job that is temporarily stored on the print server's hard disk.

A network printer can be connected directly to a print server using a printer cable or it can be connected directly to the LAN using hardware built into the printer, which requires the network printer to have its own IP address. A network printer connected directly to a print server doesn't require an IP address because documents from the print server flow to the printer over the printer cable and not over the LAN.

The network administrator grants access to a network printer. Access not only means the right to print a document, but also the right to change jobs on the print queue. The permission to manipulate the print queue depends on which network operating system is used. Most network operating systems allow every user to review the print queue and delete their own print job from the queue.

Typically, only the network administrator can delete or rearrange all print jobs on the print queue. However, the network administrator can assign these rights to any user.

Fax Server

A fax machine is an integral part of any business and, with the creation of the fax modem, every client can have its own built-in fax machine. While this might be desirable, it could create unnecessary cost to an organization because the organization must acquire a fax modem and provide a telephone line for every client.

An alternative to individual fax modems is to create a fax server. A fax server is a computer on the network that contains one or more fax modems. Its job is to receive documents to be faxed from clients on the network, then send those documents to the fax modem, similar to a print server's operations

A fax server also monitors fax modems for incoming documents. It receives the document from outside the network, then forwards it to a designated client on the network. This is called routing the fax.

Routing is a major concern when setting up a fax server because incoming faxes don't contain the network address of the client destined to receive the fax. It is up to the fax server to deliver the fax to the proper client.

There are a number of solutions to this problem. These include the use of T.30 subaddressing, Novell embedded systems technology (NEST), transmission station identification (TSI), or direct inward dialing (DID). All of these follow the same basic concept.

The person sending the fax uses a telephone number that is unique within the organization or contains the extension of the client. The fax server uses this number to identify the client, then transmits the fax to the client's network address.

T.30 subaddressing, TSI, and NEST require the sender to include a client's telephone extension. DID is a trunk line the telephone company provides that enables the organization to receive calls for multiple telephone numbers. For example, an organization might be assigned a block of telephone numbers from 555-8000 to 555-8999. Anyone calling a telephone number within that range is directed to the organization's trunk line. Software used to run the organization's private branch exchange (PBX) system (see Chapter 6) identifies the client by the last three digits of the incoming telephone number.

There are other less desirable options available to process incoming faxes from the fax server, such as manual routing, in which someone reads the recipient's name on the fax, then forwards it to the client.

Another method is to use optical character recognition (OCR) or intelligent character recognition (ICR). These are software utilities that convert the graphic file containing the faxed document into a text file. The text file is then searched to identify the client. However, this conversion process is not perfect. On the average, only 80 to 90 percent of the document is converted accurately.

THE BENEFITS OF USING NETWORK APPLICATIONS

Application software consists of, among others, word processing programs, spreadsheet programs, and customized programs that automate operations within an organization. Computer applications typically fall into two general categories based on where the application resides. These are called stand-alone applications and network applications.

A stand-alone application is the most familiar to computer users because it identifies programs that run on our computer. Stand-alone applications do not require any network resources and typically cannot be shared with other clients on the network, although data produced by stand-alone applications are commonly shared using network resources. A network application is a program that resides on the network and can be used by any network client.

For example, a word processing program such as Microsoft Word can be either a stand-alone application or a network application. As a stand-alone application, one computer can use the program because the program resides on the computer's hard disk.

However, as a network application, Microsoft Word can be used by a specific number of clients on the network. The number depends on the licensing agreement the organization has with the manufacturer. The network application resides on a server, typically an application server.

Network applications are best suited for organizations that have many clients that need the same application because the network application is more economical and easier to maintain than a stand-alone application. For example, everyone on the network receives the same version of the application from the same source and only one copy of the application must be maintained.

OVERCOMING INCOMPATIBLE NETWORK OPERATING SYSTEMS ·····································

Computer networks are discussed with the same uniformity as MS Word, MS Excel, and MS Access in that we tend to think of a computer network as a cohesive product manufactured by a single manufacturer. When you buy a copy of Word, you assume the spell checker and thesaurus will work flawlessly with every Word document.

However, this same cohesiveness doesn't exist with network clients. A client must speak the same "language" as the network operating system before the client can send and receive information over the network. No communication occurs if both the client and the network operating system speak a different language. Therefore, it is up to the network administrator to resolve the conflict using one of two techniques. These are called a client solution and a server solution.

The client solution requires that more than one redirector be installed on the client—one for each network operating system. The appropriate redirector translates the client's request for a network service to the network operating system. The redirector translates responses from the network operating system to a "language" the client understands.

The server solution requires the network administrator to install additional software, called a service, on the server to translate software running on a client and the network operating system.

A different service is required for each kind of software running on network clients. The service receives requests from client software for network resources. Before processing the request, the service translates it into a form readable by the network operating system. Likewise, transmissions sent to the client are translated from the network operating system back to the form the client's software requires.

The thought of installing multiple services or redirectors may seem overwhelming at first, but it isn't because there are three common network and client operating system providers. These are Microsoft, Novell, and Apple Computer. Therefore, services or redirectors are limited to three choices. Each of these companies provides services or redirectors to enable all three clients and services to communicate with each other.

The Client/Server Model

The term *client* is used throughout this chapter to refer to a computer that is connected to a network and requests a network resource from the network operating system. This is similar to the business model in which a client requests service from a business owner. Typical requests by clients on a network are to execute an applications program stored on the network application server, to copy files stored on a network file server, or to send or receive faxes.

These requests all have the same characteristics. That is, the client asks for a file to be transferred. Processing of the file is handled by the client and not by a network resource. This is commonly called the *file server model*, in which the server receives requests to transfer files and not to process the files.

The file server model was the first model used for computer networks and is still used today. However, enhancements made in database technology have provided another model called the *client/server model*, which requires the server to process requests for information rather than simply transfer a file to a client.

In the client/server model, the client makes a request for information, such as "sales for last Monday." A database server running a database management system, such as Sybase or Oracle, receives the request. The database management system searches its database files, then sends the client just the information the client requests. So instead of transferring the complete sales file, as in the case in a file server model, only last Monday's sales figures are sent.

The client/server model makes network operations more efficient than the file server model because less information is transferred across the network. For example, instead of 365 days of sales information, only one day is sent.

Clients and Requests

There are two components in the client/server model. These are clients, called the front end, which interfaces with the user, and the server, called the back end, which processes requests from the client and transfers the data back to the client (Figure 7.5).

Software running on the client is used to formulate a request for information by using a data inquiry screen. A data inquiry screen contains data input fields for search criteria and is unique with each application .

The user at the client enters values in the input fields, then signals the software (i.e., clicking the OK button) to find the data. The software then formulates the request using Structure Query Language. SQL has become the standard language used to request information from a database management system.

In addition to using the data inquiry screen, a user can directly write requests for information using SQL. The file containing the SQL request is then submitted to the database management system and is processed just as if the data inquiry screen generated the SQL request.

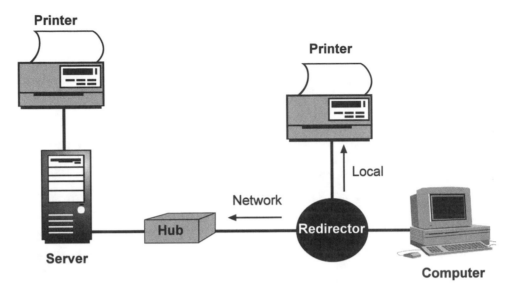

Figure 7.5
Clients on a network request the network operating system for information contained on network servers.

When the server returns the requested data to the client, software running on the client is responsible to further process the information. This might include displaying the information on the screen, in a printed report, or incorporating the data with other information already at the client.

Besides recalling information from the server, software running on the client also is used to maintain the database and can insert new information into the database, update existing information, and delete unwanted information. Each task is performed by an SQL request that is sent to the server.

Servers and Requests

The server component of the client/server model has the responsibility of processing requests from multiple clients and maintaining the integrity of the data stored in the database on the server.

A request from a client is constructed of SQL statements, which are stored in a file (Figure 7.6). The file is transferred to the server component for processing. A statement tells the server to do a task, such as "send me the first and last name data." Another statement typically follows in the file that tells the server where to find the data (i.e., which database to use). Still another statement provides the search criteria. There are also statements for inserting, updating, and deleting data. Database management software on the server reads and follows the directions of the SQL statements in the request.

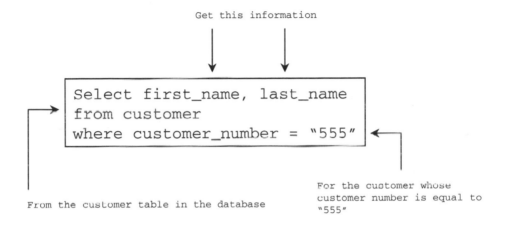

Get this information

Select first_name, last_name
from customer
where customer_number = "555"

From the customer table in the database

For the customer whose customer number is equal to "555"

Figure 7.6
An SQL query such as this is used to select, insert, update, and delete information stored in a database.

The client/server model greatly reduces the traffic over the network. As noted, clients no longer receive large files; instead they receive just the information needed to meet the user's needs.

However, eliminating the need to transmit frequently used requests can reduce network traffic even more. A request that is made often, such as for the current inventory level, can be stored on the server as part of the database. These stored requests are called stored procedures. A client can ask by name for a particular stored procedure to be run by the database management system.

Besides reducing network traffic, stored procedures also ensure control over requests. A stored procedure need only be created once, whereas an SQL request must be created every time a client requires information from the server.

The Client/Server Database

A database management system is designed to respond to multiple requests within a reasonable time frame, but requests can be delayed because the server component of the client/server model is the central point for requests. It can become a bottleneck on the network. If two requests require the same resources (i.e., data), the second request must wait until the first is processed.

A database management system is unable to accurately determine the maximum time required to process a request because every database and every request is unique. The processing of the request depends on the design of the database, which is unique to every application, and the way in which the SQL statements are written. An improperly written request can dampen the effectiveness of any database management system.

Steps can be taken to improve processing requests by properly configuring the server components of the client/server model.

Organizations typically use a single-server client/server configuration that contains a single database server on the network. One server fulfills all the requests for data from clients in addition to managing data stored on the server. If bottlenecks occur, technicians, such as database administrators and programmers, can either redesign the database and/or rewrite SQL requests to improve performance.

However, when these techniques fail, then a multiserver client/server configuration should be considered. In a multiserver client/server configuration, there is more than one database server, each containing the same data. Therefore, the high volume of requests can be divided among servers so that each client realizes a reasonable response time.

Although there is an improvement in response time, there is a drawback. All the databases must be synchronized. Changes in data on one server must be replicated on the other servers or the integrity of the data is questionable. Database management systems provide an automatic method for synchronizing databases.

Another variation of the multiserver client/server configuration is called a data warehouse configuration. Like the multiserver client/server configuration, a data warehouse configuration has more than one server, and one server contains all the data. This is the data warehouse server, sometimes referred to as the main server.

The most requested data is replicated from the data warehouse server to other database servers on the network, sometimes called intermediate servers.

Clients request data from an intermediate server. If the data isn't available on that server, then it requests the data from the data warehouse server.

Web Servers

The Internet and Intranets use the client/server model to distribute Web pages. Clients are computers connected to the network that use a browser to interact with the server. The server is called a Web server.

As described in Chapter 6, a client requests a specified Web page by either entering a URL or by clicking a hyperlink. In either case, the browser sends the request to the Web server. The Web server processes the request and sends a file that contains the Web page to the client. The Web page is then displayed by the browser.

Web servers contain static Web pages and programs that build dynamic Web pages. A static Web page is one that is created by a developer and stored on the server. A dynamic Web page is one that is created by a program at the time a client requests the page. The developer of the Web site determines if a Web page is static or dynamic based on the need to customize the contents of the page (see Chapter 6).

Web servers also contain files other than Web pages and programs that create dynamic Web pages. These files include programs that query a database server. For example, whenever a Web site prompts you to enter your membership ID and password, your response is processed by a program on the Web server that looks up your information in the site's membership database.

Some companies are using a Web server to create a light client/server application. In a typical client/server application, programmers write relatively large programs to run on both the client and the server. However, with the onset of the Intranet, programmers can take advantage of Java and browser technology to reduce the size of programs that run on the client. This is referred to as a light client/server. Typically, a light client/server application is written using Java and run using a browser located on the client.

Light client/server applications are easier to maintain than traditional ones because they are written in Java and stored on a Web server. Java, as discussed in Chapter 6, is computer independent. That means the same program can run on many different computers without having to be modified.

Since the light client/server application is stored on the Web server rather than on each client, programmers can quickly update the application. In a traditional client/server application, new versions of the application must be installed on each client. In a light client/server application, new versions need only to be installed on the Web server. This is because the application is requested by every client from the browser every time the client needs to run it.

SUMMARY ....

Client/server technology is the way information is exchanged over many networks, including local area networks and the Internet. A computer connected to the network is called a client and it can request services from another networked computer called a server. A service can be save or retrieve a file, print a document, send a fax, or run an application, such as Microsoft Word.

Servers are categorized in three ways based on the role they play in running the network. These categorizes are the primary domain controller (PDC), the backup domain controller (BDC), and the stand-alone server.

The PDC is the server that oversees network operations on a segment of a network. The BDC takes over those duties whenever the PDC becomes disabled. All other servers connected to the network are called stand-alone servers.

Stand-alone servers include an application server, a print server, a fax server, a file server, and a database server. An application server stores computer programs such as Word, Excel, and any networked version of an application. A print server manages printing documents to a network printer. A fax server is a central computer that contains one or more fax lines and manages fax transmissions to and from clients.

A file server stores files, such as Word documents and spreadsheets, that can be shared by clients that are granted access to those files. A database server stores data and runs database management software. A client who needs a subset of data sends requests written in Structure Query Language (SQL) to the database server. Database management software interprets the request, finds the data in the database, and returns the data to the client.

The network operating system (NOS) is the set of programs that manages transmissions over the network. NOS has two components: client software and server software. The client software is called the redirector. The redirector translates client requests into a form that is recognized by the NOS and translates NOS responses to the client.

Network services appear seamless to clients because of the way the redirector and the client's operating system work together. For example, a file server appears as another drive on the client's file menu screen, enabling the client to select the drive in the same manner as the local hard drive is selected. The client's operating system knows when it isn't a local drive and passes the request to the redirector, which sends the request to the NOS.

The NOS is a multitasking operating system that can process many requests from different clients simultaneously. There are two ways in which this system manages multiple tasks. These are called preemptive and nonpreemptive multitasking.

Preemptive multitasking is the kind in which the operating system controls when the CPU stops processing an application temporarily. Nonpreemptive multitasking is the kind in which the operating system requests the application to give up the CPU temporarily so another application can be processed.

Summary Questions

1. 1. How are clients and servers identified to the network?

2. What are the duties of the primary domain controller?

3. How does a fax server distribute faxes received externally from the LAN?

4. How are clients able to interact with different network operating systems?

5. How does a print spooler work?

6. What is the difference between a file server and a database server?

7. Explain the concept of a subnet.

8. What is the difference between an inclusive network operating system and an added-on network operating system?

9. What is the concept of parallel processing?

10. What is the difference between a stand-alone application and a network application?

PUTTING IT ALL TOGETHER ....

Your e-mail travels through a maze of cables and networking devices before it reaches its destination. The journey begins when you click Send and your e-mail is transformed into bits that flow from the network card inside your computer over network cables.

Cables are arranged in various ways, called a topology. Your network has one of several topologies that is likely to be a bus, a ring, or a star topology, or a combination of these. You can consider a topology like the layout of the highway over which your e-mail travels.

The network operating system ensures that your e-mail arrives at its destination quickly and securely by enforcing network rules called protocols. I like to think of protocols as the rules of the road. One of the most common protocols used today in networks is TCP/IP, which is the protocol used for the Internet and Intranets.

Depending on the topology used in your network, your e-mail is likely to make its first stop at a central point called a hub. A hub is where all network cables join together like a highway interchange. The e-mail is then routed on the fastest path to its destination.

The destination for your e-mail is identified by a unique network address called an IP address, which is similar to the address of a building along the highway. Each network device, such as a computer or a server, has its own IP address so your e-mail can't be delivered to the wrong destination unless you've placed the wrong address on it.

Whenever you e-mail, your computer requests the service of a network server. In this case, the server is an e-mail server and the service is to process your e-mail. The relationship between your computer and the server is called a client/server model in which a client (your computer) makes a request to a server to process information (sending the e-mail). Once the server completes processing, the result is returned to the client. For example, after the e-mail server delivers your e-mail to its destination, the server acknowledges delivery to the e-mail program running on your computer.

Your e-mail is divided into pieces with each piece placed in an electronic envelope called a packet. A packet contains the destination address, the sender's address, control information, and error checking data in addition to the piece of your e-mail. Packets are used so that no single network transmission ties up the network. You can think of this as a way of sharing the network because no one needs to wait for a long-winded e-mail to be sent before they can send theirs. Packets are stripped away at the destination address and the e-mail is reconstructed.

Like cars on a highway, packets traveling along a network can bump into other packets. However, network protocols minimize collisions by imposing one of several rules depending on the protocol used on the network.

Some network protocols require the client to listen for network traffic before transmitting. Other protocols require the client to send the packet, then listen for collisions with other traffic. If a collision occurs, then the client resends the packet. Still other protocols require the client to receive a token before it can transmit a packet.

One of the first things the destination computer does when it receives packets that contain your e-mail is to determine if the packet was received without errors. If there were no errors, then the destination computer acknowledges it received the packet by sending a message to your computer. However, a request to resend the packet is made to your computer if an error is detected.

Your company's network is probably comprised of many small networks called segments, each of which could operate independently of the other network segments. Network segments are joined to form a larger network by using a router. A router is similar to the town's post office that receives all letters mailed within the town, then distributes those letters destined outside the town to those other towns. In this case, the other town is the network segment.

Routers that connect network segments are joined by coaxial or fiber optic cables called a backbone. The backbone is like a superhighway that has many lanes of traffic moving in both directions.

Each lane of the backbone carries a signal much the same way multiple cable television channels are transmitted over a coaxial cable into your home. This enables multiple network users to send e-mail and other information simultaneously over the network.

The number of signals that can be transmitted over the network at the same time is called the network's bandwidth. The greater the number of signals that can be carried over a network, the higher the bandwidth.

A network can be extended beyond the walls of a building by using T carrier-lines to connect the network to the telephone company. The telephone company uses its own vast networks to transmit packets to remote computers. This is how your e-mail is sent to colleagues outside your building and how you can link to the Internet from your desk.

Although many networks are comprised of cables, there is a trend to incorporate wireless communication into a network. Wireless communication transmits information over the airwaves similarly to radio, cellular, and satellite technology. This means that you'll be able to keep up with your e-mails using a handheld computing device while on vacation.

Part 3

Preventing and Fixing Network Problems

I'm intrigued by the complexity of a computer network. The network cards, routers, cables, and other types of gizmos that you've learned about throughout this book make this electronic maze seem incredibly difficult to manage and to keep operational.

Yet, I'm one of the first to scream loudly whenever my company's computer network stops running. Like so many of us, I tend to over simplify the effort it takes for the network administrator to maintain order on the network and to respond quickly to fix any problems that arise.

Recently, I tagged along with our network administrator to observe what goes on in cyber space. I soon learned about the organizational and technical skills necessary to keep data flowing throughout our business.

The day began a few hours before the rest of us usually arrive at work. The network administrator gave the network a pre-flight check. Her objective
was to identify and address any problems
before the start of the business day.

from users. In her absence, there is a small army of network support technicians who carefully follow outlined procedures to systematically address any problem that arises.

To my surprise, most caller complaints about the network are quickly resolved after a few well-asked questions, and by using an assortment of network programs. In fact, network support technicians literally let their fingers do the walking over the network to examine every facet of the network without leaving their desks.

In the next two chapters, I'll share with you what I learned during my one-day tour and show you how your network administrator handles network administration, network security, and network outages.

8 Network Reliability and Security

In this chapter...

"My computer is reliable.
Whenever I'm on a deadline, it stops working."

Anonymous

We take for granted many things in our lives, including the computer network that helps us do our business. Barring a few hiccups now and then, most networks are reliable at distributing information throughout an organization. This doesn't happen by chance. Network administrators follow carefully crafted plans and tight procedures to ensure that nothing goes wrong with network operations.

In this chapter, you'll explore the factors that keep your network purring even in the face of serious trouble, such as a security breach or hardware failure. You learn about:

- network performance
- performance monitoring
- trends
- network administration
- network accounts
- user manager for domain
- types of accounts
- category of groups
- network security
- security measures
- security guidelines
- data recovery
- fault tolerant data recovery
- uninterrupted power supply

REALITY CHECK ....

Remember the days when you could hide from nasty memos sent by your boss by saying it got lost in transit? Those were the days when "snail mail" (the term to describe physical mail) was the only way to distribute information throughout an organization.

Today you don't have the luxury of saying you didn't get the memo, since your boss can e-mail a memo in a fraction of a second after writing it, and thanks to the reliability of computer networks, a return receipt is delivered to your boss once you open the e-mail.

A colleague of mine did everything to avoid responding to a memo his boss sent, which asked if he'd be interested in relocating to our Hong Kong office. Before e-mail became commonplace in the office, he always blamed turnaround time for not responding quickly. In those days, response memos were dictated, typed, proofread, retyped, signed, and left for the mailroom staff to shuffle throughout the office. This process was always good for stalling a response for a week or so.

My colleague's new excuse was that the e-mail server went down and his response was lost. This is like saying the computer ate his response. His boss simply smiled, picked up the telephone, and asked the network administrator if she could restore the e-mail server.

NETWORK PERFORMANCE.................................

Whenever you and I send an e-mail or save a file to a network drive (see Chapter 7), we expect our request to be executed promptly. Rarely do we think about what happens after we press the Enter key, unless the network response is unacceptable. Making sure the network response is acceptable is the network administrator's responsibility.

I'm the first to complain whenever something goes wrong with the network—and the last to give credit to the network administrator and technicians when the network purrs.

Network transmission involves a complex sequence of steps that must be performed quickly so transmission appears to happen instantaneously. First, a request must be broken into small pieces. Then, most pieces are stuffed into packets. Each packet must be addressed properly and contain control and error-checking data.

Next, the packet is handed over to the network operating system, where it snakes around network cables and routers (see Chapter 4) until it finds the destination address. If the packet doesn't arrive in time, the network operating system automatically resends it (see Chapter 7).

Once the packet reaches its destination, it is checked for errors. If an error occurs, then an automatic request is made to resend the packet. Error-free packets move on to the next step, in which the data is removed from the packet and reassembled with data from other packets to form the original text. This entire process takes place within a fraction of a second after the Enter key is pressed to send the e-mail.

A network is similar to a highway and is designed to handle a specific volume of traffic. I complain whenever I'm stuck in traffic and wonder how anyone could have designed such a highway, especially when it seems obvious that the highway is four lanes short of what is necessary.

What I assume—wrongfully so—is that the design engineer built the highway to handle today's traffic. Many roads were built before World War II, when no one could have anticipated today's growth in population and automobiles. A similar situation exists with networks.

Many networks evolve from a smaller networks, comprised of a handful of computers. Gradually, the growth of an organization increases its demands for network services. Additional servers (see Chapter 7) are installed and the handful of computers suddenly becomes 50 or more.

And just like old highways, old networks have traffic jams caused by the network's inability to handle the high volume of traffic. Instead of cars, packets are the vehicles on the network; however, the same traffic concepts apply.

A network has either a single-lane highway called baseband, or multiple lanes called broadband (see Chapter 4) (Figure 8.1). A baseband network can transmit one packet at a time, which is sufficient if only a few packets are sent over the network at the same time. However, delays become common whenever many computers attempt to send packets simultaneously.

A traffic pattern exists on every network, similar to the patterns that occur on highways. During certain hours, there is a heavy demand to transmit information and during off-peak hours the network can sit idle. As with a highway, users start to complain about poor response time during high-peak travel periods.

This is similar to me leaving my office at 5 P.M. and having to wait 15 minutes for an elevator. There is a 10-second wait for an elevator if I leave at 4:50 P.M. and the same at 5:16 P.M. However, there is a mad rush between those times that leaves most of us standing around or trying to jam into a crowded elevator.

A broadband network transmits packets over multiple frequencies called channels. I like to think of these as lanes on a highway. More than one packet can be sent over the network at the same time, each traveling in its own lane. The number of lanes is called the network's *bandwidth*.

Tech Talk

Bandwidth: the number of communication channels over which data can be transmitted simultaneously.

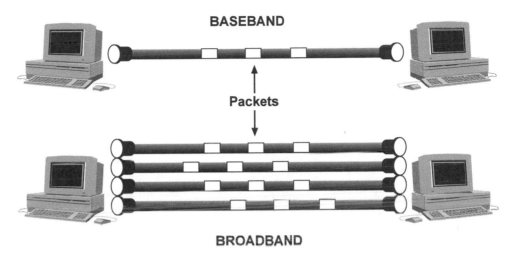

Figure 8.1
Baseband is similar to a single-lane highway and broadband is similar to a multilane highway.

Broadband networks can also become crowded, especially when many people in the company exchange information containing graphical images, which require large amounts of data.

As an example, it wasn't too long ago when the network that serviced the trading floor of a major Wall Street firm moved traffic at a snail's pace shortly after new computers were installed throughout the firm. The problem was sporadic, but typically occurred around lunch and toward the end of the day. After weeks of investigating, network engineers uncovered an attack that proved to be on the scale of a military air battle. In fact, it was an air battle that nearly brought the trading systems to a halt.

It seemed the new computers came pre-installed with a sophisticated air-to-air combat game that enabled players to challenge each other over the network. Whenever business was slow, a trading desk laid down the gauntlet and another desk met the challenge.

Regardless of how much network technicians increased the bandwidth, there wasn't adequate capacity to process trades and conduct more than 10 virtual battles at the same time. Eventually, the trading floor manager ended the war by ordering all games removed from the new computers, which gave the company more than sufficient bandwidth to process trades. However, some disgruntled traders felt that the order was given because the trading floor manager lost too many air-to-air combat battles.

Performance Monitoring

When network designers plan a new network, they estimate the anticipated demand for simultaneous access of the network. They must project the number of bytes that must be processed within a second.

Originally, I thought a network design could be created using the same rule of thumb that my brother-in-law uses to order food for his restaurant. His restaurant has 40 covers—that's restaurant talk for 40 seats—and estimates that 10 servings of each item on the menu is sufficient to meet customer demand.

Network designers don't consider the number of covers (computers) which are connected to the network, for there is little difference between having 10 computers and 70 computers on the network.

This might seem puzzling, but it's not when you consider that a computer connected to the network doesn't mean the computer is transmitting packets. Here's another way to look at this problem. Let's say I'm designing a highway for a community of 10,000 people. How many lanes should the highway contain?

Before you go scratching your head trying to remember some math formula from your high school days, I'll give you a hint. You must ask the question, "Where do these people live?". If they live in Manhattan, then you may need only a few lanes because most people in Manhattan don't own cars—they use mass transit instead. However, it's likely more lanes are needed if the people live in a Manhattan suburb.

Therefore, network designers need to know the number of packets that are likely to be transmitted at the same time, rather than the number of computers connected to the network. To estimate the network traffic, they need to analyze the business needs.

For example, a high-tech hospital requires a higher bandwidth than a small office because of the graphic information, such as X-rays, that are made available over the network.

A demand analysis of network traffic provides estimates, which become the basis for the network design. Basically, this is the expert's best guess. The network design defines the number of network segments, the network topology (see Chapter 5), and the hardware associated with the network (see Chapter 4). No one knows for sure if the network adequately meets the demand until it is operating under typical conditions for a few weeks.

Once the network becomes operational, the network administrator monitors its performance using a *network performance monitor.*

Tech Talk

Network performance monitor: software on each network device that records network traffic.

There are two kinds of network performance monitors (Figure 8.2). These are real-time monitors and batch-mode monitors. A real-time monitor records and analyzes network traffic as it occurs. Let's say that you and I send a packet simultaneously. Both packets appear on the monitor immediately when they are transmitted.

In contrast, a batch-mode monitor stores traffic information in an activity file that is recovered and analyzed at a later time. In this case, the time and date of when we transmitted packets are stored in two separate activity files on our computer. Activity files are typically recovered electronically by the network administrator at the end of the day, and then analyzed.

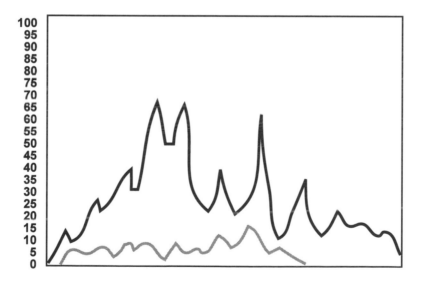

Figure 8.2
A performance monitor tracks the flow of packets throughout the network.

A network monitor reveals a device that slows transmission along the network. This is called a *bottleneck*. Let's say many requests are made to a network file server, but the file server is unable to keep pace with the requests because the file server's network card processes packets slower than the network transmits them. I like to think of this as traffic backed up at a tollbooth because toll collectors are unable to keep up with the demand.

Tech Talk

Bottleneck: a network device that processes packets slower than other network devices.

Bottlenecks slow network performance and can decrease response time, leading to complaints from network users. Whenever a network is built or redesigned, the network administrator monitors network traffic to identify and remove bottlenecks.

Once bottlenecks are removed, the network administrator establishes a baseline for the network. A *baseline* consists of various measurements of the network when it is performing at an acceptable level.

Tech Talk

Baseline: an objective metric way to determine acceptability.

The network administrator consistently measures network performance using a network monitor and compares the results to the baseline. When current network measurements stray from the baseline, then the network administrator realizes there is potential trouble with the network that could result in a decline in network performance —and a flood of complaint calls from formerly happy users.

It is rare that a network administrator sits and monitors traffic over a network. Instead, network operating systems such as Windows NT have an intelligent network performance monitor that does the watching.

When the performance monitor detects a network problem, it either sends a pager alert to the network administrator or runs a utility program that attempts to rectify the problem itself. I think of this like a fire detection system that activates sprinklers automatically while notifying the fire department.

Trends

Measuring network performance is similar to the way a physician measures your heart with an electrocardiogram. The initial visit to a physician for a complete checkup normally involves her taking an electrocardiogram reading, which is used as a baseline. Another electrocardiogram reading is taken if you're rushed to the emergency room complaining about chest pains. Any dramatic difference between a normal electrocardiogram and the one taken in the emergency room indicates a serious problem.

However, your physician is likely to take an electrocardiogram reading every year during your annual checkup. Over the course of several years, she can compare your baseline electrocardiogram to previous ones to determine if there is a gradual change that may predict future health trouble.

The network administrator performs the same task when measuring network performance. The baseline defines a healthy network. Comparing the same measurements over the course of months indicates a trend.

Measurements that teeter around the baseline show an acceptable trend. However, measurements that slowly, but consistently, move away from the baseline show a troublesome trend that requires action to reverse it.

Let's say you are asked to network 30 computers in your office and you decide all of them can reside on the same *network segment*. To everyone's delight, this baby purrs when you give it the juice.

Tech Talk
Network segment: a stand-alone network that is connected to other stand-alone networks to form a larger network.

Six months later, you notice a persistent increase in network traffic. Substantially more data packets are transmitted than during the first few weeks the network went live. No one complained, but having read this book you realize your happy campers are soon going to turn into a mean-spirited mob standing outside your office.

What course of action would you take? Looking for another job isn't the correct answer. I'll give you a hint. The correct response is to divide the network segment into two segments. This is basically creating another network and linking them using a router.

Network administrators always have an eye peeled for signs that the network design has outlived its usefulness and needs to be redesigned. It is the network administrator's responsibility to keep a few steps ahead of demand for network resources so changes can be implemented before colleagues become unhappy.

A *Behind-the-Scenes Look at a Network Monitor*

After reading the first few chapters of this book, you soon realize there are rules for every aspect of a network. So, too, are there rules for network performance monitors. A network performance monitor is a program that contains instructions that, for a fraction of a second, intercept packet transmissions.

Developers of network performance monitors adhere to specifications defined in the Simple Network Management Protocol (SNMP). As with other protocols discussed in this book, the SNMP sets forth standards to which programmers write their network performance monitor.

At the heart of SNMP is the use of special programs called agents. An agent is installed on every network device, such as clients, hubs, routers, and bridges. Packets are intercepted by the agent and stored in a management information base (MIB), which is similar to a database. The date and time of the interception are also stored in the MIB.

An administrative program polls each agent on a regular basis and copies the MIB to a file server, where an analysis program makes sense out of data in the MIB. The result of the analysis is displayed on the network administrator's screen or in a printed report.

A network performance monitor is able to identify a variety of information about the network, including the amount of packets a network device generates; the peak periods when packets are transmitted; and how long it takes for a network device to process a packet.

A device that takes too long to process packets is a bottleneck in the network and is likely to be upgraded or replaced. A device that generates a high volume of packets that clog the network is likely to be reassigned to a low-traffic network segment.

Agents provide a wealth of information for network administrators; however, they also interfere with network operations. Network performance declines slightly every time an agent intercepts a packet.

This slight delay in transmission becomes noticeable when agents are used on many devices in a high traffic network since each agent must briefly stop each packet. Therefore, network administrators are careful not to use too many agents at one time on a network.

NETWORK ADMINISTRATION ....

The technician who is responsible for a network is called the network administrator and has the job of ensuring that the network operates flawlessly. If it doesn't, the network administrator must correct any problems.

Sometimes I tease our network administrator by calling her the president of the network, then hum "Hail to the Chief" whenever she walks by. She appreciates the kind thought—and my complaints usually become her top priority.

There are similarities between a president of an organization and a network administrator in that regardless of what goes wrong, the network administrator gets blamed.

Monitoring network performance is just one of the many categories of responsibilities of a network administrator. Other responsibilities are user administration, resource management, configuration management, and network maintenance.

User administration is a combination of network secretary and cyber cop because this job records and tracks anyone who wants to access a network resource. The network administrator, when wearing her user administrator's hat, creates a network account for every user, which is referred to as a user account. You recognize your user account as the network ID you must enter to gain access to the network.

A user account is more involved than an ID and a password because it also contains information about you and your permission to access network resources. Let's say that I want to print on the network printer located on the other side of the office. I contact the network administrator and ask permission to access that printer. If approved, she grants my user account the right to use the printer.

Resource management is another of the network administrator's critical responsibilities and entails managing all the devices that are connected to the network. These include the purchase, installation, and maintenance of network printers and servers and installing and updating all the files and programs stored on those servers.

I think this is a tough job, especially when I recall the nail-biting time I have with installing new software on my computer. Running the setup program is a breeze, although responding to installation prompts can be tricky, especially when I guess the answers to those questions I don't understand.

Then there is the test of nerves that comes with every installation—clicking the Install Now button. I get that sinking feeling that a pilot must having when making his first carrier takeoff. A thumbs-up transfer control from me to the computer and I start doubting that everything is "A-OK."

The moment of truth arrives when I click the button and spend the next five minutes quietly yelling at myself for not backing up my files before going ahead with the installation.

A network administrator goes through the same agony every time software is installed and upgraded—to every device on the network! A failed installation could cause havoc in the company, especially when e-mail is lost.

Configuration management requires the network administrator to use her network designer skills to design the layout of the network and configure all devices so they can connect to the network. The network administrator determines the network topology (see Chapter 5), protocols, and the other aspects of networks that are discussed in previous chapters.

Network maintenance is the job of keeping all the cabling, network cards, and other hardware working properly. I usually get network maintenance confused with performance management because they seem to be addressing similar issues. However, I learned that performance management addresses data transmission problems such as bottlenecks, while network maintenance deals with hardware upgrades and repairs.

NETWORK ACCOUNTS ....

A user account is one of several kinds of accounts used to organize access to network resources. There are also guest accounts, group accounts, network administrator accounts, and supervisor accounts. All of these have similarities and unique features.

An account owner is called a user and assigned a user name, which you recognize as your user ID. Any set of characters can be used for a user name as long as the name follows the network operating system's rules, which can differ depending on the network operating systems.

For example, Windows NT allows up to 20 characters for a user name, except for the characters listed in Table 8.1. All user names must be unique; otherwise the network operating system isn't able to track you.

Table 8.1 Characters That Cannot
Be Used to Create a User Name

"	\
/	:
;	|
=	,
+	?
<	>

Case sensitivity is an issue with network operating systems since some, like UNIX, treat upper- and lowercase of the same letter as different characters. Windows NT considers them the same letter and is considered a case-insensitive network operating system with regard to user names.

Tech Talk

Case sensitivity: determines whether upper- and lowercase letters are treated as different characters.

Let's say that I'm permitted to create my own user name and call myself BigJim. I could log in a Windows NT network as BIGJIM, BigJim, or bigjim without any problem because Windows NT ignores the case of the letters in my user name. However, only the middle user name is acceptable to a UNIX operating system because it matches my BigJim user name.

It is common for the network administrator to standardize the format of user names throughout the organization. For example, I might be assigned the user name jk0001 and the next person whose initials are JK is assigned jk0002. Standardizing the format does dampen creativity, but it makes life easier for the network administrator, who must create hundreds of user names.

In addition to a user name, network accounts also require a unique password. Passwords are typically case sensitive, forcing you to use the proper upper- and lowercase combinations. The actual number of characters that comprise a password depends on the network operating system. Windows NT, for example, limits a password to 14 characters. Many systems require at least six characters.

Passwords are confidential. At least, the network administrator doesn't have access to passwords. Of course, nothing stops you from writing your password on a Post-it™ and sticking it on the bottom of your keyboard or in a drawer.

Passwords are stored in an encrypted file on the primary domain controller (see Chapter 7), which is the server that controls network operations. Even if you hacked your way into the password file, you'd still need to know how to decipher the password.

Don't bother asking the network administrator for your password if you forgotten it because she won't be able to help you. However, she can reset your password by using a network administration program such as Window NT's User Manager for Domains. Typically, the network administrator uses a standard format when creating a temporary password.

Tech Talk

Temporary password: a password assigned to new users and to users who forget their passwords. It expires the first time a user logs on the network.

For example, the network administrator might use the day of the week or the user ID as the temporary password. The user is then prompted to change the password when they log on the network.

Network administrators can place restrictions on your password selection and reject passwords that are easy to guess. Here are some passwords that may not be acceptable:

- user's ID
- user's first or last names, or a combination
- name of the organization
- Social Security number or employee number
- name of the computer or monitor
- name of the user's college
- name of the town where the user lives or where the organization is located
- one of the last five previously used passwords
- names of sport teams or names of sports

Security is tight on most networks. Electronic measures are taken to inhibit hackers and other unauthorized people from gaining access to the system. However, a highly insecure aspect of a network is something a network administrator finds difficult to plug. That security gap is the user—you and me.

Like me, you probably have your passwords written down somewhere on your desk and rarely change them. Anticipating this, network administrators take measures to force us to be more careful by setting a time limit after which a password expires.

The time limit is determined by the security risk. A typical user password expires every three months when the network operating system prompts the user to change the password. However, the network administrator might require a user who accesses highly classified information to change her password daily.

Special user IDs, such as a *guest account*, automatically expire after 24 hours and must be re-established by the network administrator if the user requires network access beyond the deadline.

Tech Talk

Guest account: an account given to someone who temporarily needs access to the network.

The network administrator has total control over when a user has access to the network or network resources. For example, the network administrator can disable a password immediately or never allow it to expire. She can have the network operating system temporarily disable an ID and password after a specified number of failed log-in attempts. My network administrator allows three attempts to enter the correct password before the system locks us out, requiring a call to the help desk to unlock the account.

User Manager for Domain

Every network operating system comes with software that enables the network administrator to manage user accounts. For example, Windows NT has the User Manager for Domain. The User Manager for Domain program is the tool the network administrator uses to associate a user ID with a person's name and other information.

With the click of a few checkboxes on the User Manager for Domain program (Figure 8.3), the network administrator can force the user to change the password at the next log-in, prevent the user from changing the password, and—my favorite—prevent the password from ever expiring.

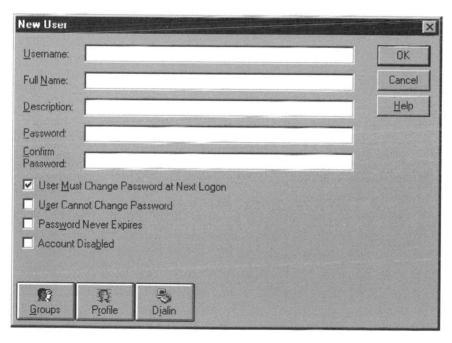

Figure 8.3
The User Manager for Domains is the tool used by network administrators to manage users on a Windows NT network. (Reproduced with permission from Prentice Hall. Keogh, Jim; Kear, Ed; Deep, John. The Complete MCSE Networking Essentials Training Course. Upper Saddle River, NJ: Prentice Hall, 1999.)

Let's say I forgot my password. The network administrator uses the User Manager for Domain to enter a new password, then selects the "change the password at next log-in" checkbox and tells me the new password and asks me to log on the network.

Whenever a breech of network security is possible, such as when an employee terminates employment, the network administrator has two choices to protect the network against unauthorized use. These are to disable the user account or to delete the user account. The decision depends on the situation.

Many organizations disable a user's account at the first suspicion of a breech of network security using the User Manager for Domain "Account Disabled" checkbox (if Windows NT is the network operating system). Access is denied the next time that someone attempts to access the network using that user name and password.

The network administrator can easily re-activate the account by deselecting the "Account Disabled" checkbox. This is a more efficient method than deleting an account because the network administrator does not have to re-establish permissions and recreate settings for the account. Information in a deleted account cannot be retrieved.

Types of Accounts

There are several kinds of accounts available on a typical network, all of which are user accounts. However, each one has different characteristics. These are the network administrator's account, guest account, regular user account, and group account.

The network administrator's account, also known as the Supervisor account on Novell networks, has access to network utilities used to manage the network, such as User Manager for Domains. The user name and password associated with this account can create, modify, and disable any account on the network. It is also used to start and configure the network operating system.

The network administrator's account is automatically created when the network operating system is installed, giving the network administrator full control over network operations.

A guest account is used to give a user temporary access to the network. Windows NT Server automatically disables this account after the session. However, the network administrator can reactivate it or create another guest account for the user.

A regular user account, which is referred to as a user account, provides general network access to a user as restricted by the network administrator. Most user accounts fall within this type.

A group account is one used to identify two or more regular user accounts. Although every user on the network is unique, some have similar characteristics, such as being within the same work group or at the same level in the organization's management. This relationship can be recognized on the network by forming a group account, then assigning these users to the group account.

For example, all users in the East Coast sales region could be members in the East Coast Sales group account. Each of them also has a regular user account. Each member of the group has the same rights as the other members.

A group account not only recognizes relationships within an organization, but also serves as a useful network management tool. Every account is granted rights to resources that are typically stored in the *account profile*.

Tech Talk

Account profile: a file that contains settings and restrictions for a user account.

If you could spend a day with your network administrator, you'd realize there is little unique about your network account because you probably have the same settings and restrictions as others in your work group. So instead of the network administrator creating those settings and restrictions for each person in the group, a group account is created with that profile. You and your colleagues' accounts are assigned to that group account.

Let's say that members of your work group use a network printer located within your work area. The right to use the printer is granted to the group's account rather than to individual accounts. If the group switches to a different printer, then the network administrator need only change the setting in the group account profile—not in the profile of each group member.

Category of Groups

There are four categories of groups that are available in Windows NT; however, other networks have similar groups. These are local, global, system, and built-in groups. Local groups are the most common kind of group set up by a network administrator. Within this category are users who work together or who have similar responsibilities within an organization.

Members of a local group can be any user on the network and any local group.

A global group consists of users who belong to the same domain. The user account of those who belong to the global group must reside on the domain's primary domain controller (PDC) server.

Only user accounts within the domain are permitted to be members of a global group. Other global groups and local groups are prohibited from joining a global group.

A system group contains all network users and is created automatically by the network operating system. The network administrator cannot modify members to this group except to delete the user name from the network.

The built-in group categories consist of the network administrator group, a server operator group, a print operator group, a backup operator group, and an account operator group. Each of these groups is used to grant limited access to a user's network. For example, the network administrator can assign duties to maintain printers and accounts and to perform backup operations by assigning a technician's user ID to an appropriate built-in group.

A group is created and modified using the User Manager for Domains. The network administrator assigns a name for the group and restrictions similarly to the way a user account is created and modified. Existing user account IDs are chosen to join the group or be removed from the group with a click of the mouse button. A user ID that is no longer a member of the group is still an active account. That user can log on the network without any problems. However, the user no longer has rights to network resources that are assigned to the group.

Here's how this works. Let's say I transfer to another work group and my previous work group has access to the printer alongside my desk. The members of the new work group have access to a printer down the hall closer to the group's location. I like where I'm sitting—closer to the elevator than my new group—so I cut a deal that leaves me sitting within my old group, yet working for my new group. I thought this was a good deal until the network administrator reassigned my user ID to the new group and I had to hike to the other end of the office every time I wanted to print a document.

NETWORK SECURITY ....

Although I hate to keep changing my passwords frequently, I appreciate the security measures that my company takes to limit the organization's exposure to people with clandestine motives, such as a disgruntled employee who wants to corrupt network resources by infiltrating the network.

A major responsibility of a network administrator is to create a network security policy that is specified in a network security plan. A network security policy consists of guidelines for protecting network resources and addresses all facets where the network is vulnerable to invasion and inadvertent destruction.

There is no blanket network security policy that will meet the needs of every organization. For example, a defense contractor typically requires extraordinary network security measures that are not required by a small real estate firm.

Even within the same organization, certain resources require greater protection than others. Take, for example, the payroll file that contains the organization's payroll records. The payroll file is likely a network resource than needs more sophisticated protection methods than a network printer, which is also a network resource.

Degrees of security for network resources are referred to as levels of security. A network security policy should specify the levels of security for each network resource.

A typical network security policy will use permissions assigned to a user account as the mechanism for enforcing security levels. For example, a user needs to enter a user name and a password before being granted access to a particular network resource. Permission to use the resource is associated with the user name by the network administrator.

Another level of network security involves physical access to network components such as cables and servers. The network security policy should classify cables according to the data that flows across them. Those cables carrying sensitive data must be placed in a restricted area.

Information carried by the cable can be copied from the network using two techniques. The first is a tap in which someone secretly connects a device, such a computer, to the cable and copies data flowing across the cable to a hard disk for later analysis.

Another technique is to listen into the transmission using sophisticated electronic devices without physically connecting to the cable. This is made possible because of the radio transmission properties of copper cable. Cables emit electronic signals, which carry data transmitted over the cable.

Therefore, all places where sensitive cables are stored, called a cable run, should be in a secured area and inaccessible to unauthorized personnel.

Servers, too, must be located in an area where they will be protected from danger, such as leaks and fire. The best way to secure a server is to place it in a locked room or closet.

Security Measures

The network administrator is usually responsible for establishing the network security policy for an organization. There are several security measures that are commonly found in a security policy. These are auditing network traffic, data encryption, and running specialized software, such as a virus protection program.

Auditing network traffic entails recording every network event into a log. These events include a user accessing specific network resources, connecting to the network, and other similar activities. Entries can be reviewed and analyzed to determine suspicious patterns or to help in an investigation into a breach of security.

Data encryption involves encoding information transmitted over the network to make it unreadable to those who intercept the data. Every client that transmits data on the network has an encryption algorithm, typically contained on the network adapter card.

Likewise, every client has a key used to decipher the data. The weakness is that the key must be transmitted to the destination address and, therefore, becomes exposed to potential interception from clandestine personnel.

Virus detection software is a critical security measure every network requires. A virus is a small program created to cause problems on a network or on a computer's hard disk. Problems can be a simple annoyance, such as writing an inappropriate message on the screen, or more serious trouble, such as corrupting files.

Virus detection software attempts to detect a known virus before it is copied to the network. Some virus protection software also repairs damage a virus causes.

Viruses typically infect a network when someone loads a program, data file, or e-mail that contains a virus onto a client or a network server. The virus then has the opportunity to spread and do its damage. Some organizations are eliminating this possibility by replacing personal computers with diskless computers. A diskless computer does not contain any disk drives, which prevents a user from loading software onto the firm's computers and from copying the organization's data from the network.

A diskless computer operates only on a network because the network card contains a chip called a *ROM boot chip*. When the diskless computer is turned on, the ROM boot chip requests the client operating system to be downloaded from the server, after which the diskless computer functions like a personal computer on the network.

Tech Talk
ROM boot chip: a computer chip that contains instructions that load the operating system into the memory of a computer.

Security Guidelines

A network security policy must conform to an organization's needs. Some situations require tighter security than others. It is the network administrator's responsibility to assess the network security needs and tailor a policy that will protect the organization.

There are two network security techniques that have proven successful and are considered a part of any network security policy. These are password protected *shares* (also known as level security for password protected shares) and access permissions (known as user level security for access permissions).

Tech Talk
Share: a shared network resource, such as a file or servers.

Password protected shares and access permissions typically are blended to restrict use of resources. Password protected shares require that all network resources be accessed after someone has entered a correct password. The password is usually entered when the user logs on the network. However, it is common for additional passwords to be entered to access restricted resources, such as a confidential file.

Access permissions restrict access to a particular function. For example, a user may have no access, read access, write access, delete access, execute, or full access to a file. These are called access permissions and are typically associated with the user name and password.

Data Recovery

The most important organizational asset that is exposed to danger on a computer network is data. Without the integrity of the data, the organization would cease to function.

Tech Talk
Data: facts used to run an organization, such as customer, inventory, and accounting information.

Data can be compromised in a number of ways including hardware failure, vandalism, a virus, and natural disasters. Every organization, including the most secured sectors of the government, has the same risk in losing data.

Whenever there is a question about data integrity, the network administrator attempts to find the cause of the problem and replace the data. Replacing the data is the first task that must be performed since this information keeps the organization operational. There are two ways in which data can be replaced: recreating the data or copying the data from another source.

Recreating the data is the least desirable choice since it is time consuming, could introduce data errors, and may be impossible to do in many cases.

Copying data, which is called restoring data, is the most desirable choice since restored data is exactly the same as what was on the server before the data problem occurred.

However, before data can be restored, the original data must have been copied to tape, CD, or disk. This is known as data backup (Figure 8.4). The most common data backup method used on computer networks is the tape or CD backup in which data and other files, such as programs stored on a server, are copied to a tape or burned onto a CD on a regular schedule.

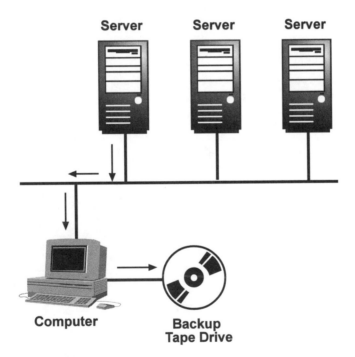

Figure 8.4
A network administrator is able to recover data by regularly backing up data.

The network administrator is responsible for creating a backup plan that ensures that the organization can recover data easily if data security is breached. The network administrator determines which data or files are at risk and the size of those files. This information is used to create the backup schedule and in choosing the backup method and equipment. When assessing the risk factor for each data or file, the network administrator must answer the following questions.

1. Can the organization function without this data or file?

2. How long can the organization function without access to this data or file?

The answer to the first question determines whether the data needs to be backed up. If the answer is no, then data is included in the backup process. The answer to the second question helps decide the schedule of the backup and the equipment used for the backup.

For many organizations, a full nightly backup is sufficient protection. The worst-case scenario is that the organization loses the current day's activity, which can be recreated once the prior day's data is restored.

If loss of a day's data can't be tolerated, then a more frequent backup schedule must be introduced. This may require a fault-tolerant data-recovery system (see "Fault-Tolerant Data Recovery" on page 272).

Equipment used for the backup must be able to reliably copy the data from the server to a tape, a CD, or a disk within the timeframe allotted for the backup process. As a general rule, the backup medium (i.e., tape) must have more than enough room to back up all the data. The backup must also be able to check for and correct data transmission errors during the backup process.

Data deemed mission critical (i.e., the organization cannot function without it) can be further categorized as requiring more frequent backup than others. For example, some data, such as new orders, may need to be backed up hourly while others, such as employee files, can be updated daily. Still others, such as program files, can be backed up monthly or when they change.

These categories help to determine which backup method will be used. There are three methods used for backing up data and files on a network: differential or incremental, copy, and full.

A differential backup, also known as an incremental backup or a daily backup, is used to back up selected files when the content of a file has changed. The backup system reviews the date and time of the file that indicates the last time the file was updated and compares it with the file. If they differ, then the backup system copies the file; otherwise the file is not backed up. Files that are backed up are not marked as backed up.

A copy backup is used to back up selected files. Files that are copy backed up are not marked as backed up. A full backup copies all the files on a server regardless of whether they changed since the last backup.

The choice of backup methods is important to the backup schedule's efficiency and the backup medium's capacity. For example, a full backup takes longer and requires the most storage capacity. The differential backup requires less time and less space because fewer files are backed up. The copy method entails the least amount of time and space because only one or a small selection of files is backed up.

A critical aspect of every backup plan is the method used to maintain backup copies of data. There are three areas that are addressed by the network administrator. These are identifying the backed up data, storage, and retrieval.

Every tape, CD, or disk used to back up data and files clearly identifies the data, date, and time of the backup, storage location, backup method, and person who performed the backup. This information should be contained on the copy of the backup tape, CD, or disk and in a backup log. A backup log is a list of pertinent information about each backup and should be stored electronically and in printed form. Many network administrators enter log information into a file (i.e., Word, Excel, or proprietary program), then immediately print out a copy of the log.

Backup copies are stored both on-site and off-site. That is, a few weeks of backups should be on-site, so the information can be restored quickly. Another copy of all backups should be sent to an off-site facility designed to protect tapes, CDs, and disks. More than two sets of backups should be made for extraordinarily sensitive data that should be stored at two or more off-site locations.

Information from either on-site or off-site locations are retrieved and restored within a reasonable time. For example, a few hours is reasonable for accounts receivable data, while a shorter time frame is reasonable for Wall Street security transaction data.

A network administrator should perform periodic tests to determine the length of time required to restore backup data and the quality of the backup tapes, CDs, and disks. The tests reveal the organization's readiness to recover from a data disaster.

Fault-Tolerant Data Recovery

There is a time lag between when data integrity is breached and when a copy of the data is restored. The lag can be less than an hour for many organizations if the backup data is available on-site, or several hours if the backup is kept off-site.

However, even a minute's delay is unacceptable for some applications, such as a stock exchange trading system. Therefore, the network administrator must take special consideration to address these needs.

Nearly instantaneous data recovery is possible if a fault-tolerant backup recovery system is employed on the network. Fault tolerant means that if a problem occurs, the operation continues unaffected. For example, a stock exchange records hundreds of security transactions a minute. A failure of data files for even a minute can have serious financial repercussions. However, a fault-tolerant system enables a security exchange to recover almost instantaneously from any breakdown.

A fault-tolerant system replicates changes to data immediately following a data change in the file. This is called redundancy. The replicated data is physically stored in a different location on the network, such as a different server called a replication server. If an application cannot access data from the primary data file, it automatically accesses it from the replication server.

The issue that faced computer engineers was how to store information on the replication server so as not to impede performance and to make the replicated data readily accessible. For example, storing data in two locations requires double the normal time required to store data—time for the primary storage and more for the replication storage. Their solution was to use redundant arrays of inexpensive disks (RAID).

RAID is a standard for fault-tolerant systems. It is divided into seven categories called levels. Levels are identified with numbers from 0 through 10. Levels 6 through 9 are not used for replication storage. Each level specifies a step in storing replication data. (Some fault-tolerant systems, such as Windows NT Server, support some, but not all, levels.) RAID requires a group of hard disks, each of which has its own disk controller to speed the storage process by transferring data to each disk simultaneously. The group of hard disks is called a disk array.

Tech Talk

Disk controller: the circuit board inside a computer that controls access to a hard disk.

Level 0, the first of the levels, specifies the technique used to divide data. This is called disk striping, which distributes blocks of data among the disks at the same time. This distribution method is called interleaved.

There are two significant advantages of disk striping. First, each disk in the array can process the transfer of data fast because each has its own disk controller. Also, disk striping makes better use of disk space because it creates a large partition from several smaller partitions. However, a major drawback of disk striping is if a partition fails, all the data stored in it is lost.

Level 1, called disk mirroring, requires data to be copied to the disk array intact. The entire partition of the primary storage device (i.e., hard disk) is duplicated to a partition on the disk array. The technique is called disk duplexing (Figure 8.5).

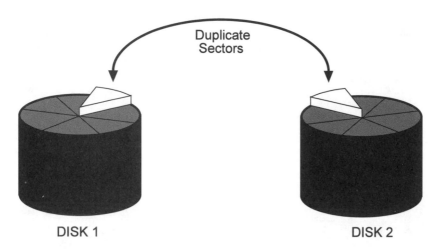

Figure 8.5
Disk duplexing duplicates a partition of a disk.

Level 2, called disk striping with error correction code, is similar to Level 0, but the software transferring the data must employ an error correction scheme to determine errors in the transfer.

Level 3, known in error correction code as *parity*, is the same as Level 2 except parity is used as the error checking technique. Data is represented as a series of 0s and 1s.

Tech Talk

Parity: a feature that specifies that there must be either an even or odd number of 1s in the data. This is called even parity or odd parity. If parity is even and an odd number of 1s is received, then a data error is assumed and a request is made for the data to be retransmitted.

Level 4, called disk striping with large blocks, is the same as disk striping except each large piece of data, called blocks, is stored on each disk in the disk array. This technique is not suited for transactional processing, such as an order entry system.

Level 5, known as striping with parity, is the most common method used by fault-tolerant systems. Data and parity information are stored on different disks and are used to reconstruct data if a disk in the array fails.

Level 10, called mirrored drive arrays, replicates data stored on another disk of the disk array.

Another common fault-tolerance technique is called sector sparing, which is used on SCSI devices. Sector sparing is contained within some operating systems, such as Windows NT Server, and automatically relocates data stored in a bad sector to a good sector on the same disk when the bad sector is detected during normal input/output operations.

Uninterrupted Power Supply

Implementing a fault-tolerant system, scheduled backup procedures, and a good data security policy will not eliminate the Achilles heal of every computer network: electrical power. Clients, servers, and other network resources are disabled during an electrical failure.

There isn't a way to either prevent power outages or predict when they will occur. However, the network administrator can keep the network operating during these times by using an uninterrupted power supply (UPS).

There are two kinds of UPS used in industry. These are battery powered and generator powered. Both supply electricity to clients, servers, and network resources.

Battery powered UPS supplies power for a limited time period. This is usually enough time for the network administrator to notify users that power has been lost. Users can then save their work and shut down their computers.

Likewise, the network administrator will shut down servers and other network resources. Battery powered UPS is not designed to power network operations for the duration of the power outage.

Generator powered UPS uses an electrical generator to provide power for network operations until power is restored. Smaller organizations use gasoline engines to generate power while large organizations, such as Wall Street firms, use jet engines. The generator power can continue until the generator runs out of fuel.

When choosing a UPS, the network administrator must determine the electrical requirement of clients and network resources. The UPS must provide more electricity than the amount required to power the clients and network.

Furthermore, the UPS should activate automatically and alert the network administrator of power events. A power event is the loss of power, the regain of power, and the impending loss of power due to low battery or low fuel.

SUMMARY ....

The task of managing a computer network is called network administration and is performed by the network administrator. The network administrator is responsible for user administration, resource management, configuration management, performance management, and network maintenance.

A user is a person who can log on the network using a client that is connected to it, and using a user name and a password. These and other information unique to the user make up a user profile and are referred to as a user account.

The network operating system contains a utility program that enables the network administrator to create, modify, and delete a user account. The User Manager for Domain is such a utility for Windows NT Server.

There are several kinds of accounts available on a typical network, all of which are user accounts and each having different characteristics. These are the network administrator's account, guest account, regular user account, and group account. The network administrator's account allows the user to have complete access of all network resources. A guest account grants access to the network for one session. A regular user account is used to perform all but administrative tasks on the network. A group account is used to associate two or more regular user accounts that have similar needs, such as to use the same network files.

There are four categories of groups that are available in Windows NT; other networks have similar groups. These are local, global, system, and built-in groups. A local group contains accounts of users who work on the same project. Global groups are users who belong to the same domain. A systems group consists of users who belong to the same network. Built-in groups typically consist of users who have some network administrative responsibilities.

A critical role of the network administrator is to monitor network operations performance to ensure that information is transmitted efficiently. As additional clients are connected to the network, there is a tendency for bottlenecks to develop. A bottleneck is a network device that processes data slower than other components on the network. It is the network administrator's job to remove bottlenecks.

The network administrator uses a network operating system tool called a performance monitor to observe the flow of data along the network. Once the network is operating smoothly, the network administrator should make note of various measurements the performance monitor reports. This creates a baseline of data that is used to compare to daily performance readings. The closer the measurements are to the baseline, the more likely the network will perform without problems.

Nearly all network performance monitors adhere to the Simple Network Management Protocol (SNMP). SNMP is a standard that requires using agents to capture network data and store it in a management information base (MIB). An agent is installed on every device that the network administrator is to monitor, such as clients, hubs, routers, and bridges. Another program polls the agents regularly and copies their MIB to the network server. Data in the MIBs is analyzed and presented on the screen or in reports to the network administrator.

The network administrator is also responsible for network security. This involves protecting network hardware, software, and data stored on network servers. The network administrator must establish a network security policy that sets rules for how network resources are accessed and protected.

There are several security measures that are commonly found in a security policy. These are auditing network traffic, data encryption, and running specialized software, such as a virus protection program.

Auditing network traffic involves tracking every user's network activity to determine if someone is a threat to network security. Data encryption is a method used to encode data transmitted on the network. This inhibits an unauthorized person who taps into the network from easily reading the data. Virus software acts as a roadblock preventing the invasion of programs that are designed to corrupt network operations and resources.

Some network administrators install diskless computers to eliminate the chances of virus infiltration and the unauthorized copying of programs and data from the network. A diskless computer does not contain any disk drives and is activated using a ROM boot chip, which loads the operating system from the network server to the diskless computer.

The first line of network security is restricting access to the network to only authorized users. There are two network security techniques that have proven successful in this area. These are password protected shares, also known as level security for password protected shares, and access permissions, which is known as user level security for access permissions. The term share refers to a shared resource, such as a file or a server.

Password protected share requires a user to enter the correct password before access is granted. Access permissions restricts access to a network resource based on the user password. For example, there are several types of permissions that can be granted to use a file. A user may be granted full permission or only a few permissions based on the user's need to access the file.

The network administrator must provide a way to restore any data or program stored on a network server that becomes corrupted. This task is called data recovery. However, before data can be restored, it must be backed up. Backup refers to making a copy of data or a program. There are three methods used for backing up data and files on a network: differential, copy, and full backup.

Differential backup is the type in which a file or program is copied only if it has changed since the last time a backup was done. If it hasn't changed, then no backup is done since one already exists. The copy method involves individual files or programs that are selected for backup. If a file or program isn't selected, then it isn't backed up. A full backup means that every file and program on the server is copied regardless of whether it has changed since the last backup.

Backups must occur on a regular schedule, typically at the end of the day. However, data can be backed up and restored nearly instantaneously by using a fault-tolerant backup recovery system. Fault tolerant means that if a problem occurs, the operation continues unaffected. In a fault-tolerant backup recovery system, data is maintained on at least two separate disk drives (sometimes two servers) that are accessible on the network. If the file fails on one drive, the network switches to the copy of the file, which allows the user to keep working.

Another threat to network operations is a power outage. The network administrator must keep the network operating during these times by using an uninterrupted power supply (UPS). There are two kinds of UPS used in industry: battery powered and generator powered. Both supply electricity to clients, servers, and network resources.

A battery powered UPS supplies power for a limited time that is sufficient for users to save their work and shut down their computers properly. Generator powered UPS supplies a continual flow of electrical power until normal power is restored.

Summary Questions

1. Why is a baseline used to measure a network's performance?

2. What is the concept of fault tolerance?

3. Why is a group account an efficient way to manage network accounts?

4. What is the source of security threats to a network?

5. Why do network administrators use various ways to enforce password protection?

6. What is the technique used to back up data?

7. Why should network cables be protected?

8. Why should a network administrator prohibit certain words to be used as passwords?

9. How does a network administrator protect the network against a disgruntled employee?

10. What are the categories of groups found in a Windows NT network?

9 How Technicians Troubleshoot a Network

In this chapter...

They Said It...

*"You're not paying for my time,
but paying me for knowing which
screw to turn to fix your problem."*

Anonymous

You probably become frustrated whenever your company's network has problems. You experience slow network response time, e-mail backs up, and periodic outages. Behind the scenes, the network administrator is in emergency mode trying to locate and fix the problem.

You can appreciate the challenge the network administrator faces, especially after you have read this book and realize the complexity of a computer network. In this chapter, you'll explore how a network administrator troubleshoots a network and you'll learn about:

- preventive measures
- standardized procedures and good documentation
- backups, maintenance, and upgrades
- monitoring network operations
- troubleshooting network problems
- researching and isolating the problem
- troubleshooting network devices

REALITY CHECK ....

It was 4 P.M. the day before a presentation to a client, when the network went down, leaving all our presentation files inaccessible in cyber space. We had an inkling that trouble was brewing because it took forever to retrieve files from the network server.

I had the same sinking feeling the day my car started to die on the highway. The car chugged along as I tried to coax it to keep going a few minutes longer until I reached the next gas station. Like my car, no matter how much I sweet-talked the network, I knew deep in my heart that the network wasn't going to make it.

To make matters worse, only our work group's network was affected. The network that served the rest of the building worked fine, and, since it was already 4 P.M., we had a strong feeling our network technicians were on their way out of the office.

We sent a 9-1-1 call to the network administrator's beeper and, to our surprise, the network administrator had already been working on the problem for most of the afternoon. Our network administrator, like most in her profession, receives an automatic alert from software that monitors network operations whenever the software detects a network problem. The alert is a message sent to the network administrator's beeper.

The network administrator used time-tested techniques to sift through what seemed to us to be a jumble of cables and black boxes to locate the trouble. In our case, the problem was isolated to our network segment and specifically to a malfunctioning hub, which was quickly replaced using a replacement hub.

PREVENTIVE MEASURES ....

The old saying that "an ounce of prevention is worth a pound of cure" holds true for computer networks. Although all the planning in the world won't guarantee that the network will keep running forever, a good plan will minimize the impact that a network failure has on the organization.

It is the network administrator's responsibility to develop a good operating plan for the network, which reduces the opportunity for mistakes to occur. This plan should consider:

- network security
- standardizing procedures
- good documentation of standardizing procedures
- backups of network resources
- regular maintenance of network components
- regular upgrades of network components

Network security involves more than preventing an intruder from accessing network resources. In fact, there are few accounts of such attacks when compared with the number of people who use networks daily.

I consider this to be like air travel. Thousands of planes fly every day and only those that occasionally fall from the sky make headlines, which convince some of us that if God wanted us to fly he'd give us wings.

Of greater concern to the network administrator is the likelihood that someone who has legal access to the network will do something inadvertently to stop network operations. This also includes the network administrator, whose mistakes can be irrecoverable.

The best way to reduce the chance of these errors from occurring is for the network administrator to establish and strictly enforce *access restrictions*.

Tech Talk

Access restrictions: restrictions that limit the network resources a person can share, and the way the person can use those resources.

One of the most exposed and most used network resources is a file server. A file server contains files of information that can be shared among network users (see Chapter 7). Typically, everyone on the network is able to access a file server.

However, each person is restricted to certain directories or folders on the server. Furthermore, the network administrator limits (Figure 9.1) a person to a particular file(s) within the directory and grants the person *read-only* or *read/write access* to those files.

Tech Talk

Read-only access: the opportunity to view information stored in a file, but not to modify or delete it.
Read/write access: the opportunity to change or delete information contained in a file, which could inadvertently corrupt the data stored in the file.

While network software such as Windows NT provides utilities to limit access to network resources, the network administrator is responsible for instituting access permissions based on the network plan.

A network administrator must strike a balance between protecting the network and impairing users like me from doing our jobs. No doubt you've experienced the same frustrations I have when denied access to a file that everyone else in the company can access. A good network administrator can foresee such problems and rectify the situation before receiving a nasty call from someone like me.

Here's how a network administrator tackles this problem. First, she identifies the owner of the network resource, then lets the owner decide which users are granted access to the resource. The owner is probably the best person to weigh the business needs against the security risks.

Let's say you created a spreadsheet file that contains sales information and you save that file on a file server. The file is considered a network resource and you are considered the owner of the file. You determine which users have read and/or write access to the file. Likewise, the network administrator takes ownership of network resources such as printers, printer servers, and fax/modem servers.

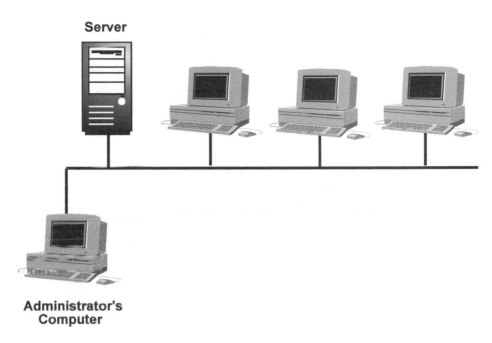

Figure 9.1
Permission for users to access network resources are physically given by the network administrator.

Getting the owners permission before being allowed to access a network resource delays access to the resource. I got caught up in such red tape when I first joined a Wall Street firm. It took two months before I could access a certain file because the owner was on a business trip followed by vacation. Although I had security clearance to log on the network, I still needed the owner to sign the approval form that granted me access to the file.

Although the owner grants permission to use a resource, physical control of the resource remains with the network administrator. That is, the network administrator can ignore the policy and grant access to any user to any network resource.

Standardized Procedures and Good Documentation

I always browse the Sunday papers for new gizmos that I can add to my computer. However, I rarely buy any because of the nightmare I envision installing them. Regardless of the sales pitch on the package, I assume the worse—my computer is the one exception that will require a few hours on the phone with a technician to get the gizmo working.

Having gone through a few nightmarish installations, I can appreciate the horror a network administrator must undergo when dealing with countless network devices supplied by various manufacturers. Installation is just the tip of the iceberg because the network administrator must train technicians to maintain these devices.

Just think for a second—a technician has only a few minutes to repair the guts of a router or other network device once it fails. Otherwise the network administrator finds herself fielding hundreds of complaints. This hodgepodge of hardware and software that we call a network becomes manageable because a network administrator minimizes the number of component variations.

Here's how it works. The network administrator finds the best of each type of component, then uses only those components to form the network. Let's say she requires 30 routers (see Chapter 4). Instead of buying an assortment from various manufacturers, the network administrator determines which is the best router, then orders 30 of them.

The network administrator and her staff of network technicians must learn how to set up and maintain each network device. So if the same make and model router is used throughout the network, then technicians need to learn just one procedure to set up and maintain a router, instead of 30 different procedures.

Procedures for each network device are stored in a handbook created by the network administrator. The handbook provides step-by-step instructions that walk a technician through the setup and maintenance processes. Most of these procedures are copied from the manufacturer's documentation. However, the network administrator also includes the *configuration* for each device in the handbook.

Tech Talk

Configuration: a listing of device settings, such as IP addresses and network protocols, that are particular to a specific network device.

The standardization of network components simplifies network administration and reduces operating costs for supporting the network. This becomes evident when an organization loses a network technician.

Whenever a network technician terminates employment, the network administrator uses the procedure handbook to train another staff person to handle routine tasks until an experienced replacement is found. In many cases, the staff person permanently fills the position because 80 percent of what a technician needs to know about the network is found in the procedure handbook. The network administrator can supplement the missing 20 percent.

The handbook contains more than procedures. It contains the physical location of network components in the organization, floor plans of each floor that identify location of departments, desks, and desk numbers. Desk numbers are referenced when a trouble call is received from a user. Also found in the handbook are names and telephone numbers of *secondary support staff.*

Tech Talk

Secondary support staff: technicians, such as manufacturer's technical representatives, who resolve problems not contained in the network procedure handbook.

Backups, Maintenance, and Upgrades

A network plan considers contingencies. What happens if something catastrophic occurs? "Look for a new job" is my network administrator's joking reply. However, she has developed contingency plans to keep the network operating smoothly when a critical component breaks down and disables the network.

Even Bill Gates can't prevent hardware and software failures, but a network administrator minimizes network down time by planning ahead. The best way a network administrator reduces network down time is to have backups available that can immediately take over for a disabled component. Backups refer to copies of software and data stored on network servers that should be copied to tape or CD regularly, as described in Chapter 8.

Backups also refer to duplicate hardware available on-site. It is not at all uncommon for a network administrator to have drop cables, connectors, hard disks, modems, network cards, and even a ready-to-run server available to go online at a moment's notice. Any network component that could fail and interrupt business is likely to have a backup on-site.

Let's say a database server crashes. The server can be replaced by a backup server immediately (assuming that you've backed up the server), then software and data files can be restored to the backup server from the tape backup. Once the replacement server goes online, technicians troubleshoot and repair the broken server.

Having backup equipment is costly and may be beyond the economical reality of small businesses. For example, it probably isn't economical for an organization that has one server to have a backup server, although software and data files stored on the server should be backed up. The network administrator conducts a risk analysis to determine which devices need to be backed up.

Managing Risk

A network administrator manages risk by conducting a risk analysis. This analysis is a review of network operations and components to assess their chances of failure and the economical cost of those failures on the organization. Risk analysis considers these factors:

1. **How much would the organization lose if a particular component (i.e., server) became disabled?**

   The network administrator must answer this question in the context of the component and the estimated length of time the network might be unavailable. For example, a five-hour down time of the network segment that supports the accounts payable department might have little effect on the organization. In contrast, the organization is deeply hurt if the telephone sales department's network segment goes offline for even an hour.

2. **How soon can the malfunctioning component be replaced?**

   An assessment is made to determine how quickly replacement parts can arrive at the site if they are not stored on the premises. As a general rule, the longer the delivery time, the more the network administrator considers having a replacement part on hand at all times.

3. **What is the failure rate of network components?**

   No one can predict when a component will break down, but component manufacturers have specifications citing their experiences, which is called the component failure rate. This rate is identified as the number of operating hours before a failure occurs. The network administrator consults the component manufacturer to determine the failure rate of each component. Once known, the network administrator estimates the timeframe until the network component is likely to fail.

4. **Is it economical for the organization to stock replacement components?**

   This isn't an easy question to answer. For example, an organization may invest $20,000 for a backup server that won't be used for years. Yet, the current network server could become disabled in six months, making the backup server a lifesaver. Here's an approach a network administrator takes when deciding whether to stock replacements.

First, she determines how much money the organization would lose per hour if a network component does not work. For example, practically no economic loss occurs if a client's drop cable or connector malfunctions. However, a drop cable connecting a router to a server could have an economical effect on the organization.

Next, the administrator determines how soon a replacement component can be delivered. If a supplier can deliver the component within the hour, then it is unlikely she'll need to have a backup component on site. However, the longer the delivery time, the more money the organization could lose.

Finally, she determines if the cost of having the replacement component in stock is less than the money the organization would lose. If so, then she seriously considers stocking replacement components.

The network administrator also develops a system for tracking replacement components. Components are usually stored in an equipment closet in an orderly manner in properly labeled boxes so a technician can find them in an emergency. Also, components are inventoried at least once a month to determine if they should be reordered.

Another aspect of network planning includes scheduled hardware maintenance. Maintenance is probably the most overlooked factor of keeping a network operational because the benefit isn't obvious.

For example, removing the buildup of dust inside a router doesn't make the router perform any better than if the dust was left to accumulate. However, dust increases the operating temperature of the router by reducing the cooling area of circuits inside the route. Eventually, the increased heat will take its toll on the router.

A good maintenance schedule includes:

- Verifying that all network cable connects are tight. A lose cable can cause intermittent network outage for a client—and a headache when troubleshooting the network.
- Removing dust from inside all electronic network components. This includes network components and clients.
- Comparing the *in-service time* of components with the failure rate of the component. A network administrator can expect a problem to occur when the in-service time is close to the failure rate of the device.
- Regularly examining the network response time from various network segments. If response time is slowly becoming unacceptable, then the network administrator plans to reorganize the segment.

- Testing all components to ensure they work. Some network components, such as a printer or a fax modem, may be underutilized by clients and may not be operational. For example, we had four network printers located throughout the office. Everyone had rights to print on all printers. However, we knew one printer was always broken, so rather than report the problem, we printed to one of the other three printers. It was a year before the network administrator realized that one printer had malfunctioned.

Tech Talk
In-service time: the length of time a component is connected to the network.

The network administrator creates a network maintenance log that contains the prescribed maintenance schedule of network devices, maintenance procedures, and information on when those procedures were performed and by whom.

I like to consider the maintenance log like a patient's hospital chart. The log details the status of components during the maintenance check, which is compared to previous statuses to determine if there is a trend. A negative trend frequently points to future trouble that can be avoided before the problem occurs.

Network administrators are careful to follow the maintenance procedures the equipment manufacturer recommends because failure to do so invalidates the manufacturer's warranty. The maintenance log actually supports claims against an equipment manufacturer since it documents maintenance procedures.

In addition to developing a good maintenance plan, the network administrator makes sure all network devices are *upgraded* as required by the equipment or software manufacturer.

Tech Talk
Upgrade: the replacement of part of a component.

Some organizations are skeptical about manufacturer-recommended upgrades since they could be a ploy by manufacturers to make more money. You and I have the same concern whenever Bill Gates tells us we need to purchase a new version of Windows—and a new version of Microsoft Office—when our existing version runs perfectly well.

Is an upgrade beneficial? This isn't an easy question to answer. However, upgrades are commonly issued to fix bugs in a product, so a network administrator cannot simply dismiss the announcement of an upgrade. Instead, discussions are held with the manufacturer to determine the differences between the upgrade and the current product. These discussions provide a rationale for upgrading the network device.

An upgrade can cause problems with network operations. In an effort to minimize exposure, all upgrades should be installed and tested on a Friday night, giving technicians the weekend to fix any problems arising from the upgrade.

Monitoring Network Operations

A good network operating plan is augmented by consistently monitoring information flowing throughout the network. Although some people tend to jump to the conclusion that the monitoring of information is like Big Brother watching, this is rarely the case. Instead, monitoring network operations provides the network administrator insight into how well the network design meets the organization's needs.

Demand for network services change slowly as network usage grows. As you learned in Chapter 8, these gradual changes tend to exceed the original design and cause degradation of performance.

Monitoring the network regularly enables the network administrator to find clues of upcoming problems and gives her time to take preemptive action before users notice a drop in network services.

Many network operating systems provide monitoring software that adheres to the ISO's five network management categories. These are:

- accounting management
- fault management
- performance management
- security management
- configuration management

The accounting management monitor tracks usage of network facilities. For example, this utility makes note every time a user logs on the network and uses a network resource.

The fault management monitor tracks the workings of network components, detects components that failed, and reports those failures to the network administrator.

The performance management monitor tracks the flow of data throughout the network and receives and counts all the data packets that flow over the network.

The security management monitor makes sure users have proper access to network resources. The configuration management monitor is used to set parameters for the network operating system and the network components.

The network monitors collect and count certain activities on the network and relate them to the time the activity occurred (Figure 9.2). The information is displayed in various ways to help the network administrator analyze network operations.

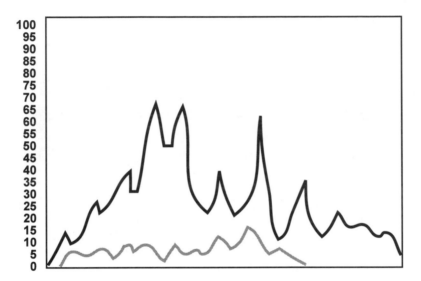

Figure 9.2
The network administrator constantly monitors network performance to quickly identify trouble.

In the case of the performance monitor, the number of data packets across the network per hour is displayed as a graph. This enables the network administrator to determine the maximum volume of traffic over the network.

Once a network is installed and has stabilized, the network administrator runs all the monitors to determine a baseline for the network (see Chapter 8). Many network-monitoring utilities provide a facility to save network statistics.

Every time the network is measured, the network administrator compares the results to the baseline. This helps to determine if current network activities conform to acceptable levels.

An acceptable level is subjective within a tolerance. For example, many users won't complain about a delay of a couple of seconds in network response. However, a volume of complaints can be expected if there is a 10-second response time.

The network administrator tracks the date and time of all user complaints and associates them with network statistics at that moment.

Network monitors are used to forecast trouble before it arises. As statistics move closer to the unacceptable limit, the network administrator can anticipate trouble and takes measures to avoid the problem.

TROUBLESHOOTING NETWORK PROBLEMS ....

The most important role of a network administrator is to be able to quickly respond to disruptions in network operations. When a network malfunction occurs, the network administrator has two objectives: locate the trouble and correct the problem.

Fixing the problem is easier than identifying the component causing the problem. Locating the troubled component is an ardent task since, in a large network, there are hundreds of network connections, thousands of feet of cable, and many routers, repeaters, and other line devices. Any one of them could be the culprit, and it is the network administrator's job to track down the problem quickly.

The first sign of trouble comes when someone like me calls the help line established by network operations support team, who are technicians that work with the network administrator to keep the network running smoothly. The help line is supported by a technician whenever the network is operating, including extended business hours and weekends.

The network administrator creates procedures to guide network technicians through the process of addressing the user's network problems. Procedures provide the most efficient way to approach a network problem. Here's what is included in these procedures:

1. Identify the caller by log-in ID and client location. This information helps to pinpoint the network address that is experiencing a problem.

2. Identify the problem. The technician interprets the user's complaint into technical terms.

3. Replicate the problem if possible. The technician tries to recreate the problem by connecting to the user's computer and asking the user to retrace the steps that lead to the problem.

4. Determine the severity of the problem. The technician determines how the network malfunction affects the business by questioning the caller.

5. Set the priority of the call. Compare the severity of the problems with other outstanding calls. The most severe problem is addressed before all others. This is call triage.

Research the Problem and Isolate the Problem

A complaint call reveals the experience the user encountered. This alone is not sufficient to address the user's network problem. Instead, information gathered from the call provides the network support technician a starting point from which to further explore the situation.

The caller typically makes a passionate plea for help that sometimes is tainted with accusations and condemnation of the technicians who run network operations. Somewhere in the midst of the frustration the caller gives the network support technician clues, some of which are pertinent to the problem.

It is the network support technician's job to sort through the information and identify clues that are helpful to track down and fix the problem. Once the information is identified, the network support technician systematically researches it. Here are few factors she considers:

1. **Has the caller complained about a network problem recently?**

   Every call should be recorded in a log with the nature of the problem listed along with detailed steps used to attempt to fix the problem. Both successful and unsuccessful steps are entered into the log. If the caller experienced previous problems recently, then there is a high probability that the problem wasn't fixed and could be an *intermittent problem*, or the remedy could have caused another problem.

   Tech Talk

   intermittent problem: a problem that occurs irregularly and is difficult to replicate.

2. **Have other callers complained about the same network problem recently?**

   A network malfunction typically affects more than one user. The call log is searched to identify recent callers who reported the same problem. This information helps to narrow the network fault to a common device, such as a router (see Chapter 4 for more on routers).

3. **What network events occurred around the time the user experienced the problem?**

   A change in the network or a specific sequence of events could be the cause of a network problem. For example, a router table could have been reconfigured and that may have influenced network failure. Likewise, network activities that occur in a certain sequence could cause an intermittent network problem. The network support technician examines call logs, maintenance records, and, in the case of an intermittent problem, reviews network monitors to determine network changes and patterns. The objective is to collect information. The network support technician who must diagnose and fix the problem will determine whether the information has a bearing on the problem.

4. **Has any network user reported a similar problem in the past?**

Rarely is a network problem unique. Many problems, such as a malfunctioning router or a loose cable connection, have probably occurred previously—although not necessarily recently. Caller, repair, and maintenance records are reviewed to identify previous occurrences and to learn steps used to solve the problem.

After a complaint is received and researched by a network support technician, the source of the problem must be identified. This is called isolating the problem. Network complaints arise from four general areas of network operations: software, hardware, user training, or network design.

Software and hardware problems can be located at either the client or the network. For example, the client requires client-side network software configured to the proper protocol, a valid network ID and password, a network card, and proper cable connection to the network. The network contains the network operating system, routers, repeaters, bridges, fax/modems, printers, servers, related cabling, and other network devices.

Analyzing the information that is known about the problem helps to isolate a network problem. Here is a procedure that helps to track down the troubled network component.

1. **Is the problem located on the client or the network?**

When more than one caller complains about the same problem, the trouble is likely located on the network rather than a client. An exception to this rule is if new client-side software was installed recently; then the network support technician suspects a configuration problem with the software installation. However, if there is only one reported incident, then the client-side is the place the investigation begins.

2. If the client-side is suspected, is the client's address active on the network?

Network operating systems provide a utility to test if a network address is active. This is called pinging the address. If the address is not active, then the network support technician suspects a problem with the client's network card, the drop cable connection, the port to which the client is connected, and possibly a router table. If the address is active, then she suspects problems with network software on the client-side.

3. If the network-side is suspected, is there commonality among clients who reported the same problem?

Typically, there is something in common with users who complain about the same problem at the same time. For example, all of them might be on the same network segment serviced by the same network device. Likewise, they might use the same network printer and be unable to print documents. The network technician refers to the network layout to trace clients to common devices, then examines shared devices beginning with the first device common to clients.

4. If client-side appears to be operating properly, is the user properly trained?

The network support technician needs to visit the user or remotely connect to the user's computer and ask the user to repeat the steps that lead up to the problem. It will become apparent if the user makes an error. For example, a network operating system may require a user to enter the proper case for a password. The user may have inadvertently activated the caps lock on the keyboard, then complain he can't log on the network.

5. If the network-side appears to be operating properly, is the design of the network causing the problem?

An organization can easily grow beyond the initial design of the network. This growth can lead to all kinds of problems, such as users complaining about poor network response time or of intermittent problems on the network.

Troubleshooting Network Devices

Once the network support technician has isolated the problem to one or more network devices, each device is examined to determine if it is at fault. Manufacturers provide guidelines showing technicians how to troubleshoot the devices.

As a general rule, the technician tries the simplest solution first to fix the problem. Let's assume one client cannot communicate with the network and the technician pinged the address to find that it is not active. The technician examines the cable connection before replacing the network card or conducting more sophisticated network tests because this is the simplest thing to do.

Network support technicians use the most efficient technique for locating a malfunctioning network device. Sometimes this involves swapping a device known to work with one that is suspected of causing the problem. This technique is at times faster than using sophisticated test equipment to locate the problem.

However, network components such as a cable cannot be easily replaced and therefore test equipment is required to determine if the component is working properly. There are a number of common test equipment used to track down network problems. These include Time-Domain Reflectometers (TDRs), oscilloscopes, a digital voltmeter (DVM), protocol analyzers, and cable testers.

A TDR (Figure 9.3) is a tool used to track down a bad cable by sending a sonar signal across a network cable, then analyzing the strength of the returned signal to determine the cable's condition.

Figure 9.3
The TDR send a sonar signal across a network cable to determine if the cable is bad.

Typically, a TDR is used with an oscilloscope to display the signal's voltage to see if the signal has decayed as it is reflected back to the TDR. The TDR and the oscilloscope are mainly used during the installation of network cables, although they can be useful in identifying a problem with an existing cable.

Tech Talk

Oscilloscope: a device that shows voltage over time in a graphical form on the oscilloscope screen.
Signal decay: the loss of power that is used to generate a signal.

A DVM is another tool commonly used by a network support technician to determine the flow of current through a cable and other network devices. The DVM measures both voltage of the signal and resistance of a device. Think of voltage as the force of the signal over the cable, and resistance as force pushing against the signal by the cable.

Although a DVM is used primarily to determine if a signal can flow across a cable, it can also be used to search for malfunctions within a network device, such as a network card. However, it is rarely used in this manner.

The TDR, the oscilloscope, and the DVM are tools used to measure the network's hardware components, but these devices do not give the network support technician any insight into the local components, such as data packets.

A protocol analyzer and an advanced cable tester are used to measure network traffic. This includes counting data packets that are transmitted, the number of collisions that occur, and the number of data packets present, and measuring the traffic flow across various segments of the network.

SUMMARY ··

The network administrator develops a good operating plan for the network to reduce the opportunity for mistakes to occur—mistakes that could disrupt network operations. The plan considers network security, standardizing procedures, good documentation of those procedures and other aspects of the network, backups of network resources, and regular maintenance and upgrading of network components.

Network disruptions typically occur by someone who has legal access to the network and inadvertently does something to halt network operations. This includes the network support technicians, whose mistakes can be irrecoverable.

The network administrator reduces these errors by establishing and strictly enforcing access restrictions to the network. Access restrictions limit the network resources a person can share and the way the person uses those resources. While network software provides utilities to limit access to network resources, it is up to the network administrator to institute access restrictions in the network plan.

Granting access to network resources begins by identifying the owner of the network resource, then letting the owner decide which users can have access to it. The owner is the best person to weigh the business needs against the need for protection.

Standardizing components before the network is installed makes supporting network operations efficient. The network administrator develops a handbook that contains setup and maintenance procedures for every network component. Each procedure is a step-by-step guide that walks a technician through a process.

The handbook contains the physical location of network components, configurations, floor plans that identify departments and desks and desk numbers used to identify a user when a trouble call is received.

The handbook also contains the names and telephone numbers of secondary support staff. These are the people, sometimes manufacturers' technical representatives, who help technicians resolve problems not contained in procedures.

The network administrator cannot prevent hardware failures, but she has developed a plan to minimize the network down time when hardware failures occur. The best approach is to have backups available that can immediately take over for the failed component.

Backups refer to duplicate software and hardware available on-site. It is not at all uncommon for an organization to have drop cables, connectors, hard disks, modems, network adapter cards, and even a configured server available to go online at a moment's notice.

A backup plan is costly and may be beyond the economic reality for smaller organizations. The network administrator should conduct a risk analysis to determine how much of a backup plan the organization needs. A risk analysis is a review of network operations and components. It assesses the chances of failure and the economic cost of those failures.

Network planning includes scheduled hardware maintenance, which extends the time between failures of network components.

Network operations must be consistently monitored to give the network administrator an insight into how well the network design meets the needs of the organization. The network administrator looks for clues of forthcoming difficulties so preemptive action can be taken before users notice a drop in network services.

Network monitors collect and count certain activities on the network and relate them to the time the activity occurred. The information is then displayed in various ways to help the network administrator analyze network operations.

Once a network is installed and has stabilized, the network administrator runs all the monitors to determine a baseline for the network. A baseline consists of statistics that represent acceptable performance and is stored for future reference. Network performance is compared to the baseline to determine if the network is operating efficiently. If not, adjustments are made to the network to bring its operations closer to the baseline.

Summary Questions

1. How does a network support technician identify the source of a network problem?

2. What is the importance of properly maintaining network components?

3. Why is using standardized network components an efficient method to run a network?

4. How are various network logs used?

5. What are the components of a network plan?

6. How are preventive measures used to maintain network operations?

7. How are tools used to troubleshoot a network?

8. How does a network administrator determine whether to upgrade hardware and software?

9. Why does the owner of a network resource determine which users have access to the network?

10. Why may a complete backup plan not be advantageous to a small organization?

PUTTING IT ALL TOGETHER ....

My first suspicion of a network problem is whenever there is a delay in receiving e-mails. This is as if the cyber space highway is closed for road repair. Sometimes my suspicion is on target and other times there is a rules violation that holds up the e-mail.

E-mail is just one of many services available on a network. Anyone using the network must receive permission to use the service; otherwise it can seem like the network is not working properly. For example, I can send e-mail, but it won't be delivered if the person's permission to the use the e-mail service is denied.

The network administrator manages access to network services by creating accounts such as a user account, then giving accounts permission to use specific network services. There are several kinds of accounts available on a typical network, all of which are user accounts, but each with different characteristics. These are the network administrator's account, guest account, regular user account, and group account. The network administrator's account allows the user complete access to all network resources, while a guest account grants access to the network for one session. A regular user account is used to perform all but administrative tasks on the network. A group account is used to associate two or more regular user accounts that have similar needs, such as to use the same network files.

Group accounts fall into four categories. These are local, global, system, and built-in groups. A local group contains accounts of users who work on the same project. Global groups are users who belong to the same domain. A systems group consists of users who belong to the same network. Built-in groups typically consist of users who have some network administrative responsibilities.

If the e-mail is still delayed although the recipient has permission to receive e-mails, then my original suspicions are true—a problem exists with the network. Problems are minimized and fixed quickly because the network administrator painstakingly develops a network administrative plan that covers configuration management, performance management, network maintenance, and network security.

Configuration management involves the design or redesign of the network and installation of network devices such as network cards, routers, and hubs. For example, it is up to the network administrator to restructure the network whenever the organization requires greater network capacity.

Performance management is a critical role of the network administrator and requires constant monitoring of network performance. A tool called a performance monitor is used to observe the flow of data along the network. Once the network is operating smoothly, the network administrator makes note of various measurements the performance monitor reports. This creates a baseline of data that is used to compare to daily performance readings. The closer the measurements are to the baseline, the more likely the network will perform without problems.

The network administrator keeps a careful watch for bottlenecks, which are devices on the network that impede the flow of data. For example, a file server that cannot keep pace with requests for files creates a bottleneck and must be upgraded to avoid unacceptable network performance.

Monitoring software, called an agent, is installed on each device that is to be monitored by the network administrator. Agents capture network data and store it in a management information base (MIB). Another program polls the agents regularly and copies their MIBs to the network server. Data in the MIBs is analyzed and presented on-screen or in reports to the network administrator.

Network maintenance management requires the network administrator to ensure that technicians properly maintain network devices. This includes regular inspections, upgrades, and adherence to manufacturers' maintenance schedules.

The network administrator is also responsible for network security, which involves protecting network hardware, software, and data stored on network servers. This requires the creation of a network security policy, which sets rules for how network resources are accessed and protected.

There are several security measures that are commonly found in a security policy. These are auditing network traffic, data encryption, and running specialized software, such as a virus protection program.

Auditing network traffic involves tracking every user's network activity to determine if someone is a threat to network security. Data encryption is a method used to encode data transmitted on the network. This inhibits an unauthorized person who taps into the network from easily reading the data. Anti-virus software acts like a roadblock, preventing the invasion of programs that are designed to corrupt network operations and resources.

The network administrator must devise a data recovery procedure and ensure the organization that corrupted data can be corrected by using a backup copy of the data. There are three methods used for backing up data and files on a network: differential, copy, and full backup.

Differential backup means a file or program is copied only if it has changed since the last time a backup was done. If it hasn't changed, then no backup is done since one already exists. The copy method means individual files or programs are selected for backup. If a file or a program isn't selected, then it isn't backed up. A full backup means every file and program on the server is copied regardless of whether it has changed since the last backup.

Data can be backed up and restored nearly instantaneously by using a fault-tolerant backup recovery system. Fault tolerant means that if a problem occurs, the operation continues unaffected. In a fault-tolerant backup recovery system, data is maintained on at least two separate disk drives (sometimes two servers) that are accessible on the network. If the file fails on one drive, the network switches to the copy of the file, allowing the user to keep working.

Another threat to network operations is a power outage. The network administrator must keep the network operating during these times by using an uninterrupted power supply (UPS). There are two kinds of UPSs used in industry. These are battery powered and generator powered. Both supply electricity to clients, servers, and network resources.

The network administrator cannot prevent hardware failures, but he or she has developed a plan to minimize the network down time when hardware failures occur. The best approach is to have backups available that can immediately take over for the failed component.

Backup also refers to duplicate software and hardware available on-site. It is not at all uncommon for an organization to have drop cables, connectors, hard disks, modems, network adapter cards, and even a configured server available to go online at a moment's notice.

A backup plan is costly and may be beyond the economical reality of smaller organizations. The network administrator should conduct a risk analysis to determine how much of a backup plan the organization needs. A risk analysis is a review of network operations and components. It assesses the chances of failure and the economical cost of those failures.

Part 4

Industry Overview

You probably have a good idea of how a network operates after reading the first three parts of this book. However, your exploration of networks isn't complete until you learn about the businesses that develop, manufacture, and market network hardware and software that enables our thoughts to be sent around the world at the speed of light.

In writing this book, I discovered that the industry that brings us networking and Internet technologies is just as complex as the largest network. I also noticed that the industry is composed of many companies that are not household words, even though they provide the technology and infrastructure used by companies we read about in the press.

Instead of creating large corporations with strong research, development, and marketing departments, businesses in the new economy create strategic alliances in which each company does at least one thing better than other companies. Collectively, they work toward the same goal of improving technology—and making a profit.

In the next two chapters (and the accompanying appendix), I'll take you on a tour of these businesses and discuss the strategic alliances that form the cornerstone of the industry. The tour begins in Chapter 10 with an overview of how the industry is organized today.

We'll then take a look into the future. I'll look into my crystal ball and project how networking will change in the foreseeable future. From there, we'll take a brief look at the leading companies that operate in four segments of the industry.

10 Network: The Industry

In this chapter...

*"Togetherness is working
as a team to make money."*

Anonymous

There is a tendency to overlook the companies that develop networking devices and software that keep our networks purring 24 hours a day, 7 days a week. Engineers and scientists devise the technology that distributes information around the globe in a fraction of a second, and a team of managers, financiers, and other professionals bring this technology to fruition.

You probably have a deeper appreciation for network technology than you did before reading this book. In this chapter, your appreciation will grow as you take a look at the networking industry. You'll learn about:

- the breadth of the industry

- the depth of the industry

- the industry today

- getting there first

- the infrastructure

- financing dreams

- growing pains

- killer applications

- incubators

- the players

- the risks

REALITY CHECK...

There is a long road between proving a scientific concept in a lab and making the concept a viable product, as in the case of fiber optic transmission. Scientists transmitted messages using light waves over fiber optic cables years before the first fiber optic cable was laid in the ground.

Long distance carriers such as AT&T and MCI WorldCom had to justify replacing existing coaxial cables with the more expensive fiber optic cables. The growth of the Internet spurred the decision to move ahead with the conversion.

Next, equipment manufacturers created new machinery to manufacture fiber optic cables, transceivers, and connectivity devices. Once the machinery was in place, the cable manufacturers and others were in the position to build the components of a fiber optic network.

Tool manufacturers were needed to develop new products used to install fiber optic cables and other fiber optic network components; and installers were required to be trained in to use these tools.

Programmers needed to write software, called firmware, to handle the translation of light signals to electronic signals. Firmware is loaded onto chips inside transmission and connection devices.

All the manufacturing and training had to be completed before any long distance carriers could begin building their fiber optic networks to meet their customers' growing demand for fast and reliable Internet service.

This is mind boggling when you think about the coordinated effort required to bring one aspect of the Internet to reality. This monumental challenge was undertaken without any guarantees that companies within the industry would recoup on their investment.

THE BREADTH OF THE INDUSTRY ....

Let's begin our tour of companies that form the networking industry by dissecting the network itself. As you have learned throughout this book, a network consists of two basic elements: the hardware and software. Hardware refers to the physical devices that connect computers and other network devices. Software refers to the programs that enable the hardware to transmit data.

Companies that form the networking industry are similarly categorized. That is, they either make network hardware components or software components. The type of hardware and software a company manufactures defines subcategories within each industry segment. The hardware segment falls into the following general subcategories:

- cabling
- network switch devices (i.e., routers, switchers, and hubs)
- computers and servers
- wireless services

The software segment is divided into the following general segments:

- network operating systems (i.e., Unix, Windows NT, and Windows 2000)
- database management systems (i.e., Oracle and Sybase)
- development tools and languages (i.e., Java, HTML, and XML)
- application programs (i.e., browsers, electronic commerce)

Defining the network industry is similar to grabbing Jell-O™. Just when you think you got it, it slips out of your hands. Let's follow the trail of the cabling subcategory to illustrate this point. Cabling is divided into two groups: copper cables and fiber optic cables. Copper cables are further grouped into solid core and twisted pair (see Chapter 3). Solid core copper cables are then classified by the thickness of the copper core.

THE DEPTH OF THE INDUSTRY ....

A general contractor is typically hired when an organization wants a network installed. This is similar to having your kitchen remodeled. You call a general contractor who assesses your needs and designs a plan around your budget.

A networking general contractor does something similar and divides the network design into a sequence of tasks that need to be performed for the network to become operational. Each task is assigned to a subcontractor.

Let's say the general contractor uses coaxial cable (see Chapter 3). She places the order for a number of reels of cable with a cable distributor. This sets into motion a series of events that resembles cascading dominos.

Another order flows from the distributor to the cable manufacturer, who in turn orders prefabricated components from suppliers. This is similar to how an auto manufacturer receives parts from various parts manufacturers.

Coaxial cable has at least two parts. These are the copper core and the insulation sleeve, each made by parts manufacturers. The parts manufacturers rely on raw materials supplied by raw material suppliers. For example, a mining company supplies copper ore that is melted and formed into a copper core, which is used as a part of coaxial cable.

Four types of companies are involved in supplying network cables: raw material suppliers, cable manufacturers, cable distributors, and general contractors. Another firm is assigned the task of installing the cables.

Other network components have a longer supply line than the cable segment. Routers are a good example. As you learned in Chapter 3, a router is a special kind of computer that performs a job similar to a post office. The router redistributes packets to other network segments based on the destination address.

Take a look inside a computer and you'll appreciate the number of parts needed to manufacturer a router because the inside of a router is similar to the inside of a computer. There's a cabinet that contains the motherboard, a power transformer, and an assortment of switches and connectors.

A different company supplies each part and uses their own network of suppliers to provide subcomponents and raw materials. For example, the manufacturer of the motherboard buys the coated board, chips, switches, and connectors from an array of vendors.

THE INDUSTRY TODAY..

The growth of the Internet is fueling the networking industry. The Internet is a network of networks over which practically anyone can sell anything to anyone anywhere in the world. The enormity is mind boggling when you consider that three electronic commerce companies (Cisco Systems, Dell Computers, and Intel) sell $100 million a day over the Internet. Electronic commerce in the computer sector alone will account for $400 billion in sales by 2002.

The global economy is in a transition moving from *brick-and-mortar* stores to electronic commerce. Both old-time companies and upstarts see vast opportunities in cyber space. Old-line brick-and-mortar companies see the Web as a way to reduce expenses.

Tech Talk
Brick-and-mortar companies: companies who do not conduct business on the Web.

No longer is there a need for middlemen in the distribution channel of the new economy. Manufacturers can sell directly to consumers. The cable distributor mentioned in the previous section isn't required if the cable manufacturer sells cables directly to the general contractor over the Internet.

Upstart companies see a dramatic reduction in cost to entering existing markets. With the help of *venture capitalists*, a company has the financial resources to form strategic alliances with companies in the supply chain that give them the depth to compete online against old-line market leaders.

Tech Talk
Venture capitalist: a company or a person that finances new companies.

Companies that have brick-and-mortar assets and ownership of time-tested supply lines are finding themselves at a disadvantage during this transition. Middlemen are critical to maintaining their existing operations, which cannot be supported by their online business.

Here's their dilemma. Many industries are moving toward e-commerce, involving the manufacturer selling directly to the consumer. However, attempting to reach the online market will disrupt existing relationships with middlemen—relationships that are vital to a manufacturer's current brick-and-mortar business. Alternatively, abandoning efforts to open an online business will cause manufacturers to loose future market share and dramatically reduce their likelihood for survival in the new electronic economy.

Practically every manufacturer wrestles with this problem. Yet, new online companies don't have this problem because they haven't got relationships with any suppliers. They simply have nothing to lose, and use the disadvantages associated with brick-and-mortar manufacturers as leverage to enter the market.

A technique used by many old-line companies is to create their own online companies independent from their main business. The association between the online and the brick-and-mortar units is not widely publicized so as not to offend middlemen in their distribution line.

Getting There First

Competing online is becoming a zero-sum game in which a company either wins or loses the market. There doesn't seem to be a middle ground. In the brick-and-mortar world, companies develop a market presence and establish their *brand*.

Brick-and-mortar companies spend millions of dollars establishing their brand in the market place. However, electronic commerce is a new marketplace where brands must be re-established.

Tech Talk
Brand: a name that consumers associate with a certain product and service quality that helps them make a purchase.

A few years ago, e-commerce was new and anyone could open shop at a relatively low cost and attempt to sell anything. As consumers went online, they quickly discovered the absence of familiar brand names that they relied upon in the brick-and-mortar economy.

Instead of finding Toys 'R'Us, they discovered eToys.com. No one knew anything about eToys. Gradually, through the marketing efforts of eToys, consumers were encouraged to make small purchases online. Favorable price, availability of hard-to-find products, and the ease of shopping motivated consumers to abandon their local Toys'R'Us brick-and-mortar store and buy from eToys.com.

Their good experience buying from eToys spread throughout the country and it wasn't too long before eToys captured the online toy market. Toys'R'Us, who once held the lead in the retail toy industry, now found itself playing catch-up.

The upstart eToys staked the first claim to the online retail toy market. As long as eToys provided good prices and availability, and gave consumers a good online experience, there wasn't any reason for their customers to shop elsewhere. All of eToys' resources were focused on maintaining their brand reputation.

Online startups such as eToys employ a widely used tactic to own an online market. Their goal is strictly to take over their market and not to make a profit. Here's how this strategy works.

Consumers tend to have brand loyalty. For example, you probably have your favorite soft drink and rarely think of switching unless there is no alternative. Venture capitalists understand this concept very well and are willing to finance an upstart that has the potential of owning an online market.

With the right *business model* and management in place and backed by venture capitalists, an upstart company invests heavily in attracting customers—even if they lose money on every sale. Their objective is to build a steady, loyal following of customers who would rather continue to deal with a company they know than risk dealing with a new company.

Tech Talk
Business model: the way a business provides goods and services in return for revenue and profits.

It may take years before this customer base is in place. However, once the company is established, it will be difficult for competitors to compete successfully in the market since it already has a reliable provider of goods and services.

The online toy market is a good example of this. Toys'R'Us was late to the online market and had an uphill battle to compete with eToys. Toys'R'Us had a successful chain of brick-and-mortar stores throughout the country whose business was being eroded by eToys.

A consumer who bought from eToys was likely a former Toys'R'Us customer who was no longer shopping at their toy stores. The Toys'R'Us management realized that online buying was going to reduce the profitability of their stores, so they decided to open their own online toy store.

Stop for a moment and imagine being the top management of Toys'R'Us. An online upstart was reducing the revenue brought in by your brick-and-mortar stores, forcing you to invest heavily in an online business that wasn't likely to be profitable for years to come.

To complicate matters, you had no experience running an online business. This meant that it was highly unlikely that your first attempt at selling online would be successful and could leave consumers with a bad experience. A bad experience drives former loyal brick-and-mortar customers to the upstart competitor.

A major rule of electronic commerce is: whoever stakes a claim to an online market and gives consumers goods and services at a reasonable price while giving them a good user experience has an advantage in the market.

Once the online retailer has a firm grip on the market, the company is then in a position to make adjustments in product mix, pricing, and negotiations with suppliers to increase their margins and turn a profit.

The Infrastructure

Companies in every industry are seeking to establish themselves as the dominant player in the new electronic economy. This drive has spurred the growth of every aspect of the network industry because before a company can make an online appearance they need an *infrastructure* to support their activities.

Picture yourself as the next Jeff Bezos—the founder of Amazon.com—who wants to create an online widget store. Let's assume that you found a venture capitalist who is willing to pour tons of money into your project. What do you need to make your online widget store a reality? You need computing and networking equipment.

Tech Talk
Infrastructure: the technological and physical assets required to do business on the Internet.

You'll require desktop computers for each employee and souped-up computers for the technical staff who are going to build your Web site. You'll also need powerful servers to handle e-mail and shared file storage. E-commerce servers are also necessary to display your Web site and handle online transactions. Cabling, routers, and other network devices and software must be acquired to link printers, servers, and computers.

Companies like Citibank can expect to handle a billion customers online within the next five years and must begin today to build the network infrastructure to give customers a good online experience in the future.

All the assets I just mentioned are for one online company. There are millions of organizations that have a Web presence and each one requires the same hardware and software. This demand has kept the midnight oil burning in every facet of the networking industry as it tries to keep up with demand.

Besides the infrastructure within each company, telecommunications companies such as AT&T, MCI WorldCom, and Qwest Communications International are enhancing the telecommunications network to handle this dramatic increase in demand to transmit data over the Internet.

In 1995, there were 21 million Internet users. Industry experts forecast there will be 411 million Internet users by 2002. In 1995, there were 5 million Web sites, which grew to 45 million in 2000 and generated 2.6 billion Web pages. The projection for 2002 is 7.7 billion Web pages.

These are impressive numbers, but their importance becomes relevant when you realize the amount of data that needs to be transmitted over the Internet. In the first chapter, you learned the meaning of a byte. Conceptually, you can think of a byte as being one character, although technically this isn't accurate.

Each month in 1995, 375 terabytes of data were transmitted over the Internet. That's 375 trillion bytes of data. In early 2000, 8.5 trillion bytes per month were transmitted, and by 2002 this will increase to an estimated 28 trillion bytes per month. An increased use of the Internet and electronic commerce, as well as the use of interactive Web pages that use video and audio to enhance their graphical offerings, generate this growth. Consumers will also use the Internet for telephone calls using IP telephone technology. Telecommunications companies must quickly rebuild their infrastructure to keep up with Internet traffic that doubles every three months.

Financing Dreams

No one doubts that networking technology and the Internet have opened the door to the world of electronic commerce, where the only location that is important is a company's dot-com name. Companies must invest heavily in networking infrastructure and an organization to ensure that they can compete with brick-and-mortar and upstart companies. Table 10.1 contains the typical functions that are needed to operate an Internet company.

Table 10.1 Functions and Infrastructure Required by an Online Company

Function	Infrastructure
Relationship applications	Fulfillment
	Supplier management
	Customer management
	Demand management
	Logistics
E-commerce applications	Internet application development tools
	Supplier-facing platforms
	Portals
	Trading exchanges
	Customer-facing platforms
	Commerce servers
Infrastructure technologies	Communications/Web infrastructure
	Middleware
	Security
	Databases/data warehousing
	Integration
	Management
Back office integration	Finance and administration
	Operations planning and execution
	Purchasing
	Product development/design collaboration
	Research and development
	Human resources
	Inventory/asset management

Traditionally, funds to acquire an infrastructure are supplied by revenue from business operations. However, this is no longer true for online companies, nearly all of whom have little revenue compared to the outlay necessary to construct the infrastructure.

There are some questions that I'm always asked whenever I talk about the infrastructure electronic commerce firms need. The first is, "Where do they get the money to finance the infrastructure?".

E-commerce companies' capital flows from investors, beginning with venture capitalists who provide seed money to private companies in exchange for a share of the business. Additional funding comes from investors when the company's stock is publicly traded on the stock market.

The second question is, "Why would anyone invest money in a company that has little chance of turning a profit anytime soon?". Even some savvy investors ask this question, especially since many electronic commerce and related networking companies are unable to provide the financial data investors traditionally use to value a company.

For example, there isn't a 5- or 10-year earnings history or ratios that can be used to predict upward or downward trends for the company's sales. Just as electronic companies are throwing away the old business rules, so too are investors discarding the old rules for evaluating an electronic company.

Investors in the companies that specialize in the new electronic commerce and related technologies are betting on the future potential of these organizations rather than immediate profit. In essence, they are hoping their company will mature in 10 years to the level of Microsoft, at which time the firm will own their marketplace.

The Internet is beyond the concept stage of development. Everyone knows the revolutionary benefits that networking and electronic commerce will have on the economy. However, they also know this will not happen unless the Internet's infrastructure and that of electronic commerce companies keeps up with the rapid demand for electronic commerce.

Therefore, investors are willing to finance building the infrastructure because they have a strong feeling their firms will capitalize on the market once the infrastructure is in place. I think of this as having your dream house built. For the year or so while the building is under construction, you're willing to live in cramped quarters and spend money for a house you can't live in yet. However, once it's completed, you'll be able to sit back, relax, and enjoy your spacious home.

Investors also know that networking and electronic commerce companies are blazing a new trail and making up rules that don't exist. They expect companies will bark up the wrong tree a few times, then backtrack and head in a different direction. These errors are costly, but are expected anytime anyone embarks on a new adventure.

For example, the complexity of the infrastructure and electronic commerce is causing companies to form *strategic alliances* to share the burden. Rarely can one company provide an end-to-end solution. Instead, companies specialize in solving a particular aspect of the problem and form alliances with similar companies that have solved other pieces of the problem. Collectively they offer a complete solution.

Tech Talk

Strategic alliance: a business arrangement in which two or more independent companies work together to provide complementary goods and services to a customer.

Most electronic commerce companies require a search engine to enable consumers to quickly find products on their Web site. Instead of a company investing resources to build a search engine, they form a strategic alliance with a firm that already developed one.

Likewise, every electronic commerce company requires a way to process credit card transactions. Instead of building this piece of the business, they join forces with a company that has a proven transaction component.

Strategic alliances appear to be similar to the *client-vendor model* that is used is most conventional businesses. Let's say a cable manufacturer requires a copper core. The manufacturer buys the copper core from a parts manufacturer. The cable manufacturer is the client and the copper core supplier is a vendor.

Tech Talk

Client-vendor model: a business arrangement in which a manufacturer purchases parts from a parts manufacturer to create an item for resale.

This is different from strategic alliances in the new economy because of the way alliance partners are compensated. In a client-vendor arrangement, the client pays the vendor for supplies. In many strategic alliance arrangements, alliance partners share a piece of the transaction.

An electronic commerce transaction illustrates this point. The alliance partner that processes the transaction retains a percentage of it or a fixed amount per transaction. This means the electronic commerce company does not pay anything to the alliance partner until a transaction occurs—and that payment is automatically deducted from the proceeds of the transaction.

Strategic alliances enable companies to preserve cash and redirect the use of cash to the core of their business. This also redistributes the risk involved in conducting business online. All alliance partners share a portion of the risk—and stand to reap substantial gains if the venture is successful.

The risk is actually minimal for many alliance partners because contributions are software-based and rarely involve brick-and-mortar investments. Let's continue with the electronic commerce transaction example so you'll have a better understanding of what I mean.

An e-commerce transaction is the step in buying online where credit card information is processed, which is the same process most online stores require. The alliance partner invests resources to build the computer program that performs the processing.

It is the computer program that is offered to alliance partners in exchange for a piece of every transaction the program processes. There is little cost involved in replicating the transaction program for each alliance partner. Ninety percent of the expense is involved in developing the program and another 10 percent used for updating and maintaining the program.

Another question I'm always asked is how savvy investors who buy networking and electronic commerce companies measure the value of these companies. There are two factors that are examined: the *target market* and the quality of the firm's managers.

At this stage in the economic development of electronic commerce, the company that gives consumers the best online purchasing experience tends to control the market. Investors attempt to identify companies that have the potential of reaching that objective, assuming the investment community provides the necessary financing to achieve that goal.

Tech Talk

Target market: the segment of the economy that the company is seeking to own.

It doesn't take a rocket scientist to determine how to value a market. Economic data that summarizes gross sales and profits for each industry are available in libraries and online. Gross sales and profits are the criteria used to set a market's value.

If the market potential is there, investors must then determine if the company's management is capable of capturing the online component of that market. Unfortunately, there isn't a sure-fire way to measure the quality of management.

THE HASSLE OF SWITCHING

The street fighter strategy for capturing and keeping a market segment might not work in the new online economy. Business schools teach future managers that to succeed in business you must differentiate your product from your competitors'.

However, the street fighter knows the winning strategy has little to do with product. Instead, it has more to do with making it too expensive or too much of a hassle for your customer base to switch to a competitor.

This strategy was originally adopted by IBM and carried through to Microsoft. Think of how much of a hassle it would be for you change to a different operating system for your computer or use a different word processor. Bill Gates banks on your lack of enthusiasm for switching to a competitor's product.

The same strategy applies to purchasing goods. Would you travel 20 miles to a competitor's store when the store you've been using for years is a mile from your house? Probably not, and merchants count on that.

However, this strategy no longer applies to online stores, in which you can buy the same product from hundreds of worldwide stores at the click of a mouse button. You can shop 'til you drop without any hassle or additional expenses.

Growing Pains

The road to an electronic economy is thwarted with mines, each of which could damage a company's efforts to stake a claim to a market. Some consumers have had bad experiences in the early days of electronic commerce and have called it a journey into e-hell.

Consumers are willing to deal with a few annoyances when doing business online in exchange for purchasing at a discount. However, there is a limit to their patience. Take, for example, the following episode involving a major airline.

A customer who frequently used the airline's Web site to book flights attempted to book a flight to New York City. She found the flight she wanted and provided her name and the other pertinent information.

When she clicked the "proceed to booking form" button, the airline's Web page rejected the form because it was missing her full name, even though her full name appeared on the form. She repeated the process 10 times and received the same result.

The experience went downhill from there. By the 15th attempt, she succeeded in booking the flight. However, in the process, she discovered she made an error. She also discovered there was no way to correct the booking online. Instead, she had to call the airline's alliance partner, which handles customer service. The error was corrected—at a rebooking charge of $75. After hours of complaining, the totally dissatisfied customer was told the problem was with the computer system and was given a travel voucher.

And her problems didn't end there. The airline required her to enter her frequent flyer number when she booked the flight online. However, the system lost her frequent flyer number. It didn't appear on the ticket and she didn't receive credit for the flight.

After three months of phone calls and letter writing to the president of the airline, all the issues were resolved and she received credit for the flight. However, the airline paid a high price. The online system gave many customers a poor experience, which resulted in defections to other airlines.

In addition, the personal care to handle customer complaints was costly because every customer who complained was contacted several times by a customer representative.

Killer Applications

As companies build the infrastructure to handle online operations, they seek to create a *killer application* that gives them a dramatic edge in the marketplace.

There are two areas in which companies are looking for a killer application. These are target marketing and convergence of legacy systems. Target marketing is the manufacturer's capability to identify a consumer for their products. Convergence of legacy systems is a company's capability to convert or link its older systems to Web systems.

Tech Talk

Killer application: a set of programs that gives a company a significant edge in the market. Windows is such an application for Microsoft.

Networking and Internet technology can be used to profile consumers who visit and purchase products online. Through a variety of techniques, such as "joining a Web site" or "registering on a Web site," a Web site owner identifies a consumer by name, address, e-mail address, and credit card number, or any other facts a consumer willingly supplies.

Tracking software is able to monitor Web pages and features that attract a consumer, thereby creating a detailed profile of the consumer's likes and dislikes. This information can be stored in a database and used to organize consumers into groups of those who have similar profiles.

A killer application will be able to sift through this information, identify potential customers for a particular product, and be able to present a sales pitch that the consumer is likely to accept. This is because the application will understand factors that convert a potential customer into one who enters into a transaction.

Currently only about 3 percent of first-time visitors to a Web site actually make a purchase. This is a slightly higher success rate than is found in direct mailings. However, profiling technologies using *collaborative filtering* and neural networks will recommend choices to users based on the user's answers to questions and other people's answers in the past.

Tech Talk

Collaborative filtering: a method used to associate profiles of others to predict a person's behavior.

Developers who use this targeting method assume that people who have agreed in the past are likely to agree in the future. Let's say Mary and Mark are friends who have similar tastes in cars. A killer application assumes that if Mary likes a specific car, then so will Mark. Therefore, the application will recommend to the Web site to display the car Mary is considering to Mark the next time Mark visits the site.

Neural network technology is at the heart of collaborative filtering. Neural networks have the built-in logic to learn by example, much the way humans learn.

Tech Talk

Neural networks: networks that make inferences based on recognizing patterns of random events, such as a consumer browsing a Web site.

Once a consumer is targeted, collaborative filtering enables a Web site owner to dynamically reconstruct the Web page to meet the projected needs of the consumer. This means each consumer will be presented with a Web site designed specifically for his or her preferences, which is expected to increase the likelihood of converting a visitor to a customer.

The other area in which the hunt for a killer application is underway is with convergence of legacy systems into those that are Web-enabled. A legacy system is a company's existing accounting, sales, inventory, billing, and fulfillment system. These are the programs that keep the company's current business operating smoothly.

Ideally, a brick-and-mortar company will need to create only the online portion of their business, which will then link directly to their legacy system. If successful, a company can reduce the cost and time it takes to go online.

Let's say a book publisher wants to sell directly to consumers on the Internet. An investment must be made in the infrastructure required to create a Web presence, display products, and transact business. The order, once received, should flow directly through the company's legacy order processing and accounting systems.

The hunt is underway to devise a killer application that makes this process seamless without requiring redevelopment of legacy systems and without interrupting current business operations.

Incubators

Who will be the next Microsoft in networking and Internet technology? If I knew, I wouldn't be writing this book. However, there are a large number of companies called *incubators* that are financing prospective startups hoping that one of them will become a key player in the online market.

These companies include Divine Interventures, startups.com, iStart Ventures, and includes some well-known companies such as Panasonic. Key executives from Disney, Earthlink, and USWeb have also branched out into the incubator market.

Tech Talk

Incubator: a company that helps launch startup companies in exchange for ownership in the company.

Using incubators is a common approach to funding technology companies. For example, Tech Farm's startup investment in eToys won it a 30 percent stake in the company, which ultimately provided a handsome return.

Traditional incubators are operated by venture capitalists whose contribution to the startup is financing. Recently, incubators began exchanging other services for stock. Services include acquiring office furniture, locating offices, hiring employees, and other necessities required to get the business up and running.

When an incubator becomes involved with a company growth is rapid. It can take as little as 10 days from the time an agreement is reached between an incubator and a startup company and the time the company is fully operational.

It isn't uncommon that an incubator works aggressively toward bringing a startup company public within a year even if its product is in final testing and it hasn't sold anything to customers. To reach this objective, incubators cut the time to develop a brand, raise funds, and recruit key employees by three-quarters of a year.

The Players

You'll find all types of companies in the networking and the Internet industry because a broad range of products and services are necessary to grow the industry. Whenever I think of networking and the Internet, I immediately think of Microsoft and other relatively new companies. However, old giants such as IBM and AT&T are also major industry players and are in the process of reinventing themselves to meet the online demand.

IBM redesigned its mainframe computing to position itself as a supplier of high performance Web servers that can handle very high traffic volumes. Likewise, IBM has transformed its customer support organization into a consulting service that helps organizations enter electronic commerce.

AT&T switched direction from delivering long distance telephone service to carrying Internet data traffic. The new demand required AT&T to replace existing co-axial cables with fiber optic cable that can transmit high-volume data required of an Internet backbone.

Companies that comprise networking and Internet industries use a variety of business models that redefine how we entertain ourselves, manage finances, shop, and communicate with each other.

Amazon.com and eToys are among the companies that use the Internet as a way to sell existing products. Other companies, such as E*Trade, eBay, and Priceline.com, introduced a new way to conduct business. E*Trade practically eliminated the need for a retail stockbroker by enabling individual investors to trade online. eBay gave a new twist to the idea of an auction. Customers and businesses alike can offer merchandise for sale to the highest bidder. Priceline.com let consumers set their price for a product and then matches them with a seller willing to sell the product at that price. Healtheon is a company that served the health industry and now uses the Internet to provide health care information and services to physicians, patients, and hospitals.

The industry also includes technology companies that are not necessarily household names. Inktomi is one of those companies. If you use Yahoo!, then you've used Inktomi's product. They built the search engine used by Yahoo!.

Then there is Exodus Communications. You probably never heard of them either. They host high-traffic Web sites for companies such as eBay. Likewise, if you've banked online, then there is a good chance you used S1's software. S1 is the former Security First Technologies, which built the online software used by major financial institutions.

A serious gap in electronic commerce exists between Web sites and back office systems that process transactions. This is where companies like Oracle and Sun Microsystems are able to step in and provide database and server products. Following right behind those well-known names is EMC. EMC is a company that uses its 20 years of data management experience to maintain very large databases, such as those used by Amazon.com and Yahoo!.

Networking and telecommunications segments of the industry are always being enhanced to meet the rapid demand for Internet services. Leading these enhancements are companies such as Broadcom, Juniper Communication, and Cisco.

Broadcom gives a shot of adrenaline to older, slower telephone systems by enabling them to handle high-speed data transmissions. Juniper Communications and Cisco manufacture routers, switches, and other network devices that send packets efficiently over the Internet. In fact, many pieces of data sent over the Internet pass through a Cisco product.

Intel and Microsoft are familiar industry names. Intel manufactures chips that are used in many computers that are used to connect to the Internet and in some of the servers used to display Web pages. Microsoft has its hands in a little bit of everything, from providing electronic commerce server software and network operating systems to operating various Web sites and electronic commerce companies.

AT&T is facing direct competition from companies like MCI WorldCom and Qualcomm. MCI WorldCom offers long distance data transmission services and Qualcomm provides wireless technology that enables various remote devices to connect to the Internet. You will learn more about these in Chapter 11.

The Risks

Everyone agrees that networking and Internet technology are providing the foundation for the new electronic economy that breaches national and natural borders to create a true worldwide economy. However, playing in the electronic economy is risky, especially in this early stage in which technology and business models are being reinvented.

Celebrities rarely violate the first rule of show business: Don't believe your own press releases. The same rule applies to the Internet; executives of networking and Internet technology companies must cut through the Internet hype and focus on the business of the Internet.

It seems that, for many Internet companies, the objective is to become the buzz on Wall Street a week or so before making an initial public offering (IPO). Rarely is becoming profitable an objective. Investors are betting that a company will survive the unprofitable years and eventually corner a market.

Since electronic commerce is new and expected to be unprofitable for years to come, many Wall Street analysts and investors are unable to quantify the value of Internet companies. This has lead to dramatic swings in stock prices. For example, E*Trade fell 50 percent at one point, and king of the online brokers Charles Schwab has seen a drop of 30 percent in their stock price. Even Ameritrade dropped 75 percent of its stock value at one point, and 87 percent of recent IPOs have fallen below their opening price.

Uncertainty exists in every aspect of the Internet even while industry experts and the press forecast a basket of gold at the end of the Internet rainbow.

SUMMARY ....

The type of hardware and software a company manufactures categorizes it in the industry. The hardware falls into the following general subcategories:

- cabling
- network switch devices (i.e. routers, switchers, and hubs)
- computers and servers
- wireless services

The software segment is divided into the following general segments:

- network operating systems (i.e. Unix, Windows NT, and Windows 2000)
- database management systems (i.e. Oracle and Sybase)
- development tools and languages (i.e. Java, HTML, and XML)
- application programs (i.e. browsers, electronic commerce)

Each subcategory is divided further. Cabling is divided into copper cables and fiber optic cables; and copper cables are further grouped into solid core and twisted pair.

A networking general contractor assesses network needs and designs a plan around the technology budget. A networking general contractor then divides the network design into a sequence of tasks and assigns each task to a subcontractor.

The global economy is moving from brick-and-mortar commerce to electronic commerce. Both old-time companies and startups see vast opportunities in cyber space. Old-line brick-and-mortar companies see the Web as a way to reduce expenses.

However, brick-and-mortar companies have a dilemma. Selling to the consumer will disrupt existing relationships with middlemen—relationships that are vital to a manufacturer's current brick and mortar business. Abandoning an online business will cause manufacturers' future market share to fall and dramatically reduce their likelihood for survival in the new electronic economy.

Competing online is becoming a zero-sum game in which a company either wins or loses the market. Consumers tend to have brand loyalty and rarely think of switching unless there is no alternative. Venture capitalists understand this concept well and are willing to finance a startup that has the potential of owning an online market.

A startup company invests heavily in attracting customers—even if they lose money on every sale. Their objective is to build a steady, loyal following of customers who would rather continue to deal with a company they know than risk dealing with a new one.

Whoever stakes a claim to an online market and gives consumers goods and services at a reasonable price while giving them a good user experience might own the market.

Companies need to build the infrastructure within their organization if they want to become players in electronic commerce. They require desktop computers for every employee and souped-up computers for the technical staff building the Web site. They also need powerful servers to handle e-mail and shared file storage. E-commerce servers are also necessary to display the Web site and handle online transactions. Cabling, routers, and other network devices and software must be acquired to link printers, servers, and computers.

Traditionally, funds to acquire an infrastructure were supplied by revenue from business operations. However, this is no longer true for online companies, nearly all of which have little revenue compared to the outlay necessary to construct the infrastructure.

Their capital flows from investors, beginning with venture capitalists who provide seed money to private companies in exchange for a share of the business. Additional funding comes from investors when the company's stock is publicly traded on the stock market.

Investors in the companies that specialize in the new electronic commerce and related technologies are betting on the future potential of these organizations rather than immediate profit. In essence, they are hoping the company will mature in 10 years to the level of Microsoft, at which time the company will hopefully own their marketplace.

In an effort to claim a stake in an online market, companies are forming strategic alliances in which each independent company contributes to the goods or services provided to the customers. In many strategic alliance arrangements, alliance partners share a piece of the transaction rather than sell their services to their partners.

Companies who play in the cyber economy are valued using two factors: the size of the target market and the quality of the firm's management. They are also seeking a killer application in either target marketing or convergence of legacy systems to give them an edge in the online market.

Summary Questions

1. **Explain the concept of strategic alliances.**

2. **What are the disadvantages a brick-and-mortar company faces when opening an online store?**

3. **Why is infrastructure so important to the success of an online company?**

4. **Why is it important to be first in the online market?**

5. **How does networking play a role in the Internet?**

6. **What are the advantages an online startup company has over a brick-and-mortar company?**

7. **How are online startup companies valued?**

8. **What are the risks involved in electronic commerce?**

9. **How is the networking and Internet industry organized?**

10. **What is the role of an incubator in the networking and Internet industry?**

11 Networks: The Future of the Industry

In this chapter...

"Life's decisions shouldn't be made with a flip of a coin when the Magic 8 Ball is available."

Anonymous

It is safe to say that we "ain't seen nothing yet" when it comes to the future of networking and the Internet. Digital communication has broken out of the hard-wired womb freeing everyone from being tied to the network with a cable. New wireless technology is in its infancy and soon you'll be able to access the Internet and private networks anytime and any place—even sitting under an umbrella on the beach.

In this chapter, you'll explore how the latest and upcoming technologies will likely change the way you work, shop, and have fun. We'll talk about:

- growth at the speed of light
- going radical
- disruptive technologies
- international outlook
- changing business climate
- customer in charge
- getting the best deals
- changing business organizations
- finance
- the law

REALITY CHECK ....

Rock 'n' roll legend Little Richard summed up how things have changed in the past 50 years in the music business when he said that the industry moved from vinyl records, to eight-tracks, to cassettes, to CDs, and to the Internet in the form of MPEG recordings.

The mother of all networks—the Internet—is becoming a global jukebox where, with a click of a mouse button, you can hear practically any song or any artist. You can download your favorite selections and burn them onto your own CD without leaving the comfort of your home.

Books, too, are on the verge of being distributed in electronic form over the Internet. Microsoft and other companies already have the technology to transform printed books into a form you and I can read on our computer or hand-held device.

I was a naysayer when I first heard about electronic books, but then so was my father when he heard about MPEG players. It took him five years to buy a CD player, which he used when jogging. Now he's an MPEG guy because the MPEG player doesn't skip when he runs around the track.

Electronic books offer convenience not found with their paper cousin. As a programmer, I'm always finding myself looking up information both at work and at home but I'm forever running into the same problems. Do I keep my books at home or in the office? How can I find the information I need immediately? How can I keep related topics in many books in one book?

The answers to all these questions are the same—an electronic book. I can buy electronic books over the Internet and store them in my own personal virtual library, which is available from any device connected to the Internet. I can even download my virtual library to my PC.

A free electronic book reader enables me to page through a book or electronically search through all my books for a particular topic. And I can copy pertinent sections of any book into a virtual binder and copy program code from a book directly into my program.

With MPEG players and electronic books, it's safe to say that we ain't seen nothing yet. The next decade is expected to change the way many of us do things. So I'm going to take my crystal ball, peer into the near future, and tell you what I think is in store for all of us, which is what this chapter is about.

GROWTH AT THE SPEED OF LIGHT.......................

Networking and the Internet are making the world smaller and changing the economic complexion of every industrialized country. I recall an economics teacher telling me that a country's labor skills and capital measures the economic power of that country. However, the Internet is changing this definition. Economic power will center on a country's capability to master information and provide services to the global market.

Worldwide trade centers on manufacturing and exchanging goods. Americans buy cars made in Germany, and Germans buy American products in return. This will change in the future when global trade expands into services such as retailing, banking, consulting, and financial services.

You don't need a crystal ball to see that the change has begun. Consulting companies in Ireland, Israel, India, and Asia that specialize in programming already have made inroads into our service industry. Many U.S. companies hire these firms to write programs for systems that are designed here.

The Internet enables programmers from anywhere in the world to log on a U.S. company's computer to write a program. The code never leaves the U.S., yet the programmer never sets foot on U.S. soil. A programmer based outside the United States interacts with a computer halfway around the world just as if the computer was on her desktop.

The Internet makes borders irrelevant for services and purchasing goods. This becomes apparent when a customer in England wants to buy a recording sold in the United States. Before the advent of the Internet, the customer had to search local retail stores hoping that the retailer or a distributor imported the recording.

Today, the customer surfs the Net and within a few mouse clicks orders the merchandise from an *e-tailer*. The customer doesn't care where the e-tailer is located. Instead the customer is interested in quality of goods, price, and delivery time.

Tech Talk
e-tailer: a retailer who sells goods on the Internet.

Follow this process to the next logical step and you can easily predict global competition among banks and other financial institutions. There will be no such thing as a local banker. Instead there will be virtual bankers available to serve you 24 hours each day of the year—and you won't know or care in which country the bank is located.

Economists predict that the Internet will combine local markets into one big market in which every business has an opportunity to compete. More than half of all U.S. residents access the Internet, which provides a vast consumer base for world merchants. Some economists estimate that this consumer base supports three-quarters of today's e-commerce.

However, the dominance of the U.S. will be challenged in the future when other countries accelerate to e-commerce. Less than one-quarter of the residents of most countries are connected to the Internet today, which means expansion is likely to occur at the speed of light.

Predicting the future, especially the economic impact of the Internet, is risky since the Internet is uncharted territory. Looking at history helps us to see if something similar has occurred before and gives us an insight into how those changes impacted the economy.

The Internet revolution is similar to the Industrial Revolution at the turn of the 1900s. Britain dominated the global economy until innovation in the United States redefined it. The U.S pushed Britain aside very quickly. The Internet revolution is likely to follow the pattern set by the Industrial Revolution in which monopolistic control over an industry erodes and changes the economic balance of power.

How long will it take before the global economy changes? That's the question economists are asking, and the answer isn't easy. A look back at history reveals that it takes 10 years for revolutionary innovations to be widely adopted throughout the world. Yet, the Internet seems to spur quicker acceptance because the cost of entering the Internet revolution can be far less than other technological advances.

For example, a small merchant in Paris can have a Net presence within a few days for a nominal expense compared to retooling by the auto industry that was necessary to adopt the manufacturing quality control developed by Japanese manufacturers.

Going Radical

The rapid development of networking and the Internet has shaken the economy and caused confusion and opportunity for radical change in almost every industry. Old, stable companies such as IBM, who seemed to always have technological answers to solve everyday problems, are challenged and surpassed by startups who were working out of their garages just a decade or so ago.

Such expansive innovation spices the marketplace and gives corporate executives an uneasiness that keeps more than a few burning the midnight oil. Industries and firms that were once predictable are now in a turmoil that many have not previously experienced.

I like to equate this to an ocean liner captain who makes the milk run between New York City and Bermuda once a week. Except for a random storm, each trip is predictable. However, market changes require abandoning Bermuda for European excursions, leaving the comfort of a weekly routine by the wayside. Customers want to vacation in Europe not Bermuda.

Are the captain's skills ready to handle the unpredictable Atlantic crossing? Will customers abandon the cruise line for more economical and convenient air travel? This shift in demand leaves the old sea captain in uncharted waters where he faces greater risk that cannot be managed based upon old experiences.

Networking and the Internet are revolutionizing how business is conducted and are leaving behind captains of those old-line companies who are unwilling or unable to manage the change. These captains are asking themselves:

- Is the Internet a fad or the new way everyone must do business?
- Must we reinvent our products and business models?
- When must decisions be made to ensure that we remain competitive?

These are tough questions to answer, especially when the old way no longer applies. Traditionally, managers used industry and corporate historical data to forecast future performance. However, historical data is useless in predicting revolutionary changes because the fundamental components of the industry are different.

Disruptive Technologies

Economists call developments such as the Internet "disruptive technologies" because they change the fundamental way business is conducted. Most changes evolve and occur incrementally. Disruptive technologies take a revolutionary approach by agitating the waters, opening opportunities for those on the bottom to quickly displace those on the top.

I've always been taught that history has a way of repeating itself, so I look back to see how similar problems were addressed whenever I come across one of those "head-scratcher" problems. Economic, industry, and company data provides insight into how common problems were handled in the past. However, these sources rarely provide any clue on how to deal with revolutionary changes caused by disruptive technologies. For this, we must look back to other times when such radical changes occurred.

If you take this trip back in history you soon discover that networking and the Internet aren't the only disruptive technologies that the world economy has experienced. As you look at each of these, you'll see how it spawned industries that we take for granted today:

- Railroads replaced horse-drawn carriages. The market for goods expanded from the area around manufacturing plants and farms to across the country, which gave birth to large manufacturing operations.

- The telephone replaced the pony express and the telegraph to become the foundation for electronic commerce. Along the way the telephone enabled instant communication and management of control over business operations over vast distances.

- The Internal combustion engine replaced horses as the means for transportation and created new industries for fuel, auto parts, and highway construction. Workers found themselves expanding their employment opportunities by traveling a greater distance to work—and returning home the same day.

- Electrical power replaced oil lights and changed every aspect of the economy. Some have compared the impact of networking and the Internet to that of electrical power because both enable people to become more efficient in the way they work. Electrical power enabled businesses to take a fresh look at how to do business.

- Radio replaced newspapers as a major source of information and entertainment and gave birth to television and the large-scale entertainment industry.

- Air travel replaced the railroad and the automobile for long distance transportation. Traveling across country or to other parts of the world took weeks for trips that today take hours.

- The transistor and integrated circuit replaced the manual processing of data. Today, we think a computer that performs a million calculations per second is slow, but we rarely stop to think the same activity required a million people at least two seconds to perform a few decades ago.

So where will the network and Internet revolution take us next? The answer I give students in my classes at Columbia University is the three Vs—video, voice, and virtual reality. The Internet will converge with televisions and provide a rich distribution pipeline that expands the creative limitations of today's *content providers*.

Tech Talk

Content provider: a person or a company that supplies information such as books, magazines, television, or radio shows over the Internet.

Voice is expected to replace the keyboard and enable us to issue voice commands to a computer—or any other device, such as televisions and appliances. You can already purchase software that recognizes your voice commands and can be used on a limited number of programs.

Virtual reality brings game technology into practical uses, such as examining conditions from a remote location. I think that doctors will once again make house calls through a convergence of cyber space and virtual reality. There are devices now in their infancy that will scan you, measure you bodily functions, and present a physician with a virtual reality image of you that is sufficient to make a diagnosis.

Tech Talk

Virtual reality: a computer simulation of something that is real.

If you're like me and become frustrated when totally irrelevant information is returned from searching the Internet, then your troubles will soon be over. New search engines are being developed that can eliminate worthless results.

Likewise, software agent technology is about to make surfing the Net unnecessary. Soon you'll be telling your computer to find you the best price for a car and software agents will do all the searching for you.

International Outlook

Consumers such as you and me tend to be country-centric in that we rarely consider buying goods that are sold outside our own country. This seems to be true whether we're from the United States or Ireland. We're not necessarily against purchasing goods made abroad as long as we have the convenience of buying them from a local store.

The Internet is rapidly changing this consumer mindset because quality information about products that are available outside a country is a mouse click away on the Internet. A consumer looking to buy a watch can go to the Web to consider offerings from around the world. Likewise, cyber garage sales and auction sites will enable merchandising to a global market.

Businesses will also find it easier and more economical to form strong partnerships with new and nontraditional countries located abroad because of the ease with which they can communicate with them over the Internet.

While consumers and firms can expect to pay higher delivery costs, such expense is likely to be offset by local economic advantages. For example, the disparity between domestic and foreign labor cost, currency fluctuations, and raw materials can make up much of the additional cost for delivery.

The expansion of competition will also enable the global buyer to set the price of goods. Today, a consumer uses the Internet to receive bids from domestic businesses. Tomorrow, global bidders will enter the competition, driving prices down.

Likewise, industries that today are not considered to have an exportable commodity will be able to enter the international marketplace through the Internet. Higher education is one of the many industries that will take advantage of this new opportunity. Today, foreign students must spend time in the United States to gain an education at an American institution. Tomorrow, the same institutions will offer distance-learning programs that enable students and faculty to hold quality classes on the Internet.

Over the next five years, experts forecast that the Internet will expand three-fold outside the United States. European and Asian countries are expected to "chip" away at the United States lead in the online market.

There will be two attacks on the United States' domination of the Internet. The initial front will be in the *business-to-consumer* market, which is what most of us consider electronic commerce. The second front will be in the *business-to-business* (B2B) market, which is expected to be far more valuable than the business-to-consumer market.

Tech Talk

Consumer-to-business: the traditional retail business model in which a consumer purchases goods from a retailer.
Business-to-business: a market in which a business purchases goods or services from suppliers, which are used to supply products and services to the consumer.

Being first has its advantages because you can corner the market and dictate the rules in the marketplace. However, you also must develop a successful business model through trial and error. I like to compare being the first to do anything similar to the pioneers. Many pioneers were wounded and died while trying to discover the way to the New World.

Those who come later have the advantage of avoiding the mistakes of the pioneers. They know what works and what does not. They also begin where the successful pioneers leave off and typically quickly move ahead of the pioneers. The United States is pioneering the Internet and Europeans and Asians are the come-latelies who will capitalize on the United States' successes and avoid its failures.

Taking advantage of the United States' successes and failures will not guarantee success abroad because local factors tend to resist rapid changes. Internet and electronic commerce growth occurs in a *local market* before serious inroads are made in the *global market*.

Tech Talk

Local market: a market within a country.
Global market: a market outside of a country.

Two factors can stymie quick acceptance of the Internet in a local market. First is the cost of starting a professional electronic Web site. Experience in the United States has shown that the startup cost is the same regardless of the country and that companies need to recover this expense from the local market before moving into the global market.

The United State has a much wider local market than other countries, which means it is easier for a domestic firm to recover cost faster than its counterpart in a foreign country.

The other factor is the economic model used for telecommunications. United States telecommunication firms charge a monthly fee that usually includes an unlimited number of local telephone calls. This enables consumers to call their local Internet Service Provider for free and stay on the Internet as long as they want.

In contrast, many European telecommunications companies charge consumers for every minute that they are connected to the Internet Service Provider, which discourages using the Internet.

Assuming these economic and technological issues are resolved, there are cultural issues that must be addressed before the visions of a global Internet marketplace become reality. Local culture and language must be reflected in Web sites designed for the international community. Consumers in each country expect to see the Web site in their own language and designed in such a way to reflect their local preferences.

These cultural barriers will take a toll on local companies' economic capabilities to enter other local markets. Each local market requires its own Web site designed to local preferences. Companies that move aggressively into multiple local markets will find themselves creating and maintaining many Web sites.

CHANGING BUSINESS CLIMATE ....

It seems that just when you think you've grasped the latest technology, a whiz kid takes it a giant step into the future. I recall a television show that perfectly describes this situation. It showed a car slowly rounding a racetrack. The car traveled at a mile an hour, then doubled its speed with each revolution. It is easy to lose track of the impact of this statement without sitting and doing the math. It takes the car six laps to reach 32 miles per hour and another four to reach 256 miles per hour. By the 11th lap the car is traveling at 512 miles per hour.

This scenario bests describes the speed at which I think business needs to change to take advantage of improvements in network and Internet technology. If you still have doubts, then compare the technological changes that occurred between the periods of 1800–1899 and 1900–2000.

The 1800s gave us the railroad, telegraph, internal combustion engine, and electricity. The 1900s gave us flight, television, satellites, space travel, and the Internet. It doesn't take a rocket scientist to recognize that the next hundred years will bring technological changes that will completely modify the complexion of all industries.

The rules of business are dramatically changing and at lightning speed. Traditionally, managers, through trial, error, and borrowing ideas from competitors, develop a way to do business called a *business model*.

Tech Talk

Business model: a description of how an organization creates profit by providing goods and services.

However, these tried and tested models are no longer meaningful in the cyber economy. College dropouts who never learned the old way of doing business—but have mastered the new technology—have created their own way of doing business, and their methods have left major corporations frozen in their tracks as they try to figure out what is happening.

Instead of spending years market researching an idea—as prescribed by business textbooks—cyber entrepreneurs go out and do it, then toy with the business until they receive public acceptance.

The Internet is very much like cable television infomercials in which you broadcast your offerings and if the phones start to ring off the hook, then you know you got it right. If the phones are silent, then you try something else. Of course, in Internet terminology, the Web sites get "hits" and not phone calls. When the hits start coming, so does the money. It took two years for Yahoo! to exceed the worth of CBS television.

The old boys business network has an unwritten rule that keeps each out of the others' territory. Instead of a fight to the death, each carves out a piece of the market and then lives together amiably. Their control of the market and the capital required to enter it is a natural barrier to competition. However, the good old boys easily got too comfortable and discarded technology—and now are being blasted out of their own marketplace by startups.

Venture capitalists supply the high stakes capital that creates limitless computer connections and databases that are available 24 hours a day, 7 days a week for free to anyone who has access to the Internet—regardless of their location in the world.

The old boys network simply cannot comprehend what is taking place because it doesn't make sense in today's market—but makes perfect sense for tomorrow's market. I recall a banker telling me that the guy who was starting our local cable company was crazy. Who in the their right mind would invest money in hanging cable from every telephone poll? The guy he was talking about was a former attorney for CBS who had the foresight to realize the potential of cable television.

In five years, cyber business has sales $50 billion shy of the $350 billion auto industry. Every industry is undergoing a rebirth and could see today's market leaders extinct unless they redefine their business model. This has already occurred in the financial sector, where consumer financial broker Merrill Lynch saw dramatic erosion of its market by upstart online brokers who offer similar service at a drastically lower cost. Merrill Lynch quickly got on board the Internet express.

Customer in Charge

Technology has introduced an element into the economy that switches the existing axiom in which business leaders tell customers what they will purchase. Customers are now in charge of their own destiny.

In the past, marketing executives used psychology and advertising to convince customers to buy their product. Logistics limited customers' choices and influences. Customers were limited to a select few stores within their area where they could comparison shop. Likewise, learning about other customers' experiences with a product was limited to friends and acquaintances. So there was a low probability that a customer would take the time to comparison shop and learn about other customers' dissatisfaction.

The Internet has made this a moot point because a cyber customer uses various technological tools before buying a product. Online stores are visited at the click of a mouse, and exited at the same speed. Price-finding software is used to seek out comparison prices for the same product without the consumer needing to visit a cyber store.

To further complicate matters, consumers are encouraged by many Web sites, such as Amazon.com and other auction sites, to comment on their experience with a product or with a vendor. Consumer feedback is shared with nearly every consumer who is a potential customer.

Companies looking to do business in cyber space can't just say they have the best product for the price; they must deliver on their claim or they'll be out of business at the click of a mouse button.

The ramifications of placing the consumer in charge of goods and services will have a dramatic impact on the way business is conducted today and to the phrase "we're lean and mean." No longer are companies able to hide behind such puff statements. They have to be lean and mean to survive because they won't have prices to support their large organizations.

Once major corporate leaders realize they can no longer sit back on their tried and true methods of doing business, they'll harness networking and technology to offer customers a level of products and services that few can imagine today.

Cyber businesses know much more about their customers than any brick-and-mortar business because technology enables businesses to watch every movement of their customers in real-time. For example, a cyber business knows exactly how each customer explores its Web site, where they came from, what pages they looked at and for how long, and what pages they didn't look at. The business can associate this information with a customer by placing a cookie on the customer's computer, asking the customer to register when entering the Web site, or whenever they make a purchase.

Information gathered by the cyber business is stored in a database as it is received from the consumer—and it can be retrieved just as quickly. Let's say you were looking for a new car and you browsed a business' Web site, stopping to read about a Mercedes Benz and staying longer on that page than other pages. The cyber business pops up a Web page that encourages you to take a look at a Lexus. The assumption was made by the computer that customers who are interested in a Mercedes Benz would also be interested in a Lexus. In fact, the computer will also determine the model and add-ons that a consumer is interested in, then use up-selling techniques to purchase a more expensive product.

Tech Talk

Up-selling: a technique used by merchants to encourage people to buy a more expensive product.

Coupons and other sales incentives that are used today to attract a broad range of customers will now be targeted to each customer. Let's say a customer favors a cyber supermarket and purchased a box of cereal every week. The supermarket's computer tracks the amount of units and when the customer bought cereal. On the next purchase, the supermarket might recommend that the customer buy a larger box of cereal and show a box that will last two weeks and save the customer money.

Networking and technology will change the way goods are manufactured. Today, manufacturers estimate consumers' needs and design products they feel fit those needs. Tomorrow, customers will tell manufacturers their specific needs and receive custom-made goods in return for this information.

For example, you'll be able to go to a clothing store where your body will be scanned by a computer—or a scanner might be an attachment to your computer. You then select the material and style of clothes. Your selection and your measurements are sent electronically to the manufacturing plant where a computer drives plant equipment to create customized garments at the same price as off-the-shelf clothes.

Who needs *middlemen*? The supply line between manufacturer and consumer is eroding and is causing a headache for every industry. A manufacturer can offer its wares directly to the consumer or at least to an online reseller without having to flow through normal distribution channels.

Tech Talk

Middleman: the person or company that distributes merchandise from a manufacturer to a retailer.

However, the transition from today to the day when there will be fewer middlemen is fraught with danger. Businesses cannot abandon the existing distribution channels until their cyber business flourishes. Yet if they don't exploit new cyber channels, some upstart will take over their market share.

Getting the Best Deals

"Have I got a deal for you!" That's a phrase that you won't be hearing too much in the future because the way we agree on a price for anything is changing. At one point most goods were purchased the way most of us buy cars—through negotiations. We would go to the market and haggle with the merchant to arrive at the best deal.

Haggling over price was seen as a cost-effective way to determine the fair market value of goods. Good negotiators spent less than poor negotiators for the same goods. Businesses also negotiated for everything; however, the results of poor negotiations could lose a competitive advantage and maybe lose the business.

Negotiating prices was seen as being too volatile except for high-price or high-volume purchases, which were traditional. By the turn of the 20th century, the economy moved to fixed pricing. Merchants set prices based on competition in the market rather than negotiate prices with each customer.

At the beginning of the 21st century, the way goods are priced will change once again to a more dynamic pricing method in the form of *auctions*, *cooperatives*, and *bartering*. For example, some experts estimate that 15 percent of all e-commerce is conducted at auctions in which the quoted price is the starting position for negotiation.

Tech Talk

Auctions: the place where a merchant sells goods to the highest bidder.
Cooperatives: a place where consumers join together to buy a large quantity of the same good at a lower price than if they bought the merchandise individually.
Bartering: a process in which goods or services are exchanged in place of currency.

And even the traditional auction process is undergoing a revolution that moves bargaining power away from the seller and to the buyer. Some Web sites such as Mercata form an instant cooperative group that agrees to purchase the same product. The Web site then uses this volume purchase to drive prices down.

Still other Web sites, such as Priceline.com, can elicit lower than publicized prices by agreeing to strip away conveniences. Let's say a customer is flexible in departure time; he could purchase an airline ticket at below advertised prices.

Shopping for the best price is going by the wayside. Today, Internet-savvy consumers needs to visit auction and reverse-auction sites to find the best deal. In the future, the best deals will find the consumer. Automatic shopping agents will take a consumer's request for a product and wander the Internet searching for the best price.

Price will be the only factor that differentiates merchants. Factors that are now considered competitive assets are liabilities in the future. We only need to look at the book industry to see how *fixed asset* is an anchor in the race to capture consumers. Barnes and Noble has fixed assets of $472 million, while Amazon.com has $56 million in fixed assets. This difference alone enabled Amazon.com to be in a better position to offer more competitive prices for longer periods than their competitors.

Tech Talk

Fixed asset: a physical object, such as an office building, a manufacturing plant, or a warehouse.

Sales and support staff also become a liability in the cyber economy because businesses don't need them. Instead of hiring an army of people, cyber businesses will computerize nearly all business operations and outsource labor-intensive operations to business partners.

Cisco Systems, the maker of routers and other network devices, is an example of how businesses will function tomorrow. Seventy-eight percent of all orders are received over the Internet and employees touch half of those. Orders flow directly from the customer to one of Cisco's 30 plants, only two of which are owned by Cisco. The remaining plants are owned by business partners. These partnerships can be formed and dissolved quickly based upon quality and demand. This is called *dynamic trade*, in which the lines between corporations are blurred.

Tech Talk

Dynamic trade: trade in which a corporation forms strategic alliances to meet market demands. Realignments are made based on changes in demand.

Industries will be transforming themselves into new lean and mean operations in which price and quality are the only things that will keep them competitive. No longer will bulk and market share be sufficient to dictate terms of sale.

Remember how "Big Blue" (IBM) thought they were the only game in town when it came to computer power, until a few college dropouts started Microsoft. No doubt the gray suits at IBM laughed when they first heard of Bill Gates' efforts.

The same is true in all industries. Both mom and pop and major retailers are fearful of giants like Wal-Mart coming into town. Yet they probably give little thought to online grocery upstarts who are building massive warehouses in strategic areas of the country, which can be used to deliver groceries to any house.

Price is the game and fixed assets are liabilities and because firms don't require a large fixed asset to offer cyber merchandise, it is difficult for established companies to recognize their future competition.

Changing Business Organizations

Some large companies, such as Sears, recognized the influence computer networks could have on their business operations and decided to link their entire supply chain. The process began with merchandising managers in each store who determined the quality of various products they wanted to sell.

Their requests were placed in an *Electronic Data Interchange (EDI)* system, which distributed them to the distribution center, to the manufacturing plant, and to raw material suppliers. If the distribution center was running low on the product, then a request to replenish stock was sent to the manufacturing plant, which in turn sent the request for raw materials to suppliers. All transactions were conducted by the EDI system.

Tech Talk

Electronic Data Interchange (EDI): the process by which corporations link computer systems to suppliers.

While this streamlined operations, it was also very expensive to build and maintain. Only very large corporations could afford an EDI system and even those firms could link the system to only 20 percent of their business partners.

The Internet will change this because each business partner is already connected to the Internet and can exchange information with anyone else who is connected to it without the expense of an EDI system. We can expect that a manufacturer who is not conducting business on the Internet will not be in business in the future.

Custom manufacturing will replace mass production because organizations such as Cisco use networks and the Internet to redefine how goods are sold and manufactured. The process begins with a customer who enters an order by visiting the Cisco Web site. Software prompts the customer through the selection process and verifies that all the necessary information is provided on the order.

Next are the manufacturing and the accounting systems. Software routes the order to the appropriate vendor, who assembles the product and ships it directly to the customer. Once shipped, the accounting system completes the transaction. There are no sales representatives, clerks, or anyone else except for a customer service representative who is sitting by the phone to help the customer through the process if necessary. Cisco monitors every aspect of the manufacturing process using the Internet.

Automobile manufacturers such as Volvo (a subsidiary of Ford) are testing the viability of collecting sales orders over the Internet. Today this is limited to Belgium, but soon it could be the way all of us buy cars.

The future will see industry change radically from fully integrated operations to business partners that need only do one thing very well. Let's say that you have an idea for a product. Instead of creating a large business operation to design, manufacture, and market your product, you build alliances with business partners. One partner designs the product. Another manufacturers it, and still another markets the product. Your role is to supply the capital and coordinate their efforts. Distributing the effort among business partners introduces flexibility that isn't available in today's economy. And networking and the Internet make this feasible.

Henry Ford's statement that a customer can buy any color car as long as it was black no longer holds true in cyber technology. The new slogan—actually this is a bit old—is "Have it your way." Customization must be the objective of every company, for not only does it please customers, it also saves money.

Ask yourself this question: Is it better to have products sitting in the warehouse or in the consumer's hands? The answer is obvious, yet the auto industry warehouses weeks' worth of cars every day on dealer lots because they don't have the product the customer wants.

Move ahead a few years in cyber space to a time when you choose from a range of options the exact car you want, on the Internet. A week after you click your mouse button, the car is delivered to your house.

Every car manufactured this way is already sold, eliminating the need to have cars sit idly on dealers' lots waiting for the right buyer. Experts claim that companies could increase profit by 30 percent—or pass the savings along to customers.

Organizations will be powerless to compete in the cyber economy without the right technology and a talented technical staff. Capital and strategies aren't sufficient to keep pace with the Internet marketplace. Instead, firms must have a technologist who can create and implement technological solutions quickly.

There are three factors that are guaranteed in life: death, taxes, and today's technology becoming obsolete within two years. To complicate matters is that talented technologists are in short supply. Companies looking to remain competitive must develop a strategy for attracting, retaining, and training employees; firms that do will take market share.

The future will see a shift in jobs. The Internet directly links customers with manufacturers. Those positions that form that link today will no longer be necessary. We could see technical jobs going wanting along with unemployment rising in non-technical areas.

Finance

Changes that the Internet brings to the global economy have far-reaching effects on the stability of the financial markets. Each country controls its financial markets through regulation and manipulation of economic factors by central banks. When the economy becomes sluggish, financial controls are activated to get it moving again. When the economy overheats, central bankers pull in the reins. Local economies have a direct bearing on global economies through import regulations that are negotiated by financial representatives of each government.

However, the Internet will cause turbulence in what seems to be controlled local and global economies because it has no country boundaries. Financial needs, such as loans and investments, will be fulfilled by the global market rather than a local banker or a broker. Customers will deal directly with issues of securities and notes instead of going through middlemen as they do today.

The trend will be toward consumers doing everything themselves rather than getting advice from the experts. For example, consumers will take hold of their retirement funds and use the Internet to invest.

The transition from slow moving, predictable economic mobility to one that moves at the speed of light will be tumultuous, to say the least. Consumers will have the same power as professional Wall Street traders, and be able to invest 24 hours a day in markets throughout the world. Such global trading will grow local economies, but at a steep price.

Rules that control local economies must be expanded to consider global influence, otherwise international consumers will take their business elsewhere. Most governments will be unwilling to give up their rights to set rules governing their local economy.

Furthermore, market stability is in jeopardy because consumers will be making financial decisions based on herd mentality instead of sound financial thinking. For example, when stocks begin to dip, consumers intuitively sell out their positions, which of course causes stocks to fall, causing more frenzy.

Unlike professional traders, consumers lack the knowledge and the financial strength to stay the course in a market downturn. And to further complicate matters, consumers will have the power through the Internet to trade in all world markets. Therefore, a dramatic drop in the London market will keep dropping in the United States and then through Asia.

New regulations must be created in all world markets to coordinate efforts to control any waves of consumer optimism and pessimism; otherwise we'll lose the market order that was established after the stock market crash of 1929.

The Law

The factors that will hinder rapid growth of networking and the Internet aren't technologies, but rules of each country that govern various aspects of business. The Internet crosses both local and national jurisdictions and is causing havoc with those seeking to enforce existing laws.

The story of a French model illustrates this point. Her nude photos were reprinted on the Internet without her permission, which is a clear case of copyright infringement. She brought the issue to court and won. The company that hosted the Web site was fined $70,000 by a French judge.

The company that hosted the site claimed it was not responsible for the content because another company owned that. It only provided disk space and connection to the Internet. In response to the fine, the Web site hosting company shut down its servers, putting 4,000 French e-businesses out of business. In addition, the company threatened to open business outside the country and bring with it the 4,000 e-businesses.

Web site owners around the world came to the defense of the Web site hosting company by reprinting the model's photo on thousands of Web sites, most of which were outside the jurisdiction of the French court. A truce was eventually made when the hosting company agreed to give $7,000 to the model's favorite charity.

The Internet is considered the Wild West of cyber space because legal ramifications of the Internet parallel those of the unsettled old West, where anything goes regardless of the law. Lawmakers in every country are now seeking to tame the Internet, but its growth is far outpacing the legal machinery.

Problems stem from distribution of pornography to minors, to copyright violations, to all-out electronic fraud. The problem is so immense that governments alone can't bring law and order to cyber space without the full participation of its residents, such as Internet providers, Web site operators, and Web site hosting companies.

There is a huge incentive for self-regulation because the Internet is going to become a $3 trillion global marketplace if consumers feel safe conducting business in cyber space. The stakes are high.

It is easy for everyone to say that something must be done, however, achieving the objective is more complex than the Internet itself. Think of the time that you tried to get four of your friends to agree on a place to go on a Saturday night. It takes me a whole week to get everyone in agreement and there is usually one guy who backs out at the last minute.

Now imagine trying to get the governments of the leading countries in the world to agree upon rules to govern the Internet. It's a nightmare. The Organization for Economic Cooperation and Development in Paris has been doing just that for years and hasn't ironed out even the most basic Internet laws.

Here's a typical problem. A United States Web site hosted by a French Web site defrauds a customer in Japan. Which country has jurisdiction? This is a tough problem and an agreement was reached that the seller's home country had jurisdiction. However, who sold the merchandise? Was it the Web site or the Web site hosting company? Do they really expect a Japanese customer to be able to take legal action half way around the world? The expense alone would probably cost more than the merchandise.

Then there is the tax issue. Sales over the Internet are not taxed, although many states have laws requiring its residents to pay sales tax on any merchandise they receive through the mail. Of course, this is on the honor system.

Internet sales will have a serious impact on the financial stability of many locales since sales taxes funds many government operations. Should a sales tax be imposed on merchandise bought over the Internet? Probably. However, collecting the sales tax is a problem. A national commission in the United States is deadlocked on how to do so after studying this problem for years.

There are more than 50 sales taxes currently imposed on various merchandise. Who is going to identify where each applies and how are they going to collect the sales tax? Let's say a New Jersey resident buys an item from a California company whose Web site is hosted in New York City. Does the customer pay New Jersey, New York, or California sales tax, or a combination? And who collects those taxes?

Some suggest the federal government collect an Internet sales tax and distributed it to each taxing jurisdiction. This is a logistic nightmare because local sales taxes are not uniform. Also, few trust the federal government to forward all the taxes without keeping a few pennies for itself.

Others suggest that an independent, nonprofit organization be formed to oversee an Internet sales tax. This, too, sounds like a good idea, but one only needs to look at the Internet to see a problem. The Internet Corporation for Assigned Names and Numbers (ICANN) is doing all it can to manage Internet addressing. These are addresses that contain two pieces of information: a name (i.e., *www.keogh.org*) and an IP number, both of which are uniform.

Another legal hurdle is privacy. Web site owners gather information about every customer's buying habits along with financial information such as a credit card number. Credit card information can be correlated with personal information stored in credit reports and linked to medical records stored electronically by insurance companies.

Before the Internet took hold of companies, government agencies could easily assemble a profile of anyone who bought on credit because we voluntarily provide vast amounts of personal data to the credit bureau.

Few of us stop to realize that we have little privacy, which is about to evaporate totally when we enter cyber space. Here's what the government can find out about you without having to speak with you:

- Telephone records identify everyone you call, including the time, date, your location, and the other person's location.

- Credit card records identify what you buy, where you shop, when you shop, and the amount you pay.

- Gasoline credit card or any credit card used to fuel your car reveals where you purchase fuel and how much. When this is compared with motor vehicle records, it can be estimated how far you traveled from the last place you received fuel.

- Cellular telephone can pinpoint your exact location when you receive a telephone call, as well as the date and time the call was received.

- The banking system tracks nearly every penny you earn and save. Your employer reports your pay to the government. Bank records can easily be used to trace deposits and withdrawals.

- Insurance claims detail your medical condition.

If all of these records are combined and organized in sequence, anyone looking at these records has a complete picture of your finances, buying habits, daily routine, and health without notifying you.

Now let's fastforward a few years and bring the Internet into the picture. No one tells you that information is being collected about you every time that you visit a Web page or send an e-mail, but it will be happening.

Your computer is assigned a temporary IP address when you connect to your Internet Service Provider (ISP). The date, time, IP address, and your account number are saved in a file. Every Web site you visit electronically stores the pages you view and how long you visit each page. This information will be able to be linked backed to your temporary IP address and to you even if you don't "sign in" to a Web site or make a purchase from the site.

This means that all of your movements on the Internet can be tracked and stored in an electronic file that can be used by anyone who has access to the file to develop a profile of your habits. They'll be able to assemble a list of your interests at the click of a mouse button.

Many believe the Internet gives everyone freedom of speech because you can post any comment for all to read. However, Web site operators, Web host operators, employers, and government agencies will one day monitor Internet communications.

Software that looks for keywords and phrases in e-mail chat rooms and other kinds of Internet communication will perform the monitoring. This will be like having someone reading your mail without your permission—and without your knowledge.

You may think I'm one of those radicals who feel Big Brother is watching my every move. I assure you, I'm not. However, privacy will be eroded under the claim of national security and efforts to stop criminals.

Wouldn't you want the government to prevent terrorism? Of course, but to do so the government must read all e-mail in an effort to identify terrorists. If you think I'm exaggerating, then consider Japan, which is expected to give police the right to intercept e-mail without any suspicion of criminal activity.

Keep in mind that I'm not simply talking about the United States government. Remember, the Internet is global, so laws in one country might prohibit snooping, but laws in another might encourage it.

Two of the biggest electronic commerce economies, the European Union and the United States, are seeking to create a self-regulatory body that prohibits the export of data that doesn't adhere to their standards. However, a number of e-commerce businesses refuse to obey these rules, which only increases the lawlessness of cyber space.

Cyber law is something everyone can agree to in principle, but there isn't agreement on the details, and that will continue to prevent an orderly structure of electronic commerce. In the absence of cyber police and cyber courts, businesses that are taking leadership roles are trying to establish market standards that ensure customers, investors, and business partners a secure place to conduct business. These standards will become the unwritten law of the land that is enforced by consumers who take their business to only those merchants who adhere to these standards.

A major legal hassle of doing business online is a signature. Purchases of substantial value or services with a duration of more than a year typically require both parties to sign a binding contract. However, the legal community is wrestling with how to obtain these signatures electronically over the Internet.

Technologists have devised digital codes that uniquely identify an individual and deem the code an electronic signature.

So those looking to do business on the Internet will find a growing audience for their products and services along with a mine field of legal trouble that could scuttle their operations or ruin customer confidence the first time a deal sours.

SUMMARY ....

My crystal ball tells me that networks and the Internet are disruptive technologies that will change the economic and legal framework of every industrialized country. This technology makes country borders irrelevant in the purchase of goods and services. As long as goods and services can be delivered to a customer, the merchant's location is no longer meaningful.

The ability to make purchases around the clock on any day has an enormous ramification to the way we live and work. For one thing, competition for consumers will be fierce because purchasing decisions will be based on price and quality rather than on market share and advertising.

Consumers, businesses, and governments will have to change the way they interact with each other. Consumers can comparison shop at the click of a mouse button and will soon employ BOTs, which are programs, to impartially search the corners of the Internet for the best deals.

Businesses can no longer count on investments in fixed assets and capitalization to hold on to market share. Factors that give businesses advantages today will become liabilities on the Internet because traditional barriers to startups entering the market no longer exist. With an investment of a million dollars anyone can open an online business that gives him or her the same opportunity for customers that established companies have.

A new way of doing business will be sweeping across industries. Rather than form large, fully integrated companies, online upstarts create strategic alliances with business partners to form a dynamic, yet fully integrated operation that supplies consumers with goods and services. The combination of low cost of entry into mature markets and strategic alliances places startup businesses on the same footing as the old-line conglomerates.

Governments will quickly see a loss of power in three fronts: legal, economic, and financial. The Internet collapses local markets into one global market in which transactions cross oceans in the same vein as you and I make purchases at our local grocery.

Therefore, local and national laws governing how we transact business must be enhanced to address multiple jurisdiction that cross language and cultural barriers. How will a consumer in Japan who purchases goods from a French online merchant whose Web site is hosted in the United States, enforce a commercial agreement?

There is no easy answer. Governments have been trying to address such concerns for years and have yet to make any headway toward a resolution. This has left cyber space lawless, which can make consumers uneasy about participating in the new global market.

The Internet gives local economies a new face and poses new problems. The global economy is a delicate balancing act between the well being of each country's economy and international trade. Central banks and governments within each industrialized country influence economic growth by adjusting interest rates and government spending.

If an inflationary trend is seen, in which too much money is chasing too few goods, then higher interest rates are used to bring money and prices back in line. Likewise, if there are more goods for sale than consumer demand, government spending is increased to stir economic growth.

Governments control the world economy by influencing the rate of exchange of currencies and by imposing import and export taxes. Let's say that you want to purchase a Japanese-made automobile and you live in the United States. The Japanese auto manufacturer wants yen in exchange for the car. However, you have dollars.

Therefore, somewhere along the transaction process (usually handled by the United States importer of Japanese cars) dollars must be converted to yen. The number of yen that is exchanged for one dollar is called the exchange rate.

The exchange rate increases whenever United States consumers want to purchase Japanese goods because more consumers require yen than dollars—unless Japanese consumers purchase an equivalent amount of United States goods. In this case, the demand for yen moves into a balanced position with dollars.

However, as the exchange rate increases, it reaches a point at which the price of the merchandise in dollars is higher than a similar domestic product. The price for the Japanese product is too high. Governments can influence exchange rates by purchasing more of the currency or by imposing an import or export tax, which in effect raises the price of goods.

The Internet will increase the volume of exported goods to levels that have not been seen before. Exports will become a major portion of domestic economies and require a coordinated effort among governments to provide a balance of trade; otherwise, exports could plunge domestic economy into a depression.

To a great extent, local governments are funded through sales taxes on goods sold within their locale. Sales tax is not collected on Internet sales, although consumers are on the honor system to pay such tax. The anticipated rapid increase in Internet sales is expected to cause havoc on funding local governments —and there is no easy way to collect sales tax on Internet sales.

Few economy, business, or government leaders disagree with the forecast that networking and the Internet will revolutionize our daily lives. However, the question that remains unanswered is "When will the full effect of the Internet be felt?".

My crystal ball tells me that it will take about 10 years before the way we do things today becomes old fashioned. This projection is based on fact. Looking back to other disruptive technologies and revolutionary innovations, we see that a decade passes between their onset and becoming widely adopted throughout the world.

Therefore, 10 years from now when you prepare this book for a garage sale you'll be thinking back and saying, "I remember the good old days when I couldn't find a parking space at the mall and when books were printed on paper."

Summary Questions

1. What is the concept of disruptive technologies?

2. What are the difficulties creating and enforcing laws on the Internet?

3. How would you solve the Internet sales tax problem?

4. Why would a consumer not purchase goods on the Internet?

5. What is the concept of the business-to-business model?

6. What is the concept of the business-to-consumer model?

7. How could major corporations lose market share to Internet upstart companies?

8. Why are foreign corporations at a disadvantage creating a Web site as compared to corporations in the United States?

9. How do cultural differences affect Web site design and operation?

10. What effects do fixed assets have on operating an online business?

Appendix A

Network: Profiles of the Major Players

There is a revolution afoot by network and Internet technologies that is going to change how each of us conducts business. No longer will we need to drive to a shopping mall and battle for a parking space because all merchants will be just a telephone call away.

The revolution is being lead by a group of companies, many of whom you've probably never heard of because they are quietly doing their magic out of sight of the press. In this appendix, you'll find a brief introduction to 33 of these companies. I've included their URLs so you'll be able to quickly find out more about each of them. They are grouped into four categories: electronic commerce, network software/services, network hardware, and network communication.

ELECTRONIC COMMERCE SEGMENT ....

Electronic commerce is changing the way consumers and businesses make purchases. Today you can review offerings of competing vendors online, make a purchase with the click of a mouse button, and receive the goods a few days later.

Online e-tailers have penetrated about 20 percent of the brick-and-mortar retail market and have clear plans to capture the rest. However, the most promising online market is the business-to-business sector, where businesses can tap into a vast array of suppliers online to find the best deal.

Here are important players in the electronic commerce segment of the industry.

CMGI   www.cmgi.com

CMGI is in the business of creating and managing the largest, most diverse network of Internet companies in the world. The firm consists of a network of diverse yet interconnected companies all holding leadership positions, or the promise of leadership, in Internet-related businesses.

CMGI owns and invests exclusively in business-to-business and business-to-consumer companies that fall into one of four core areas of the Internet economy: marketing/advertising, e-commerce, content and community, and enabling technology.

The company began 30 years ago in the business-to-business market selling mailing lists and direct marketing services. It then formed an affiliated venture capital division focused on the Internet, which later developed into its major market.

DoubleClick   www.doubleclick.net

DoubleClick sells online ad space, delivers online ads, and markets ad-tracking software that is used by 10,000 Web sites. Among its major clients are Microsoft and IBM. The company's objective is to provide a global Internet advertising solution.

The DoubleClick network is a network of networks and is made up of six leading networks of premium content in the following areas: auto, business, entertainment, technology, travel, and women/health.

The company offers a product called DART that matches advertiser-selected target profiles with individual user profiles and delivers an appropriately targeted ad. Another product called DoubleClick Local allows advertisers to precisely target their advertisements to the states, zip codes, and area numbers in which they do business.

EarthLink Network   www.earthlink.net

EarthLink Network is an Internet service provider (ISP) that connects three million users to the Internet and provides DSL services to its customers. It is one of the nation's largest ISPs. The company began when its founders realized consumers had difficulty accessing the Internet because of the difficulty in installing Internet software and the lack of technical support. They created a user-friendly and reliable Internet connection.

The company is the default Internet service provider for Packard Bell and NEC computers. It is also the default Internet software for Apple computer's iMac. In addition, the company is expanding its exposure with alliances with Sprint and the National Football League and is the official ISP for CompUSA, one of the nation's largest computer retailers.

Knight/Trimark Group www.knight-sec.com

Knight/Trimark Group is the company that handles much of the back office for online trading. The company brought together a consortium of more than 25 securities firms to pool their trading volume for execution.

Knight/Trimark Group's trading methodology is focused on real-time analysis of market activity and price movements. This enables them to manage risk better and quickly adjust trading strategy in an effort to maximize trading profits. Throughout the business day, they continually analyze your trading positions in individual securities and monitor your short and long positions and your aggregate profits and losses. They use this information to assess market trends and adjust its trading strategy on a real-time basis in an effort to maximize its trading profits.

The company, which is the number one execution destination for trades originating over the Internet, is the unseen "processing power" behind the explosive growth in online securities trading.

RealNetworks www.real.com

RealNetworks is the pioneer and market leader in streaming media technology on the Internet and its products enable Web sites to broadcast music and videos over the Web and Intranets.

In 1995, the company launched its first RealPlayer, which is used by consumers to receive music and videos on their browser. There are currently more than 95 million RealPlayers in use and 175,000 RealPlayers are downloaded for free every day.

RealNetworks' software is sold to Web broadcasters and is used to transmit 145,000 hours of live sports, music, news, and entertainment each week. Web broadcasting is expected to make major inroads once every home and office is connected via fiber optics.

VerticalNet www.verticalnet.com

VerticalNet operates 50 trading communities that provide a place where vendors can sell goods to industrial audiences. Each community is individually branded by industry and caters to individuals with similar professional interests, giving business professionals the best value for their time on the Web.

In addition to being an online marketplace, each community also contains editorial content and career centers that foster a community atmosphere instead of just an e-commerce store. VerticalNet has partnered with content providers and information and technology distributors.

VerticalNet communities contain high-quality content, including product information in buyers' guides, supplier and product directories, daily industry news and articles, job listings, and classifieds. In addition, VerticalNet's sites enable business-to-business exchanges of information, supplementing existing trade shows and trade association activities. When combined, these factors create user communities unique to the Internet and are a catalyst for heightened information exchange among experts in these individual fields.

NETWORK SOFTWARE/SERVICES SEGMENT...........

Electronic commerce requires network software and services to flourish, otherwise Web site operators are unable to display their offerings and provide the "bells and whistles" that attract visitors to their sites.

The network software/service segment of the industry provides various products and services that ensure a good consumer experience whenever an online store or Web site is visited. The future for this segment of the industry is bright because of the ever-increasing demands by Web site operators to keep their site state-of-the-art.

Here are key players in the network software/services segment of the industry.

BroadVision   www.broadvision.com

BroadVision markets software that enables users to tailor Web sites to manage order fulfillment, billing, payment, and customer service. Their products are suited for high-volume Internet retail e-commerce sites and business-to-business e-commerce sites.

Two key factors in BroadVision's products are personalized service to consumers and rapid deployment of secure and scalable e-business applications. Broad-Vision's target markets are firms that want to create a Web presence quickly and give their customers a personalized experience.

BroadVision provides a personal financial portal application for banking, brokerage transactions, and billing, as well as cross-sell and up-sell campaigns. In addition, it offers a personalized electronic billing, payment, and customer self-care solution that enables efficient relationship management for e-business.

Citrix Systems   www.citrix.com

Citrix Systems develops Internet application server software and has a client list that includes Microsoft, Cadbury Schweppes, and the United States Navy, among other leading companies. A key factor in Citrix Systems' services is digital independence, which is the ability to run any application on any device with any connection. This includes wireless connection to the Internet.

Applications are installed and updated on servers instead of on each client and this reduces the complexity, time, and resources required to manage the applications. Citrix Systems' products accelerate application deployment, provide predictable service with centralized management, and work independently of bandwidth.

In 1997, Microsoft licensed Citrix Systems to create a multi-user version of Windows NT Server 4.0, which is incorporated in Windows 2000 Terminal Services. Other licensees of Citrix Systems' products include Compaq, IBM, Sun Microsystems, Hewlett Packard, and Motorola.

Concentric Network   www.concentric.com

Concentric Network provides an assortment of Internet services for companies like Microsoft's WebTV Networks and AT&T. These services include Web hosting, Internet telephony and virtual private networks.

The company's services rely on a high-performance, Asynchronous Transmission Mode (ATM) based network that covers North America, backed by constant customer support. It has strategic alliances that extend their reach to South America, Europe, and the Pacific Rim.

Concentric Network targets small- and medium-sized businesses for high-speed dedicated and DSL access, Web hosting, and e-commerce services. They also customize virtual private networks for large organizations.

Exodus Communications   www.exodus.net

Exodus Communications hosts servers and manages Web sites for major e-commerce Web sites that include CBS Sports and eBay. The company has pioneered the Internet data center market where it provides scalable, flexible, and secured servers for high transaction, mission-critical Internet operations.

The company offers a sophisticated system and network management solutions, along with technology professional services to provide optimal performance for customers' Web sites. Exodus Communications manages its network infrastructure via a worldwide network of Internet data centers located in the United States, Europe, and Asia.

Within these facilities Exodus Communications is able to deliver the highest levels of reliability. It does this through a number of redundant subsystems, such as multiple fiber trunks coming into each Internet data center from multiple sources, fully redundant power on the premises, and multiple backup generators.

Inktomi   www.inktomi.com

Inktomi develops high-performance networked information and infrastructure applications and has built the search engine technology used by Yahoo! and Lycos. Its customers are Internet service providers and backbone carriers.

The company built the first large-scale commercial network cache, called the traffic server. The traffic server reduces massive congestion over the Internet, increases overall network efficiency, and can handle more than a terabyte of data.

Inktomi's search engine handles massive data and large user bases without requiring expensive multiprocessor supercomputers. Its features include regional or global Internet searching, retrieval systems for large text archives, and powerful online search support for published archives. The company has also developed a shopping engine that enables users to compare merchandise on price, reviews, and user commentary.

Macromedia   www.macromedia.com

Macromedia markets an assortment of tools that enable designers to easily publish Web pages, CD, video, and graphics on the Internet. The company's software tools are used to design major Web sites.

The company's objective is to add life to the Web and transform the Web experience by delivering a completely new generation of Internet products. Its tools are used to build interactive Web sites and sophisticated animation.

Macromedia is expanding beyond shrink-wrapped software to include systems and servers that focus on Web publishing and Web learning. They are bringing Web learning solutions to corporations.

Microsoft   www.microsoft.com

Microsoft provides the operating system used by most personal computers and many servers including those used to host Internet applications and e-commerce. The company offers a wide range of products that include the SQL Server used to store and retrieve data, a communications server, WebTV, the Microsoft Network, and a commerce server.

Others products include operating systems for personal computers and networks, server applications for client/server environments, business and consumer productivity applications, interactive media programs, and Internet platform and development tools. Microsoft also offers online services, personal computer books and input devices, and it researches and develops advanced technology software products.

Microsoft products, available in more than 30 languages and in more than 50 countries, are available for most PCs, including Intel microprocessor-based computers and Apple computers.

Network Associates   www.networkassociate.com

Network Associates is the manufacturer of the number one encryption and anti-virus software and is the world's largest independent network security and management software company.

Its brands include McAfee anti-virus, PGP encryption, Gauntlet firewall, Magic Help Desk applications, and the Sniffer family of network analyzers, which serve 60 million customers around the world.

Network Associates' strategy is to empower clients to move from responsive and reactive to strategic and proactive by leveraging the interactive, open architecture and enabling individual security products to operate in concert, actively communicating alerts and adapting security policies for real-time response when threats are detected.

Network Solutions   www.netsol.com

Network Solutions is the world's largest registrar of Internet domain names and is expanding into other information technology services. The company has issued more than 8.1 million domain names since 1993.

The company has mastered the technique of scalability, which it shares with clients. It took four years to register the first one million domain names. However, Network Solutions now takes 11 weeks to register a million domain names by employing scalable technology.

The government has forced competition in the domain registry market, so Network Solutions has branched out to other areas, such as developing the largest find engines on the Internet and Web design services for budget-conscious small businesses.

Oracle   www.oracle.com

Oracle manufactures database software used by many e-commerce companies. Oracle is the first software company to develop and deploy 100 percent Internet-enabled enterprise software across its entire product line: database, server, enterprise business applications, and application development and decision support tools.

The company offers its database, tools, and application products, along with related consulting, education, and support services, in more than 145 countries around the world. This includes professional services for help in formulating e-business strategy, as well as in designing, customizing, and implementing e-business solutions and a comprehensive suite of Internet-enabled business applications.

Oracle is also exploiting the Intranet market and is helping companies replace expensive, unwieldy client/server computing applications with innovative applications that can be accessed with a Web browser.

Razorfish   www.razorfish.com

Razorfish is an e-commerce consulting firm that advises major organizations on Web strategy and systems integration. Its clients include Charles Schwab, Time Warner, and the Smithsonian Institution.

The company plans, designs, and builds products and services that make it seamless for an organization to gain a Web presence. The firm uses a holistic approach to a client's problem and reinvents the client's entire operation rather than concentrate on a client's Web operation. This is what makes Razorfish stand out from other e-commerce consultants.

Razorfish developed a proprietary process for conceptualizing, planning, and executing solutions to complex business problems that centers on five phases, which are business strategy, marketing and branding, technology, and user-centered design.

Security First Technologies   www.s1.com

Security First Technologies provides software that enables financial institutions to put their banking operations online. The company started out as one of the first online banks, but this failed so it capitalized on its experience and the technology it developed by offering a turnkey operation for major financial institutions.

Security First Technologies' client list includes financial institutions in 11 countries. Some of its clients include ABN AMRO, Banque Nationale de Paris, Chase Manhattan, Citibank, Huntington Bancshares, Net.B@nk, Royal Bank of Canada, Wachovia, and Wingspanbank.com.

The company's software provides a variety of services, including consumer electronic bill payment and business cash management. Scalability and customization are key aspects of its products. Security First Technologies is able to handle small and large clients and meet their unique needs by modifying their software.

TMP Worldwide   www.tmpw.com

TMP Worldwide provides various locator services for businesses. Services include online recruiting, physician locator and information service, online Yellow Pages, and customer prospecting and servicing.

The company operates Monster.com, the Internet's leading personnel recruiting service, which records 6.7 million visits per month. Monster.com is expanding to Australia, Canada, England, France, Belgium, and the Netherlands. It is also targeting industries with Monster Campus, Monster Mid-Career, Monster Executive, Monster Technology, Monster Healthcare, Monster HR, and Monster International.

TMP Worldwide maintains the electronic version of the American Board of Medical Specialties Public Education Program's physician locator and information service. This enables people to search for a physician free of charge by specialty and geographic (zip code) location.

USWeb/CKS   www.uswebcks.com

USWeb/CKS develops Web sites, e-commerce applications, and advertising campaigns for major e-commerce companies. Its client list includes Charles Schwab, Apple Computer, and Levi Strauss. The company has built and implemented strategic branding and advertising, systems integration, network design, and e-commerce solutions for Fortune 500 companies.

USWeb/CKS is capitalizing on its time-to-value strategy by reducing the amount of time a client requires to become an e-commerce player. Clients use the company's expertise to reduce the time to get both the physical Web site and market recognition working.

The company has proven methods for a client to differentiate its products and build integrated marketing and branding campaigns. These campaigns deliver consistent messages to break through the Web chatter that bombards e-commerce consumers.

NETWORK HARDWARE SEGMENT ....

Cables, high-speed modems, enterprise servers, and switches are a few of the hardware components that keep the Internet humming. There is a heavy demand on the network hardware segment to provide broadband networking components that can transmit audio, video, and data at acceptable levels.

The demand for new and improved network hardware devices has opened vast opportunities for corporations in this industry segment that will last for decades. Here are important members of the network hardware segment of the Internet industry.

Broadcom   www.broadcom.com

Broadcom is a chip maker whose products are used in cable modems and high-speed networking circuits that are used to connect locations to the Internet. Broadcom's products enable the high-speed transmission of data over existing communications infrastructures, most of which were not originally intended for digital data transmission.

You'll find Broadcom's chips in cable set-top boxes, cable modems, high-speed office networks, home networking, direct broadcast satellite and terrestrial digital broadcast, and digital subscriber line. Broadcom has strategic customer relationships with 3Com, Nortel-Bay, Cisco Systems, General Instrument, Motorola, Panasonic, and Scientific-Atlanta.

At the heart of Broadcom's success is its capability to develop advanced digital signal processing hardware architectures, new communications systems algorithms and protocols, and high-performance analog and mixed-signal circuit design using industry standard CMOS processes.

Cisco Systems   www.cisco.com

Cisco Systems manufactures routers, switches, and other network devices that manage data traffic on networks and on the Internet. The company offers end-to-end enterprise network solutions for such applications as connecting branch offices to the home office and providing the network backbone for corporations and college campuses.

Its technology provides intelligent network services and scalable architectures that make it efficient to operate large networks. The company has three prime markets. These are the enterprise market, such as large organizations that have complex networking needs; service providers, which are companies that provide information services such as telecommunication carriers, Internet Service Providers, and wireless communication providers; and small- and medium-sized businesses that require data networks and connections to the Internet and to business partners. Cisco Systems has a network of consultants who are able to incorporate the firm's productions into customized network solutions.

Dell Computer   www.dell.com

Dell Computer manufactures computers and network servers that are offered over the Internet and through telephone orders. Michael Dell, the founder of Dell Computer, was one of the first e-merchants to master the art of selling merchandise on the Internet. IBM followed his lead when deciding that IBM computers would no longer be sold in stores.

Although Dell Computer is known for providing consumers with desktop and laptop computers, the company also manufactures a line of network servers, some of which run the company's e-commerce Web site.

EMC   www.emc.com

EMC is a key player in the market for intelligent enterprise storage systems, software and services that are essential data-storage systems used to make the Internet efficient. The company's products store, retrieve, manage, protect, and share information from all major computing environments, including UNIX, Windows NT, Linux, and mainframe platforms.

Major customers include the world's largest banks and financial services firms, telecommunications providers, airlines, retailers, manufacturers, governments, universities, and scientific institutions. These industry leaders rely on EMC's storage solutions for such applications as online reservation systems, transaction processing, customer billing, the Internet and corporate Intranets, data mining, and data warehousing.

EMC became the first company to provide intelligent storage systems based on arrays of small, commodity hard disk drives for the mainframe market, which had developed in today's redundant array of independent disks (RAID) technology. Its unique mirroring software made EMC the world's leading storage-based solution for business continuity and disaster recovery.

IBM   www.ibm.com

IBM is known as the mainframe computer king that was over taken by PC manufacturers. However, IBM is one of the leading e-business solution providers and provides many businesses with complete e-commerce solutions.

The company's mainframe business also found new interest from larger corporations that are entering e-commerce. Consumers who purchase goods on the Internet require quick responses from e-merchants. The volume of visits and transactions place a strain on many servers. However, IBM's retooled mainframe computers easily handle this demand.

As e-commerce grows, so will the need for high-performance servers able to manage massive databases. IBM's mainframes are the likely choice to handle this job.

Intel   www.intel.com

Intel manufactures computer microprocessors and circuit boards used in the majority of computers used to connect to networks and to the Internet and run about 60 percent of the Web servers. Its products include the Pentium III Xeon processor, used in mid-to high-end network services; the Pentium II processor, designed for use in entry-level services; the Celeron processor, used in value PC desktop systems; and the Mobile Pentium II processor for use in mobile PC systems.

In addition to these central processors Intel manufactures motherboards, which are the main circuit board in computers and servers. Intel also makes flash memory. Flash memory is reprogrammable memory that retains data when the device, such as a mobile phone, is turned off.

Another aspect of Intel's business is the manufacture of embedded control chips. These are chips specifically designed for used in automobile engine and braking systems, hard disk drives, laser printers, input/output control modules, cellular phones, and home appliances.

Juniper Networks   www.juniper.net

Juniper Networks manufactures high-performance Internet routers that enable service providers to meet demands of the growing Internet. Its family of routers delivers performance that is easily scalable and gives technicians manageable control over traffic while maintaining optimal bandwidth efficiency.

Juniper has targeted its routers to transmit IP packets across the Internet backbone by combining a new class of integrated chip with software-based routing systems.

Lucent Technologies   www.lucent.com

Lucent Technologies is the forerunner of Bell Labs, the company that invented the transistor, among other technologies. Today, Lucent Technologies has its sights on bridging old telephone technology with tomorrow's Internet networks.

The company has more than 125 years of networking experience and created the existing telephone network. Lucent Technologies is developing ways to transmit digital transformation that blends voice, data, and video into a seamlessly networked flow of information over public and private networks.

Wireless systems, messaging systems, call centers, optical networking, semiconductors, data networking, and communications software are all Lucent strengths. Lucent Technologies is leading the way for the ultra high-speed optical transmission of voice and data.

Network Appliances   www.netapp.com

Network Appliances makes cache systems that retain frequently viewed information over the Internet. Prior to Network Appliances, data was stored on an application server, which slowed the response time to deliver data over the Internet.

The Network Appliances' solution is to move data to a special service it calls a special network appliance, which is responsible for serving data at high speeds. Network Appliance was the first to devise this high-performance network appliance concept.

Its network file servers and Web caching solutions deliver fast, simple, reliable, and cost-effective access to data stored on the network or across the Internet, which is an extension of the industry trend toward dedicated, specialized products.

The Network Appliances' data-access solutions are used by businesses across a variety of industries and applications including the Internet and e-commerce, computer-aided design, engineering, manufacturing, electronic design automation, software development, and financial services.

Network Appliances' products are used by corporations and ISPs, including 3Com, Adobe Systems, Tripod, John Deere, NationsBanc, and GTE to reduce the cost and complexity of managing mission-critical data.

Qualcomm   www.qualcomm.com

Qualcomm manufactures the next generation of Internet-enabled cell phones. It is also the pioneer of Code Division Multiple Access (CDMA), the technology of choice for next-generation wireless communications.

More than 65 leading communications manufacturers have licensed the CDMA technology because it has unsurpassed voice quality, system capacity, privacy, and flexibility by using digital wireless communications products.

Qualcomm has various satellite businesses that place it in a strategic position to benefit from global wireless Internet access, which is expected to be available through most cell phones.

Sun Microsystems   www.sun.com

Sun Microsystems manufactures services that are used to host Web sites. The company first made a name for itself building high-powered workstations that were quickly adopted by major Wall Street firms. As the Internet and e-commerce began to grow, Sun Microsystems retooled its products to meet the needs of Internet companies.

Web performance is up 400 percent and performance of Java applications, a language developed by Sun Microsystems and used to develop Internet and Intranet applications, is up 1,400 percent with the redesign of Sun Microsystems' Solaris Operating Environment.

Sun Microsystems has made its products scalable, which enables e-commerce companies to easily grow in synchronization with the e-commerce market.

NETWORK COMMUNICATION SEGMENT ....

New and existing communication carriers are building the Internet infrastructure that enables visitors to travel through cyber space at nearly the speed of light. Telecommunications networks that formed the first electronic superhighway are being retrofitted with improved technology.

As demand for speed along the Internet increases, so does the demand for better communication networks. This results in new opportunities for the network communication segment to develop new products and tap into new revenue sources. Here are the major players in the network communications segment of the Internet industry.

AT&T   www.att.com

AT&T is the granddaddy of long-distance telecommunications companies. It had its empire divided and opened to competition by an act of Congress. AT&T has managed to rebuild itself and fight off competition by developing new technologies at its research and development lab.

Although AT&T has a strong position in telecommunications, 80 percent of revenue is from voice communications. Competitors are either concentrating on data communications or a combination of voice and data communications.

AT&T is the largest digital wireless network in North America and is one of the leading direct Internet access services for customers. Through acquisitions, AT&T is enhancing its network capabilities and is able to offer broadband video, voice, and data services throughout the United States.

On the international front, AT&T has joined with European partners to offer seamless domestic and international telecommunication services to corporate clients.

Global Crossing   www.globalcrossing.com

Global Crossing is playing a key role in making the Internet worldwide by laying undersea cables and providing the media to transfer international data. Its digital fiber optic cables handle transmissions of voice telecommunications as well as broadband applications such as the Internet, Intranets, and video conferencing.

A concern of many corporations who seek to link local networks internationally is to deal with one vendor that offers a complete service and that can increase or decrease telecommunications services as needed for business. Global Crossing is a global telecommunications carrier that provides one-stop shopping for international telecommunication services.

Although telecommunications companies are gradually replacing copper cables with fiber optic cables, most of these upgrades take place on land. Few upgrade initiatives are in undersea fiber optic cables. This is where Global Crossing is making inroads with more than 97,000 miles of fiber optic cables connecting five continents, 24 countries, and 200 major cities.

MCI WorldCom   www.wcom.com

MCI WorldCom is a telecommunications company that offers fully integrated local, long-distance, international (65 countries), and Internet services to homes and commercial customers. Although MCI WorldCom handles voice communications, its primary objective is to transmit data-intensive telecommunications.

MCI WorldCom's goal is to provide local-to-global-to-local telecommunication services throughout North America, Latin America, Europe, and the Asia-Pacific region without relying on local telecommunications companies. Its system will be fully integrated and self-owned.

In addition to offering a seamless, complete telecommunications package, MCI WorldCom also offers customers virtual private networks, Web hosting, and e-commerce services.

Qwest Communications   www.qwest.com

Qwest is an Internet communications company that uses fiber optics to carry voice, data, and images. In the U.S., it reaches 18,815 miles and connects to 150 cities across the country and 1,400 miles into Mexico.

The Dutch Telecommunications Company, KPN, joined with Qwest to create a 9,100-mile fiber optic network that connects 40 European cities. Qwest is also a member of a consortium that is building a 13,125-mile cable from California to Japan and other Pacific Rim countries.

In addition to long-distance fiber optic networks, Qwest has created its own local networks in 19 cities in the United States where they offer homes and businesses fast access to the Internet through their Digital Subscriber Line Services.

Qwest also offers services other than providing a fast connection to the Internet and Intranets. These include Web-based paging, Internet calling, and online faxing. For businesses, Qwest offers dedicated Internet access, Web hosting with high-bandwidth connections, outsourcing resources for corporation Internet services, and virtual private networks.

PUTTING IT ALL TOGETHER ....

There are hundreds of companies that are working toward the same common goal of using networking and Internet technology to make our lives more interesting and productive. Chapters 10 and 11 gave you a brief tour of the networking and Internet industry. I list Web sites in Appendix A for important players in the industry, which you can use to continue your industry tour.

The networking and Internet industry falls into two major categories called hardware and software. The hardware sector is generally grouped into cabling, network switching devices, computers and servers, and wireless services. The software sector generally falls into network operating systems, database-management systems, development tools, and languages and applications.

This new technology is dramatically changing the way people do business. We are moving from brick and mortar commerce to electronic commerce. Both old-time companies and startups see vast opportunities in cyber space.

Old-line brick-and-mortar companies see the Web as a way to reduce expenses by selling directly to the consumer. However, this is done at a risk of disrupting existing relationships with middlemen in the distribution chain.

New online companies invest heavily in attracting customers even if they lose money on every sale. Their objective is to build a steady, loyal following of customers and stake a claim to an online market. The first online company that gives consumers goods and services at a reasonable price while giving them a good user experience will own the market.

Companies who go online require the infrastructure to support their online business operations. Infrastructure includes cabling, routers, servers, and other software and network devices that keep data flowing throughout the company and over the Internet.

New companies finance their infrastructure with funds supplied by incubators and venture capitalists who provide seed money to private companies in exchange for a share of the business. These investors are betting that the new company will eventually own the online market of a particular segment of the economy.

Companies are forming strategic alliances in which each independent company contributes to the goods or services provided to the customers. Alliance partners share a piece of the transaction rather than sell their services to their partners.

We are at the beginning of a cyber space and Internet revolution. It is difficult to predict with any certainty how this new technology will affect our lives in the future because networking and Internet technology is a disruptive technology—technology that changes the economic and legal framework of every industrialized country.

This isn't the first time that the world has seen a disruptive technology. Electricity, the internal combustion engine, and the airplane are just a few technological inventions that have influenced every aspect of life.

If history is any predictor of the future, then we can safely assume that the full impact of the Internet will not be felt for 10 years because it took that long for other disruptive technologies to take hold of the economy.

When that happens, consumers, businesses, and government all will have changed their way of interacting with each other. Consumers can comparison shop at the click of a mouse button and will soon employ agents to impartially search the corners of the Internet for the best deals.

Businesses can no longer count on investments in fixed assets and capitalization to hold on to market share. Factors that give businesses advantages today will become liabilities on the Internet because traditional barriers to upstarts entering the market no longer exist. With a minimum investment anyone can open an online business that gives him or her the same opportunity for customers as established companies.

Governments will quickly see a loss of power in three fronts: legal, economic, and financial. The Internet collapses local markets into one global market in which transactions will cross oceans in the same vein as you and I make purchases at our local grocery.

One of the major obstacles posed by a cyber economy is the law. Local and national laws the govern how we transact business must be enhanced to address multiple jurisdiction that crosses language and cultural barriers. How will a consumer in Japan who purchase goods from a French online merchant whose Web site is hosted in the United States, enforce a commercial agreement? There is no easy answer.

Another obstacle is how to maintain a stable economy. The global economy is a delicate balancing act between the well being of each country's economy and international trade. Central banks and governments within each industrialized country influence economic growth by adjusting interest rates and government spending.

The cyber economy has no natural or national boundaries. There isn't a central government in cyber space to ensure a stable economy. And to further complicate matters, there is no easy way for the major industrialized countries to agree on ways to control a cyber economy.

The future of financing governments is also in flux because of this new technology. It doesn't take a rocket scientist to foresee a dramatic increase in cross-border sales of goods and services. The borders I'm speaking about are between and within each country.

Governments must revisit import and export taxes before the pressures of the cyber economy force them to make untimely decisions. Likewise, local governments must revisit the way they are financed through sales tax. There is simply no easy way to collect sales tax on the Internet.

I'm hopeful that reading the previous two chapters and appendix gave you an insight into the business of networking and the Internet. I also hope you appreciate the challenges that are facing old-line companies, startups, and local, state, federal, and national governments.

A decade from now we'll all look back at the cyber revolution and remember today—the good old days—when you drove five miles and waited an hour in traffic to shop at a mall.

Glossary

10Base5	An Ethernet standard that transmits packets at 10 megabits per second (MBPS) using baseband technology and thick coaxial cable.
10Base2	An Ethernet standard that transmits packets at 10 megabits per second (MBPS) using baseband technology and thin coaxial cable.
10BaseT	An Ethernet standard that transmits packets at 10 megabits per second (MBPS) using baseband technology and twisted-pair cable.
Access Restrictions	Limits network resources a person can share and how the person uses those resources.
Account Profile	A file that contains settings and restrictions for a user account.
Application Layer OSI Reference Model	The layer of the Open Systems Interconnection (OSI) Reference Model that specifies the protocols used to transmit and receive information over a network.
ASCII Code	Assigns characters and symbols found on the keyboard to a unique set of eight binary (zeros and ones) values called a byte.
Asynchronous Communication	Divides information into pieces and transmits each piece separately to the remote PC. The remote PC acknowledges each piece before the next piece is sent. The pieces are reassembled at the destination.

Asynchronous Transfer Mode (ATM)	A new and improved way to transmit information over long distances. I use the term information because ATM technology is designed to carry voice data as well as video and multimedia all at speeds up to 2.5 gigabits per second.
ATM	*See* Asynchronous Transfer Mode.
Attenuation	The weakening of the network signal over a network media.
Back Door	A term used to described an entrance to a server that bypasses ID and password security measures.
Backbone	A central network path that interconnects other networks much like how our backbone houses the central nervous system, which links together nerve branches.
Bandwidth	The number of communication channels over which data can be transmitted simultaneously.
Base I/O Port Address	The address that identifies the location of the network card to the network device's operating system.
Baseband Technology	One bit at a time is transmitted on a digital signal.
Basic Input Output System (BIOS)	Software located in a special chip that copies the operating system software from the hard disk into random access memory (RAM).
Basic Rate Interface (BRI)	A flavor of ISDN service that consists of three channels called B1, B2, and D. B1 and B2 are commonly called the B channels and each is used to transmit and receive either voice or data at 64 KBPS. The D channel is used to control the call.
Baud Rate	The number of bits that can be transmitted per second using any means of transmission
Binary Based Numbers	Contains only two digits—zero and one
BIOS	*See* Basic Input Output System.
Bit	A binary digit used to reflect the state of a switch: on or off.

Bottleneck	Any network device that processes packets slower than other network devices.
Bounce Back	Occurs when a signal reaches the end of the cable, reverses direction, and continues along the cable. This term is also used to describe e-mail that is returned as nondeliverable.
BRI	*See* Basic Rate Interface.
Bridge	A device that connects two or more network segments.
Broadband Technology	Multiple bits are transmitted at a time on an analog signal.
Broadcast Infrared Network	Allows an infrared beam to disperse in various directions.
Broadcast Storm	The transmission of many packets to all nodes on every segment of the network thereby causing degradation in network performance.
Brouter	A device that can operate as a bridge or a router depending on the protocol used by the network architecture. Brouters join together unlike network architectures and therefore must be able to handle both routable and nonroutable protocols.
Bus	A collection of wires etched into a circuit board used to transmit information among electronic components.
Bus Topology	One cable connects each node to the network, which causes all network-traffic flows across a single cable.
Byte	A set of eight bits.
Cable	A cable consists of two or more wires shrouded in sleeves to insulate the wires from the elements.
Carrier Sense Multiple Access with Collision Avoidance Media Access Method (CSMA/CA)	A network access method where a network device sends a packet only if no traffic is on the network.
Carrier Sense Multiple Access with Collision Detection Media Access Method (CSMA/CD)	A network access method where a network device transmits a packet then listens for a collision.

Carrier Signal	A radio signal that is transmitted at a consistent frequency used to establish a connection with a radio receiver.
Case Sensitivity	Determines whether or not upper- and lowercase letters are treated as different letters. A case sensitive search, for example, considers "CAR" and "car" two different words.
Client	A computer connected to the network that can request access to network services such as a request to send a document to a network printer.
Coaxial Cable	A solid copper core surrounded by insulation similar to cable TV cables.
Communications Channel	A pathway used to transmit information.
Communications Closet	A room where all the network connection terminates.
Compression	A technique for reducing the number of bits to represent information.
Concentrator	Concentrates network traffic to a central location, then send packets to all nodes on the network. The network card on each network device determines if the packet is addressed to its device.
Configuration	A listing of device settings that are particular to a specific network such as IP addresses and network protocols.
Connectionless Protocol	Transmits packets without first making a connection with the destination node. That is to say, packets are sent regardless of whether or not the destination node is ready to receive them.
Connection-Oriented Protocol	Creates a virtual circuit connection with the destination node before a packet is transmitted.
Contention	When two or more PCs attempt to access a network resource at the same time.
CPU	*See* Central Processing Unit.

Crosstalk	Interference from a signal generated by an adjacent cable.
Crystal	A chemical formation of molecules into a distinct pattern. Salt is a crystal that we come in contact with every day. When certain crystals are charged with electricity, the crystal vibrates at a constant frequency and some crystals vibrate within the radio spectrum.
CSMA/CA	*See* Carrier Sense Multiple Access with Collision Avoidance Media Access Method.
CSMA/CD	*See* Carrier Sense Multiple Access with Collision Detection Media Access Method.
Data	Are facts such as customer, inventory, and accounting information.
Data Link Layer OSI Reference Model	Send bits to the physical layer and receives incoming bits from the physical layer. The Data Link Layer groups data into frames.
Data Size	The amount of data that the destination network card can store in memory before the destination computer processes the data.
Datagram	A packet of information that is transmitted over the Internet.
DDS	*See* Digital Data Service.
Decode	A method used to translate information carried on a signal back to our words.
Dedicated Service	A permanent connection between two points on the telephone network. The connection remains intact after each call is completed.
Digital Data Service (DDS)	Was one of the first services offered by telephone companies to carry digital information. DDS used a special device called a Channel Service Unit/Digital Service Unit (CSU/DSU) to connect together remote computers using a dedicated line.

Digital Subscriber Line (DSL)	A service that uses a special DSL modem to transmit data using frequencies above 4 Kilohertz. You could think of this as using the shoulder of the road to increase the number of vehicles that can travel over the highway at the same time. Frequencies above 4 Kilohertz are divided into 256 subchannels, each of which can transmit 32 Kilobits of data per second. Half the channels are used for transmission and the other half for receiving data. This technique is called Discrete Multi-tone Modulation.
Direct Memory Access (DMA)	The ability of the network card to directly use memory of the network device.
Direct Sequence Modulation	Bits of a packet are sent over multiple frequencies that the same time. The receiver reassembles the packet.
Disk Controller	The circuit board inside a computer that controls access to a hard disk.
Drop-Cable	The name given to the cable that extends from a node to the bus cable.
DSL	*See* Digital Subscriber Line.
Electromagnetic Interference (EMI)	The likelihood that a network media will detect stray signals generated by other devices such as fluorescent lights and power cables
Electromagnetic Spectrum	Organizes frequencies of waves into ranges called a spectrum. For example, sound as we know it is actually a spectrum within the electromagnetic spectrum. That is, a range of frequencies which can be detected by our ears.
Electromagnetism	The phenomenon that changes a metal bar into a magnet when electricity travels over a coil of wire that is wrapped around the bar
EMI	*See* Electromagnetic Interference.
Emissions	Some network media has a tendency to leak the signal to the area surrounding the media (i.e., cable), which provides an opportunity for a technician using the proper electronic device to eavesdrop on the transmission.

Encode	A method used to translate our words into a form that can be carried by a signal.
Encryption Method	A method used to secure information by jumbling characters and numbers. A key is used to decrypt encrypted information.
Ethernet	A network architecture with roots going back to the late 1960s when Xerox, Intel, and DEC got together to develop a way to transmit computer information over a cable. Ethernet standards described how to provide traffic flow over the network and how to layout a network so to assure there is sufficient energy to send packets to every segment and node.
Expansion Slot	A socket that connects an add-on circuit board to the etched wires on the motherboard. This makes it possible for information to flow back and forth between the add-on circuit board and the motherboard.
Fast Ethernet	An enhanced version of Ethernet that increases the speed of the network from 10 MBPS to 100 MBPS by requiring the use of two pairs of category 5 twisted-pair cables or four pair of category 3 twisted-pair cables.
Fault Tolerant	A method to assure that the network continues operation in the face of a network failure.
FDDI	*See* Fiber Distributed Data Interface.
Fiber Distributed Data Interface (FDDI)	A fast, long distance highway that supports up to 100 MBPS with up to 62 miles (100 Kilometers) between nodes. FDDI networks are commonly used as the backbone that links together several smaller networks.
Fiber Optic Cable	A thin glass or clear plastic fiber within a sleeve that prevents the light signal from escaping and prevents stray light from interfering with the signal.
Fiber Optic Transmission	Uses light waves to transmit a signal over a fiber optic cable.
File Server	A computer on the network that uses its hard disk to store files from network clients.
File Transfer Protocol	FTP is the Internet process used to transfer files between two computers.

Firewall	A computer that filters every piece of information within the organization that is received from and sent to the Internet.
Frame Relay	Transmits information fast by requiring routers at the receiving site to determine if an error has occurred in transmission rather than requiring each router along the transmission path to check for errors.
Frequency	The number of complete sine waves that occur within a second.
Frequency Hopping	Sends a packet over a rotating set of frequencies.
FTP	*See* File Transfer Protocol.
Gateway	A device that translates network signals between unlike networks such as between a PC network and a mainframe network or between a mainframe network and a UNIX network.
GBPS	Gigabits per second.
Guest Account	An account given to someone who needs access to the network for one day.
Handshaking	Requires that each network card determine the data size that can be transmitted, transmission timing, data confirmation, and data transmission rate.
Home Page	The first Web page that is displayed when you visit a Web site.
Hop	The transmission of a packet to a router or final destination.
HTML	*See* HyperText Markup Language.
http	Refers to hypertext transfer protocol, which is the Internet service used to transmit Web pages.
Hub	A central point on the network used to connect together cables leading from nodes.
Hybrid Topology	A topology that uses two or more other types of topologies.
Hyperlink	The connection between hypertext and other text or documents.

Hypertext	Text or a graphic that is associated with other text on the same page or associated with another Web page
Hypertext Markup Language (HTML)	A language that uses embedded tags to describe how a document is to be displayed in a browser and how to the document is to be linked to other documents.
Impedance	The measurement in ohms of the resistance of a molecule to being placed in motion.
Infrared	A band of frequencies within the electromagnetic spectrum that use a specific range of light waves to transmit a signal through the air.
In-Service Time	The length of time a component is connected to the network.
Instruction	A series of commands written in a programming language that are executed in sequence typically in the form of a computer program.
Integrated Circuit	A network of transistors connected by microscopic wires similar to a bus inside the computer and uses much the basic concept used by mainframe computers to linked together microscopic components built into circuits on the chip.
Interference	A stray radio signal that interferes with a transmission signal.
Intermittent Problem	A problem that occurs irregularly and is difficult to replicate.
Internet	A network of networks.
Internet Service Provider	An organization that provides inexpensive accesses to the Internet backbone.
Internet Services	Various methods that are available to exchange information over the Internet and include e-mail, telnet, FTP, and newsgroups.
Internetwork Pack Exchange (IPX)	IPX is the connectionless protocol for NetWarc Networks.

Internetworking	Divides the Data Link Layer into the Logical Link Control (LLC), which manages flow control and error corrections between network devices, and the Media Access Control (MAC), which controls how the network card accesses the network.
Interrupt	A signal that interrupts the CPU from processing information.
IP Address	Internet Protocol address, which is the unique address assigned to each network device.
IPX	*See* Internetwork Pack Exchange.
Iron Oxide	A chemical compound that contains elements of iron that would retain a magnetic charge over long time periods.
IRQ Number	Assigned to the interrupt line used to tell the CPU that data is received and needs to be processed.
ISDN	An alternative to the analog telephone network, which is designed for voice communication rather than data transmissions. ISDN divides the communications line into channels much like we have television channels. Each channel can handle a transmission at the same time.
Local Printer	A printer that is directly connected to a computer.
LocalTalk	The network architecture developed by Apple Computer for the Macintosh computer and supports both Ethernet and Token Ring architectures called EtherTalk and TokenTalk.
Logic Bombs	Booby-traps that sit quietly on the server until someone inadvertently triggers the logic bomb, then instructions in the logic bomb does the dirty deed on the server.
Logical Operation	A method used to compare two settings and answers such questions as, "Do switch A and switch B have the same settings?". You see this technique used when someone tries to find your information inside a computer by searching for your Social Security number.
Log-In	The process by which a remote computer or network operating system grants or rejects access to resources.

Malicious Applet	A small program written in the Java™ programming language that is embedded into a Web page. The Web page seems like any other Web page to you and I, but once the page is opened, the Java applet can do all kinds of mischief such as send erroneous emails or search for ID and passwords stored on your computer.
MAN	*See* Metropolitan Area Network.
MAU	*See* Multistation Access Unit.
MBPS	Million bits per second.
Mesh Topology	A network that uses redundant links to connect network devices as a way to provides fault-tolerant security.
Metropolitan Area Network	The term that describes a computer network that covers a metropolitan region.
Microphone	Translates sound waves into electrical waves.
Microwave	A band of frequencies within the electromagnetic spectrum that travel in one direction; relatively difficult to intercept and is less susceptible to interference from with a stray single than other wireless networks.
Multiport Repeater	A device that receives signals from any one of multiple nodes on the network, then relays the signal to all nodes.
Multistation Access Unit (MAU)	A hub used in the Token Ring architecture.
Multitasking	The ability of the operating system to perform many tasks at the same time.
NetWare	One of the first networks used in corporations, primarily as a way to share files among computers.
Network	An interconnection of devices to form a pathway on which to exchange a signal encoded with information.
Network Architecture	Defines the standards used to communicate over a network.
Network Broadcast	The transmission of a packet to all nodes on every segment of a network.

Network Card	Consists of circuitry that, among other things, takes information from memory and encodes it into a signal that is transmitted over the network cable.It is the circuit board that connects a computer to the network.
Network File System (NFS)	Works on the application layer and makes files on a remote computer appear as a subdirectory on a local computer.
Network Layer OSI Reference Model	Responsible for defining the logical addresses of the destination and originator resource. The Network Layer works with routers.
Network Media	The general term that refers to the network cable.
Network Operating System	A set of programs that assure reliable data transfer and handles a host of other functions that gives a network administrator tools to manage the network.
Network Performance Monitor	Software that records network traffic.
Network Resource	Any device or file available on a network. This includes a file server, printers, modems, and other such devices.
Network Segment	Stand-alone network that is connected to other stand-alone networks to for a larger network.
Network Topology	Defines the network media (i.e. wiring) and how the network media is configured.
NFS	*See* Network File Systems.
Noise	The term used to describe interference in the transmission, similar to how noise in a room can drown-out a conversation.
Nonpreemptive Multitasking	The operating system requests the application to give up the CPU temporarily so another application can be processed. The application can ignore the request.

Number System	Defines the way in which we count. We use the decimal system to count. This is called a base 10 system because there are ten digits– -0 through 9. Once we exceed the last digit, we carry-over one value one place and begin counting from 0. So after 9, 1 is placed in the next position and we begin over with 0 in the first position. You and I recognize this as the number 10.
Open Systems Interconnect Reference Model	OSI divided network communications process into seven components called layers. Each layer consists of protocols for communicating with the preceding and succeeding layer.
Operating System	A group of programs that are used to handle events that occur within the computer. In other words, the software that makes those switches function together to process information.
Oscilloscope	A device that shows voltage over time in a graphical form on the oscilloscope screen.
OSI Reference Model	*See* Open Systems Interconnect Reference Model.
Packet	An electronic envelope that contains the address of the destination network resource, the address of the computer making the request, and either all or a piece of the request along with information that controls the packet.
Packet Switching	The technique of dividing information into small pieces and placing each piece into an electronic envelope called a packet, which is transmitted over the network.
Parallel Processing	The ability of a computer to process more than one instruction simultaneously.
Parity	Specifies there must be either an even or odd number of 1s in the data. This is called even parity or odd parity. If parity is even and an odd number of 1s is received, then a data error is assume and a request is made for the data to be retransmitted.
Party Line	Similar to today's extension telephone except the extensions were located in different houses.

Permanent Virtual Circuit (PVC)	A predefined, permanent virtual circuit that connects two sites for a fixed monthly fee.
Physical Layer OSI Reference Model	Responsible for translating bits into signals that is transmitted over the network.
Pixels	Picture elements used to create an image on a television screen.
Point-to-Point Protocol (PPP)	PPP, which an improved version of SLIP. PPP offers security, data compression, and error control. In addition, PPP dynamically assigns network addresses to nodes as they log on to the network.
Point-to-Point Infrared Network	Carefully focuses the infrared beam to a particular receiver.
Polling	Describes the regular transfer of data between a series of computers located in remote locations. A central computer systematically calls (polls) each computer to initiate the exchange of data.
PPP	*See* Point to Point Protocol.
Preemptive Multitasking	Where the operating system controls when the CPU stops processing an application temporarily. The application cannot inhibit the decision.
Presentation Layer OSI Reference Model	Reformats data into the form required by the network and the Application Layer. It also handles data compression and encryption.
PRI	*See* Primary Rate Interface.
Primary Rate Interface (PRI)	A flavor of ISDN service that contains 23 B channels and a D channel, which enables 23 phone calls to be made at the same time over the same line. Those calls can transmit voice or data. The D channel in PRI is also used to control the calls.
Private Branch Exchange	A subnetwork of the telephone system that is privately owned by an organization. The public telephone network is divided into smaller subnetworks, called an exchange. Organizations save considerable money by having a private exchange that is linked to the telephone network.

Profile	Information stored by a Web site owner that describes products you purchase and Web pages you frequently visit. Profiles are used to display products and other information that might be of interest to you.
Program	Consists of a specific set of tasks that are performed in a particular order to achieve a desired result.
Programming Language	Consists of a set of words and symbols that can be translated into machine language, which a computer can understand.
Protocol	A set of rules that determines the method that will be used to do something such as to send and receive information.
Protocol Suite	A set of compatible protocols, such as TCP/IP, used to communicate over the network.
Public Switch Telephone Network	A network of cables and switches that route signals to any telephone on the network based on the telephone number dialed by the caller.
PVC	*See* Permanent Virtual Circuit.
Queuing Documents	Similar to standing in line at the checkout counter. The first person in line is served first, while others wait their turn. That is, the first document received by the switch is the first document printed.
RAM	*See* Random Access Memory.
RAM Buffering	A network card that contains its own memory used to temporarily store incoming packets.
Random Access Memory (RAM)	Computer memory that is erased when the computer is powered down.
Read Access	Enables a person to view information stored in the file, but not to modify or delete the information.
Real-Time Communication	What we experience in a telephone call where someone speaks then waits for the other person to respond.
Real-Time Switching	The ability of the telephone network to connect to any point in the telephone system when someone makes a call.

Reengineering	The process of redesigning and/or redeveloping a process or device.
Repeater	A device that receives a signal then retransmits the signal giving it a boost in power.
Retransmission	The process of sending a previously sent packet because the destination network resource suspects the data within the packet is corrupted.
Ring Topology	A network topology where each node in the network is connects to two other nodes. Collectively, nodes form a ring. This is identical in design to a wedding ring except instead of diamonds embedded in the ring there are network devices such as computers, and the gold band is the network cable.
Risk Analysis	A review of network operations and components to assess the chances of failure and the economical cost of those failures on the organization.
ROM Boot Chip	A computer chip that contains instructions that loads the operating system into the memory of a computer.
Routable Protocol	A set of network architecture rules that enable packets to retransmit across network segments by a router.
Router	Similar to a bridge and used to divide a large network into segments with the router connecting segments together. Routers, too, have addresses on each segment and redirect a packet to other segments based on the network address, but routers do not broadcast packets and, therefore, cannot cause a broadcast storm.
Satellite Networks	Use microwaves to send and receive packets between a satellite ground station and a satellite.
Scanning	A method of dividing an image into a series of pixels, each of which are encoded into a radio wave
Secondary Support Staff	Technicians such as manufacturer's technical representatives who resolve problems not contained in the handbook.
Sequenced Packet Exchange (SPX)	SPX is the connection-oriented protocol for NetWare Networks.

Sequencing	A method used to track the order of packets. When packets are received, the destination node reassembles data contained in the packets by referencing the packs' sequence number.
Serial Line Internet Protocol (SLIP)	The first protocol used to access the Internet using a dialup access. SLIP works on the physical layer of the OSI Model, but does not provide security.
Server	A computer connected to the network that provides network services, such as printing services to network clients.
Session Layer OSI Reference Model	Opens and maintains a connection between the destination and originator resources and handles security issues for the communication.
Share	Refers to a shared resource such as a file or servers.
Shielded Twisted-Pair Wires (STP)	A shield is a foil or wire mesh sleeve that is sandwiched between the copper strains and the plastic sleeve that absorbs any stray signal from entering the cable.
Signal	The transmission of electrical waves that carries information.
Signal System 7	A third communications channel in the telephone network used to manage telephone calls.
Sine Wave	A wave that has flowed from the baseline through its positive and negative heights, then returns to the baseline.
SLIP	*See* Serial Line Internet Protocol.
Sniffer Program	Software that examines datagrams transmitted over the Internet looking for confidential information.
SONET	*See* Synchronous Optical Network.
Source Code	The name given to the instructions that tells a browser how to display a Web page. You can see the source code by placing the cursor on the Web page, clicking the right mouse button, then select ing View Source from the popup menu.
Speaker	Translates electrical waves into sound waves.

Spoofing	Occurs when an illegitimate Web site pretends to be a specific legitimate Web site.
Spread-Spectrum Wireless Radio Network	An alternative to the single-frequency networks and uses multiple frequencies to transmit the signal.
SPX	*See* Sequenced Packet Exchange.
Star Topology	A network shaped like an octopus with a hub as the body and cables connecting to computers as its tentacles.
Store-Forward Technology	A method of saving information to a file then sending the file to a remote computer where the file is stored until the person is available to read the file.
STP	*See* Shielded Twisted-Pair wires.
Subnet	The portion of an IP address that identifies the network.
SVC	*See* Switched Virtual Circuit.
Switched Virtual Circuit (SVC)	A temporary virtual circuit that exists for the duration of the connection and for which the business is charged a charge for the time of the connection.
Sympathetic Vibration	With each vibration the vibrating object pushes the air molecules surrounding the object causing the air molecules to vibrate at the same rate as the object.
Synchronous Optical Network (SONET)	Used to transmit data using fiber optic cables .
T Carrier-Line	A high-speed transmission line that can carry both data and voice at the same time..
T1	A T carrier-line that transmits over 24 channels.
T2	A T carrier-line that transmits over 96 channels.
T3	A T carrier-line that transmits over 672 channels.
T4	A T carrier-line that transmits over 4,032 channels.
T-Connector	A device used to connect cables to a network and looks like the letter "T." The top of the T is inserted into the cable much like how a plumber taps into a pipe. The vertical bar of the letter screws onto the network card.
TCP/IP	Are protocols used to transmit data over the Internet.

TCP/IP Protocol Suite	Used for Internets and Intranets.
Teen Line	A second telephone number assigned to a household, typically used by teenage family members and used to reduce competition to use the family's main telephone number.
Telephone Exchange	A subnetwork of the telephone network used to connect together telephones located within the same general area.
Temporary Password	Assigned to new users and to users who forget their passwords and expires the first time a user logs on to the network.
Terminal	Consists of a monitor and a keyboard that could be placed anywhere in the building. A cable from the terminal runs to a connector box inside the computer room to form a primitive computer network.
Terminator	A device connected to the end of a bus to absorb the signal and prevent bounceback.
Terrestrial Networks	Use microwaves to transmit signals across a terrain, such as between two buildings in an office complex.
Thick Coaxial cable	A thick copper core, a higher transmission rate (i.e., bits per second) and is less flexible than thin coaxial cable.
Thin Coaxial cable	A thin copper core, a lower transmission rate (i.e., bits per second) and is more flexible than thick coaxial cable.
Throughput	A measurement of how many bits can be completely processed within a second.
Tier 1 Provider	Telephone companies that have large networks that connect ISP and corporations directly to the Internet.
Token	An electronic envelope that does not contain data and is passed to each node on the network. A node that receives the token can insert data into the token and transmit data across the network to another node. A node that does not receive the token cannot transmit data over the network.

Token Ring	A network architecture that uses a ring topology and requires a network device to obtain a token before transmitting over the network.
Topology	Defines how nodes are linked to each other using wire or wireless connections.
Transceiver	A component of the network card that sends and receives signals over the network.
Transistor	A sandwich of two elements that contains two circuits. If electricity flows through the first circuit, then no electricity flows through the second circuit. If electricity does not flow through the first circuit, then electricity does flow through the second circuit. Chip technology reduced the size of a transistor from a small, bug-like device to a submicroscopic size etched into a chip.
Transport Layer OSI Reference Model	Responsible for the creation and sequencing of packets, acknowledging the receipt of packets and handling retransmissions.
Trojan Horse	A program that uses the same program name as a safe program, but inside contains instructions that once executed could destroy files on the server.
Twisted-Pair Wires	The telephone wire with many fine strains of copper twisted together within a plastic sleeve of insulation.
Unshielded (UTP)	Twisted-pair wires without a shield.
Upgrade	The replacement of part of an entire component.
UTP	*See* Unshielded.
Virtual Circuit	A temporary connection between two points on the telephone network that disappears once the call is completed.
Virtual Private Network	A private wide area network maintained by the telephone company and connects together multiple business partners.
Voltage	The measurement of power used to transmit a signal.
WAN	*See* Wide Area Network.

War Dialing	The technique of having a program dial sequential telephone numbers, trying to detect telephone numbers that are attached to modem.
Wide Area Network	A term that describes a computer network that covers vast terrain rather than localized within one area, such as within an office building.
World Wide Web	A standardized way of accessing content on computers connected to the Internet.
Write Access	Enables a person to change or delete information contained in the file, which could inadvertently corrupt the data stored in the file.

Index

Architecture, network, 114

ARCnet, 133

Area code, 149

ARPANET, 188

ASCII, 22, 53

Asynchronous communication, 33

Asynchronous transfer mode, 167, 170

AT&T, 190

ATM, *See* Asynchronous transfer mode

Attenuation, 90

Auditing network traffic, 268

B

B channel, 160

Back door, 210

Backbone, 130

Backup domain controller, 230

Backups, 285

Bandwidth, 60, 252

Barrel connector, 117

Base 10, 22

Base memory address, 85

Base station, 174

Baseband, 64, 101

Baseline, 56, 256

Basic Input Output System, 77

Basic Rate Interface, 160

Baud rate, 59

BDC, *See* Backup domain controller

Bell Labs, 25

Bell, Alexander, 147

Berners-Lee, Tim, 40

Binary, 22

Binary numbering system, 49

Binary values, 22

BIOS, *See* Basic Input Output System

Bit, 48, 53

Bluetooth Technology, 172

BNC T Connectors, 130

Bolt Beranek and Newman, 188

Bottleneck, 83, 256

Bounce-back, 119

Brand, 310

BRI, *See* Basic Rate Interface

Brick-and-mortar, 309

Bridge, 103

Broadband, 64, 56, 253

Broadcast, 18

Broadcast packet, 104

Broadcast storm, 104

Brouters, 105

Buffer, 85

Bus, 21, 25, 80, 83, 115

Bus mastering, 84

Bus topology, 116

Business model, 311

Byte, 48

C

Cable, 6, 64, 86, 99

    television, 58

    thick coaxial, 86

    thin coaxial, 86